CHOOSING
a SCHOOL for
a CHILD with
SPECIAL NEEDS

of related interest

Making the Move
A Guide for Schools and Parents on the Transfer of Pupils with Autism Spectrum Disorders (ASDs) from Primary to Secondary School
K.I. Al-Ghani and Lynda Kenward
Illustrated by Haitham Al-Ghani
ISBN: 978 1 84310 934 1

Alphabet Kids – From ADD to Zellweger Syndrome
A Guide to Developmental, Neurobiological and Psychological Disorders for Parents and Professionals
Robbie Woliver
ISBN: 978 1 84310 880 1

Challenge Me!™
Speech and Communication Cards
Amanda Elliott
Illustrated by David Kemp
ISBN: 978 1 84310 946 4

Fun with Messy Play
Ideas and Activities for Children with Special Needs
Tracey Beckerleg
ISBN: 978 1 84310 641 8

Helping Children with Complex Needs Bounce Back
Resilient Therapy™ for Parents and Professionals
Kim Aumann and Angie Hart
Illustrated by Chloe Gerhardt
ISBN: 978 1 84310 948 8

What Did You Say? What Do You Mean?
120 Illustrated Metaphor Cards, plus Booklet with Information, Ideas and Instructions
Jude Welton
Illustrated by Jane Telford
ISBN: 978 1 84310 924 2

What is Friendship?
Games and Activities to Help Children to Understand Friendship
Pamela Day
ISBN: 978 1 84905 048 7

CHOOSING a SCHOOL for a CHILD with SPECIAL NEEDS

RUTH BIRNBAUM

Jessica Kingsley Publishers
London and Philadelphia

First published in 2010 by
Jessica Kingsley Publishers
116 Pentonville Road
London N1 9JB, UK
and
400 Market Street, Suite 400
Philadelphia, PA 19106, USA

www.jkp.com

Library of Congress Cataloging in Publication Data
Birnbaum, Ruth.
  Choosing a school for a child with special needs / Ruth Birnbaum.
    p. cm.
  Includes bibliographical references and index.
  ISBN 978-1-84310-987-7 (pb : alk. paper) 1. Children with disabilities--Education--United States. 2. Children with disabilities--Services for--United States. 3. School choice--United States. 4. Education--Parent participation--United States. I. Title.
  LC4031.B487 2009
  371.9--dc22
                              2009020344

British Library Cataloguing in Publication Data
A CIP catalogue record for this book is available from the British Library

ISBN 978 1 84310 987 7

Printed and bound in Great Britain by
Athenaeum Press, Gateshead, Tyne and Wear

THIS BOOK IS DEDICATED TO MY FATHER,

SIMON KRITZ (1919–2005),

WHO NEVER GAVE UP ENCOURAGING ME
IN MY AMBITIONS AND SHOWED, BY EXAMPLE,
THAT SELF-LEARNING IS AVAILABLE TO EVERYONE.

Contents

Part 1 – Looking at Specific Definitions of Special Educational Needs

Part 2 – Understanding the Background

Part 3 – Setting Up a Visit

Part 4 – Looking at Specific Provision/Intervention

Part 5 – Other Important Issues to Consider

Part 6 – Different School Models

Part 7 – Summary

Acknowledgements

There are some people without whom this book would not have been possible.

On a personal level, I thank my family who, over the years, have respected my need to work and discover and follow new ideas. I believe that they have all inherited the drive and ambition which has made them all, in their own ways, follow successful paths (yes, I give in to pressure and will mention them by name – Yoni, Dov, Abi, Sami and Doron). Above all, my husband, Wayne, who has not only supported me but also inspired me to always move forward and recognize my strengths even when I had self-doubts. I thank my mother, Bernice Kritz, who effortlessly has the natural skills to make everyone feel comfortable. I believe what I observed during my formative years gave me the tools to develop as an Educational Psychologist – thanks Mum!

On a professional level, I would like to thank contributors to this book, all of whom I hold in the highest regard – Elisheva Birnbaum, BSc (Hons) MAR – Occupational Therapist; Deborah Hay, BA (Hons) – Barrister; Myra Pontac, BSc (Hons), MRCSLT, MASLTIP, reg HPC – Speech and Language Therapist; Sally Wright, MCSP HPC – Physiotherapist.

I also thank my loyal PA, Caroline Levey, who gave of her time day or night.

Finally, I thank hundreds of schools who have opened their doors to me over the years.

My grateful thanks are also due to the following, who kindly granted me permission to quote from their work:

- Advisory Centre for Education (ACE)
- Anaphylaxis Campaign
- Association for All Speech Impaired Children (Afasic)
- Association of Child Psychotherapists (ACP)
- Association of Speech and Language Therapists in Independent Practice (ASLTIP)
- Asthma UK
- Bristol Healthy Schools Programme
- British Association for Art Therapists (BAAT)
- British Association for Counselling and Psychotherapy (BACP)
- British Association for Play Therapists (BAPT)

- British Association for Drama Therapists (BADth)
- British Association of Teachers of the Deaf (BATOD)
- British Council for School Enivornments (BCSE)
- British Society for Music Therapy (BSMT)
- Council for the Registration of Schools Teaching Dyslexic Pupils (CReSTeD)
- Diabetes UK
- Dyspraxia Foundation
- Friends of Landau Kleffner Syndrome (FOLKS)
- GL Assessment Ltd
- Joseph Rowntree Foundation
- Mentoring and Befriending Foundation (MBF)
- Morgan Ashurst
- National Autistic Society (NAS)
- National Deaf Children's Society
- National Society for Epilepsy
- Professional Association of Teachers of Students with Specific Learning Difficulties (PATOSS)
- Raymond Lloyd Richmond
- Royal College of Speech and Language Therapists (RCSLT)
- Royal National Institute for the Blind (RNIB)
- Royal National Institute for the Deaf (RNID)
- Royal National Institute for Deafblind People
- WCS Pearson, Inc.
- Young Foundation (Launchpad)

Explanatory Terms

1. The word **child** applies to anyone under the age of 19 years. When the UK government initiative on Every Child Matters (ECM) was launched in 2003, which led to the Children Act 2004, the word child was applied to anyone under the age of 19 years. This policy has, therefore, been followed in this book, although it is recognized that for secondary-aged children it may have been more appropriate to use the term student, but a decision had to be made.

2. The term **learning difficulties and/or disabilities** refers to children who have either a learning difficulty in acquiring new skills or who learn at a different rate to their peers. Research suggests that approximately 2 per cent of the population may have learning difficulties. This terminology transcends professional boundaries between education, health and social services so that the same language is used to explain the needs of children aged 0–19 years. The Disability Discrimination Act 1995 Section 1(1) defines that:

    > a person has a disability for the purposes of this Act if he has a physical or mental impairment that has a substantial and long-term adverse effect on his ability to carry out normal day-to-day activities.

    Physical or mental impairments can include sensory impairments and learning difficulties. This definition also covers medical conditions where there is long-term and significant impact on children's everyday lives. Those children designated with **special educational needs (SEN)**, under the current education legislation, all have learning difficulties and/ or disabilities that make it harder for them to learn compared to most learners of the same age.

    When does a learning difficulty become significant? This is often an inexact measure, but usually it needs to be pervasive, occurring in different settings and of at least moderate severity. In most cases, the impact of the difficulty will not be restricted to academic performance alone, but include self-esteem, social interactions, behavioural difficulties and possible development of co-morbid symptoms.

    There is no attempt to describe every possible learning difficulty or medical condition. Some examples have been given to give a flavour of the range of difficulties that any teacher may meet within schools. A child, even with a diagnosis, will be a unique individual with their own personality and strengths and weaknesses. It is not possible to fit a child into a box or state what any typical child needs, even when diagnosis is clarified. Whilst there may be typical and common features of a syndrome or diagnosis, the way these play out and the way the child functions, may be quite different.

3.   There is no official definition of the term **inclusion**. It is generally understood to be a process whereby children are educated in the general/mainstream classroom for the majority or totality of their day, and supportive services are brought to that classroom wherever possible. Inclusion aims to remove the barriers to learning so that children can participate in all aspects of school life. There is generally a continuum practised in mainstream schools, which ranges from full inclusion, where all children attend mainstream classes, despite the severity of their difficulty, to unit-based provision or teaching for some of the school day outside of the mainstream class. It is not always the severity of the difficulty that determines what level of inclusion is beneficial for the child, and some children with less complex difficulties, such as dyslexia or language impairment, may, in fact, benefit more from unit or group settings than the more complex child with severe learning needs. What is agreed is that most children (but not all children) with difficulties benefit from 'a more normal experience', if this is possible.

4.   The term **parent** is used to include all those with parental responsibility for the child, including carers and those acting as corporate parents for looked-after children.

5.   The term **school** is used in this book as a generic term for any place where children are educated, unless otherwise specified. The use of the term school will, therefore, apply to early years settings, infant and primary schools and secondary schools, but not the further education sector. It may also refer to special schools and unit provisions. The term will apply to all educational settings irrespective of how they are funded and it includes part-time education. For the legal definition of a school, reference should be made to the Education Act 1996, Sections 4, 5 and 6.

IMPORTANT NOTE

Various specialized programmes are described throughout this book. The author does not recommend nor accept responsibility for any of the programmes or therapies listed, but merely seeks to alert the reader to their existence and provide an idea of the range of interventions that are available. It is not a definitive list and new ideas are emerging all the time. The author does recommend the reader to look at the research available and make their own informed choices about whether the intervention meets the child's needs and preferably discuss the approach with their therapist, doctor and/or other professionals involved with the child.

Introduction

No one is prepared for having a special needs child, and as many of us know, whether you live on an Estate or an estate, developmental difficulties know no boundaries. Parents, in particular, have to learn that after coming to terms with the initial shock (and for some parents that can last a long time), they must also grapple with the machinations of Local Authorities, Children's Services, social services and, in some cases, Legal Services. However, even for professionals, schools can be challenging places to visit and it is therefore hoped that this book can be of use not only to parents but also to professionals who may be considering a particular school and who may not have the educational background or experience to understand whether provision is appropriate or not.

This book plans to address questions that may arise and steer parents and professionals through the confusing world of school life. It is hoped that professional colleagues will find the questions helpful when visiting schools, whether their background is in education, health or social services. My view is that Local Authorities should also be asking themselves some of the key questions about their own schools and, of course, schools themselves can use the book to be self-critical or self-congratulatory by looking at the service and provision they offer against the questions and criteria.

My single aim in writing this book is to try and make education as accessible as possible for the children who often rely on others to be their advocates. For many children, this will be a 'best fit' school or learning situation, and may not be perfect. However, I hope that by alerting parents and professionals to the sort of questions they may need to ask and the types of provision which will be suitable, the children will benefit.

The author does not advocate any one approach. Every child is different and every family and professional needs to make their own informed choice about how best to help the child along their developmental journey. We only have one opportunity at education; we need to make sure nothing is overlooked.

Note: Information was accurate at the time of writing, but details change, so please always check for up-to-date content on websites, etc.

PART 1

LOOKING at SPECIFIC DEFINITIONS of SPECIAL EDUCATIONAL NEEDS

CHAPTER 1

The Definition of Special Educational Needs

The Special Educational Needs (SEN) Code of Practice, which was written to give practical guidance to Local Authorities and governing bodies of maintained schools and early education settings to carry out their functions under the Education Act 1996, sets out three definitions of special educational needs, and a child may fall within one or more of the definitions.

Children have special educational needs if they have a *learning difficulty* which calls for *special educational provision* to be made for them.

Children have a *learning difficulty*, if they:

a. have a significantly greater difficulty in learning than the majority of children of the same age; or

b. have a disability which prevents or hinders them from making use of educational facilities of a kind generally provided for children of the same age in schools within the area of the local education authority

c. are under compulsory school age and fall within the definition at (a) or (b) above, or would so do if special educational provision was not made for them

Children must not be regarded as having a learning difficulty solely because the language or form of language of their home is different from the language in which they will be taught.

Special educational provision means:

a. for children of two or over, educational provision which is additional to, or otherwise different from, the educational provision made generally for children of their age in schools maintained by the LEA, other than special schools, in the area

b. for children under two, educational provision of any kind.

(see Section 312, Education Act 1996)

Definitions in the Children Act 1989 and the Disability Discrimination Act 1995:

A child is disabled if he is blind, deaf or dumb or suffers from a mental disorder of any kind or is substantially and permanently handicapped by illness injury or congenital deformity or such other disability as may be prescribed.

(Section 17 (11) Children Act 1989)

A person has a disability for the purposes of this Act, if he has a physical or mental impairment which has a substantial and long-term adverse effect on his ability to carry out normal day-to-day activities.

(Section 1 (1) Disability Discrimination Act 1995)

It is important to stress that not all children will require special educational provision, even if they have special educational needs, and the graduated response that schools should make to children with special educational needs means that only a very small percentage will require a Statement of Special Educational Needs and provision under the Act.

The SEN Code of Practice, whilst not assuming hard and fast categories of special educational needs, recognizes that there are specific needs that usually directly relate to particular types of impairment. These categories are described, in more detail, in other chapters, although there is recognition that many children will have a combination of these needs and will be described as complex.

The government has set out early learning goals for the Foundation Stage of education for children from 3 to 5 years old. For children from 5 to 16 years old, the National Curriculum sets out what most children will learn at each stage of their education. Teachers are expected to take account of the fact that children progress at different rates and have different ways in which they learn best. By organizing their lessons, the classroom, books and materials they give to each child and the way they teach, teachers will consider a number of different methods and this is often described as *differentiating the curriculum* (making it different and individualized, according to the children's levels and needs).

Children who make slow progress or have particular difficulties in one area may be given extra help or different lessons and there are also national literacy and numeracy strategies, including special 'catch-up' work and other kinds of support. It should not be assumed that a child has special educational needs just because they are making slower progress than expected or receiving some support. However, if parents or a school, despite offering extra support or help, are still concerned, they may well begin the process towards the graduated response by placing the child on one of the early phases of the Code of Practice; such as School Action or School Action Plus. This may lead to the Local Authority carrying out a statutory assessment of the child to assess their educational needs and, where necessary, make additional provision within the educational setting to provide support. The majority of children with Statements will continue to have their needs met in a mainstream school, with the help of outside specialists.

The range of needs which fall under the category of SEN might include a child having difficulties with:

- all of the work in school
- specific areas of work – reading, writing, number work or understanding information
- expressing themselves or understanding what others are saying
- making friends or relating to adults
- behaving appropriately in school
- organizing themselves
- having some kind of sensory or physical need which may affect them in school
- emotional responses.

An alternative to the concept of special educational needs is the idea that children encounter 'barriers to learning and participation' (Booth and Ainscow 2002, p.4). These barriers 'may be found in all aspects of the school, as well as within communities, and in local and national policies' (p.5). Barriers may arise from a complex combination of several disabilities, the interaction between children and what, and how, they are taught. Barriers to learning can prevent access to a school or limit participation within it. This shift to a different way of thinking about educational difficulties should look at strengths as well as weaknesses. The learning environment itself is scrutinized so that curricular options, provision of teaching methods, resources, targeted support, appropriately adapted equipment or models of provision, such as units or schools, can be altered to minimize the barriers and overcome the child's difficulties.

There are no definitive categories of SEN, but there are four areas described in the SEN Code of Practice, as follows:

- **Communication and interaction** – 7:55 **(p.86).**
- **Cognition and learning** – 7:58 **(p.86).**
- **Behaviour, emotional, social development** – 7:60 **(p.87).**
- **Sensory and/or physical needs** – 7:62 **(p.88).**

There is no definition of **complex needs** within the Code of Practice, although, in 7:53 (p.85) it states:

> Although needs and requirements can usefully be organised into areas, individual pupils may well have needs which span two or more areas. For example, a pupil with general learning difficulties may also have behavioural difficulties or a sensory impairment. Where needs are complex in this sense it is important to carry out a detailed assessment of individual pupils and their situations. However, the accumulation of low-level difficulties may not in itself equate with a school being unable to meet the child's needs through school-based provision. In some cases pupils will have needs that are not only complex but also severe.

The Code of Practice states that a medical diagnosis or a disability (**medical conditions** – 7:65, pp.88–89) does not necessarily imply special educational needs. It then goes on:

> Medical conditions may have a significant impact on a child's experiences and the way they function in school. The impact may be direct in that the condition may affect cognitive or physical abilities, behaviour or emotional state. The impact may also be indirect, perhaps disrupting access to education through unwanted effects of treatments or through the psychological effects that serious or chronic illness or disability can have on a child and their family... The effects of a medical condition may be intermittent and their impact on the child's function in school can vary at different stages of their school career. This may reflect changes in the school curriculum, changes in the individual child and changes in the peer group, for example, with the onset of puberty.

CHAPTER 2

Communication and Interaction

Children who do not develop speech and language as expected are said to have speech and language impairments. These impairments may range from physical difficulties from moving the muscles which control speech to the ability to understand or use language at all. Speech and language impairments can range from mild to severe and be short or long term. Sometimes, these difficulties are unrelated to any other difficulty or disorder and are, therefore, called specific language difficulties. For some children, language difficulties are part of their other disabilities or learning needs.

The Association for All Speech Impaired Children (Afasic) states that 6 in 100 children will, at some stage, have a speech, language or communication difficulty. One in 500 children experiences severe long-term difficulties.

There is often confusion with the terms used and reference will be made to developmental language delay, developmental language disorder and specific language impairment. It can be helpful to ask a speech and language therapist to clarify the description.

Specific language impairment is the most widely used term. It describes children whose difficulties are only with speech and language. It does not include children who do not develop language because of cognitive (intellectual) or physical difficulties, hearing loss, emotional problems or environmental deprivation.

Specific language impairment typically includes the following types of difficulties:

- the child seems to understand what is said, but people cannot understand what the child is trying to say
- the child speaks clearly and at length, but often fails to get the point of a conversation, making inappropriate comments and replies

- the child speaks clearly in single words, but has difficulties linking them together to make sentences, often leaving words out
- the child understands almost no spoken language and says only a few words.

Most speech and language therapy assessments will distinguish between understanding language (comprehension) and using language (expression). Many children will be better in one area, although they may have difficulties in both.

Children who have a difficulty with their speech apparatus, i.e. the co-ordination of the muscles around the mouth, tongue, nose and with their breathing are often quickly identified as having a speech and language impairment. However, there are many areas which can also contribute to a specific language impairment, for example, phonology – the sounds that make up language; syntax (grammar and morphology) – the way that words and parts of words combine in phrases and sentences; intonation and stress (prosody) – the rhythm and 'music' of the way we speak.

A child may have difficulty in the semantic–pragmatic area. Semantics is the meaning of words, bits of words and phrases and sentences, whilst pragmatics is how a child uses language in different situations, how feelings are conveyed and when and how things are said to other people. Many children with autism may be described as having semantic–pragmatic disorder. All of these areas may affect comprehension, expression or both.

There is an important distinction between developmental language delay and developmental language disorder, although these are often used interchangeably for children who are not developing language as expected for their age. Children's language is described as *delayed* when they continue to make common mistakes and when their language is developing more slowly compared to the usual order of language development. In contrast, children's language is *disordered* when they make odd mistakes or when their language is developing in an unusual order. A delay might be mild or severe, but once it begins to develop, it develops normally in sequence and pattern. When language develops in children with a language disorder, it is delayed but also atypical and uneven. The disordered nature of their language makes it more difficult for language to continue developing and so they have additional problems in coping with communication and learning at school and at home. Inevitably, having a language disorder will mean that language is also delayed, but having a language delay does not necessarily mean that there is a language disorder.

EXAMPLES OF COMMUNICATION AND INTERACTION PROBLEMS

Semantic and pragmatic disorders

Children who are identified with semantic and pragmatic disorders frequently show signs of limited social development and play as a result of their communication disorder. Children with semantic–pragmatic disorder may have difficulties in:

- understanding the listener's needs
- taking turns in a conversation and knowing what is being talked about
- maintaining a topic of conversation without going off at a tangent
- knowing how to end a conversation without being abrupt or rude
- knowing when it is appropriate to talk and when to keep quiet
- saying more than they are capable of understanding which may include using learnt phrases or scripts in one situation, but having fluent well-formed sentences in another situation
- being verbose.

Dysarthria

Dysarthria is a condition affecting speech production which results in slurred speech due to weak or imprecise movements of the speech organs. Frequently, the speed of speech production is affected and is usually slow and more limited in range. Dysarthria can be associated with a number of neurological conditions or as a result of brain injury. If it occurs with cerebral palsy or a head injury, there may also be difficulties in understanding language or general learning. Sometimes, dysarthria is called Worster–Drought syndrome, which is also associated with mild general motor difficulties and some general learning problems. Children with Worster–Drought syndrome may have sucking and swallowing difficulties and poor control of the movement of muscles around the mouth.

Selective mutism

Selective mutism (a more recent term for elective mutism) is a term used when children who are able to talk quite freely in some situations, are persistently silent in other situations. Selective mutism is relatively rare and is more prevalent in girls than boys. It is beyond normal shyness and is thought to be a psychological problem when the child freezes or becomes unable to speak which is often a kind of social anxiety, coupled with an excessive sensitivity of the reactions to others. Children with selective mutism are represented in all levels of intelligence, but are more likely to have other speech and language difficulties compared to other children.

Autistic spectrum disorder

This term describes a group of children who demonstrate similar styles of behaviour, thought and communication. The spectrum includes terms such as autism; high functioning autism; Asperger's syndrome; semantic–pragmatic disorders and pervasive developmental disorder (not otherwise specified) which is the terminology used in the USA. The distinctive features of ASD are:

- difficulties interacting socially
- difficulties in communication
- rigid thinking.

The social communication aspects of ASD are apparent even in children with high functioning autism or Asperger's syndrome who can acquire very good speech and linguistic structure but yet continue to have difficulty with the social use of language.

Other areas of communication difficulties

Other areas of communication difficulties which may arise, and form areas of work for speech and language therapists, are:

- dyslexia/specific learning difficulties
- articulation
- stammering
- higher level language disorders
- cleft palate
- voice disorders
- specific difficulties in sound production
- phonological disorders
- phonological problems
- aphasia/dysphasia
- dyspraxia
- Fragile X syndrome
- Down's syndrome
- comprehension or receptive language difficulties
- Landau–Kleffner syndrome/epilepsy
- auditory sequential memory

- specific memory disorders
- short-term and long-term memory.

Children with a hearing impairment will also usually have speech and language difficulties.

Language and communication underpins our educational system and it is, therefore, a crucial area which crosses a number of boundaries. Language impaired children may develop behavioural problems, but these are often precipitated by breakdowns in communication and so may be quite different to the behaviours associated, for example, with the autistic spectrum. For many children, because language is a complex interactive system, problems in one area will have consequences for the development of literacy skills. Much research attributes specific literacy problems to early, possibly unrecognized phonological difficulties and so children who experience language problems are at risk for later problems in the acquisition of reading and spelling skills.

The implications of speech, language and communication difficulties can be far-reaching. Establishing and maintaining attention can be related to understanding language. Attention to auditory information and attention control can be linked directly to a child's language development in school. Auditory perception or listening is important if a child has to learn the different speech sounds, and memory is also part of the complex process that occurs in young children acquiring language.

Children who experience difficulties with communication are at risk of social exclusion because of difficulties in forming social relationships due to reduced participation in social groups and, as a result, they can, perhaps, physically respond to a situation with aggressive behaviour instead of using language. Communication and interaction, therefore, often go hand-in-hand as set out in the Code of Practice.

CHAPTER 3

Cognition and Learning

This chapter looks at a range of difficulties from profound learning difficulties to more specific learning difficulties where cognitive skills are intact. Learning difficulties are usually expressed in relation to average intelligence, as measured by a cognitive test; such as the Wechsler Intelligence Scale for Children – Fourth Edition (WISC-IV) or the British Ability Scales – Second Edition (BAS-II). These tests base scores on a standardized normal distribution with an average intelligence quotient (IQ) or conceptual ability being 100 (rather than an age-based quotient). The normal distribution or 'bell curve' yields a range of scores and, as a result, individuals with low or high IQ scores will feature at the tail end of the bell curve. The terms, moderate, severe and profound learning difficulties are still used to describe children at the lower end of the normal distribution. Gifted children, who would appear at the higher end of the distribution, are not considered as children with special educational needs. Children with difficulties in learning are described as having special educational needs. The categories for description of whether learning difficulties fall within the moderate, severe or profound category have changed over time as more and more children, who previously would be found in special schools are managing very successfully in mainstream schools. It must also be stated that IQ measures and other psychometric tests are open to interpretation, so the whole child must be considered.

Depending on which cognitive test is used by the educational psychologist, different descriptive categories will apply.

Learning disability is a descriptive diagnosis or concept; not a disease or illness. It does not infer a particular ideology and social functioning is an integral part of the diagnosis. It is important to understand that it is different from mental illness; a person with a learning disability can also develop mental illness. Learning disability as a concept is also different from learning difficulties which generally refer to specific learning problems rather than a global impairment of intellect and function.

TABLE 3.1 IQ RANGE GENERALLY USED TO IDENTIFY LEARNING DIFFICULTIES IN THE UK

IQ	Category	Educational term
50–70	Moderate or mild learning disability	Moderate learning difficulty (MLD)
20–49	Severe learning disability	Severe learning difficulty (SLD)*
Less than 20	Profound learning disability	Profound and multiple learning difficulty (PMLD)

* Some children with an uneven profile, whose overall IQ falls in the SLD category may be described as having MLD if some scores are higher.

TABLE 3.2 CLASSIFICATION OF GENERAL CONCEPTUAL ABILITY (GCA) SCORES IN THE BAS-II*

GCA Scores	Category
130 and above	Very high
120–129	High
110–119	Above average
90–109	Average
80–89	Below average
70–79	Low
69 and below	Very low

*British Ability Scales – Second Edition (BAS-II). Copyright © Colin D. Elliott, 1996. Reproduced by permission of GL Assessment Ltd.

TABLE 3.3 QUALITATIVE DESCRIPTIONS OF COMPOSITE SCORES IN THE WISC-IV*

Composite	Classification
130 and above	Very superior
120–129	Superior
110–119	High average
90–109	Average
80–89	Low average
70–79	Borderline
69 and below	Extremely low

*Wechsler Intelligence Scale for Children – Fourth Edition (WISC-IV). Copyright © NCS Pearson Inc., 2003. Reproduced with permission. All rights reserved.
'Wechsler Intelligence Scale for Children' and 'WISC' are trademarks, in the US and/or other countries, of Pearson Education, Inc. or its affliates(s).

Statistically the prevalence of individuals with an IQ of less than 70 should be 2.5 per cent. Actually, the prevalence of individuals with learning disabilities is 1–2 per cent because of:

- differential mortality (the more severe the degree of learning disability, the higher the mortality compared to the general population)
- diagnostic changes over time; not all cases are classified
- the role of functioning; those individuals with IQs of less than 70 but who have no problems functioning within their environment would not be defined as having a learning disability.

The prevalence of individuals with an IQ less than 50 is 0.35 per cent.

MODERATE LEARNING DIFFICULTY

Children with moderate learning difficulties (MLD), also sometimes described as global learning difficulties, have a general developmental delay. They have difficulties with learning across all areas of the school curriculum.

Children with moderate learning difficulties comprise the largest group of children with special educational needs in mainstream schools. Many of these children have a delay of over three years compared to their chronological age, and an IQ of less than 70. They need a high level of support in the mainstream classroom which will involve differentiation of the curriculum. Children with moderate learning difficulties may:

- have difficulties with comprehension
- need a high level of support with problem-solving activities or generating thinking
- have poor verbal and non-verbal reasoning skills
- have immature listening/attention skills which will affect their concentration
- have immature social skills
- have difficulties applying what they know to new or novel situations
- usually have a poor auditory and visual memory
- have difficulty acquiring basic literacy and numeracy skills
- have some motor co-ordination difficulties which will affect written skills
- rely on a teaching assistant, teacher or peers to direct them within the classroom situation.

Children with moderate learning difficulties may also suffer from low self-esteem and lack of motivation. In view of their failure at school, they may become resentful, refuse to attempt new work or perceive themselves as a failure even before a task begins. Generally, children with moderate learning difficulties require praise and encouragement to persuade them to adopt new strategies and to develop greater independence both in their learning and general skills.

SEVERE LEARNING DIFFICULTY

Children with severe learning difficulties (SLD) have a significant cognitive delay which has a major effect on their ability to access the school curriculum without support. Children with severe learning difficulties are likely to have problems with mobility and motor co-ordination, speech, language and communication and a delay in their self-help and independent skills. While many can hold simple conversations, others will need the use of signs, symbols or augmentative communication. Children with severe learning difficulties will need support in all areas of the curriculum. For much of their schooling, attainment will be in the upper P Scale range (P4–P8) of the national curriculum and IQs will generally measure between 20 and 49, but standardized assessments are often inappropriate for these children and functional, developmental or dynamic assessment are preferred methods of assessment.

There are children with severe learning difficulties within mainstream schools, particularly at the younger ages. The Special Educational Needs Co-ordinator (SENCo) will need to consider, together with parents and other professionals, the appropriateness of a mainstream place with regard to the efficient use of resources and the amount of time that a particular child might take up within a mainstream class, compared to other children. There are many schools which have special within school units. Some mainstream schools share a site with a specialist school where inclusion can then occur during the school day. The success of such a provision will be informed by monitoring the child's progress.

Clearly, most of these children will be working at levels typically of much younger children, whilst teachers need to ensure that activities are age appropriate. There is likely to be an emphasis on therapeutic input and the classroom needs to be organized to ensure that it is appropriate for a child who may have sensory or visual difficulties.

If a parent wishes their child to be educated in a mainstream school, then there is now specific legislation on this.

PROFOUND AND MULTIPLE LEARNING DIFFICULTIES

Children with profound and multiple learning difficulties (PMLD) require a high degree of supervision in their daily life because they are functioning at very early levels of development. Such children may have little or no spoken language, may be barely ambulant or non-ambulant and have difficulties in manipulating objects. They may be unable to feed, dress or toilet themselves independently. Most of these children will also have additional difficulties in physical, auditory or visual areas, including the functional use of these abilities.

Most of these children are operating at the very early stages of the P Scales, usually between P1 and P4. These children will usually be in special schools, which have developed multi-sensory environments. However, with the advent of information technology, emphasis is gradually moving from sensory environments and relaxation to new pedagogic approaches, as switch technology now allows these children to interact, be stimulated and feedback their responses to adults, enabling them to exercise a degree of control over their environment and experiences.

SPECIFIC LEARNING DIFFICULTY

Specific learning difficulty (SpLD) covers a number of difficulties and is used to describe dyslexia, dysgraphia, dyscalculia and, even, dyspraxia. There are also terms such as specific memory loss or specific comprehension difficulty which have also been described in the literature under the umbrella of SpLD.

Dyslexia

Dyslexia is a specific learning difficulty that affects the ability to read and spell. The controversy about the definition of dyslexia rumbles on. Dyslexia affects children across all levels of intellectual ability, usually more boys than girls and it often runs in families. It is a complex neurological disorder which can cause difficulties with general literacy skills, word interpretation and perception, basic maths, organizational skills, short-term memory, sequencing and processing information. However, children with dyslexia are often found to be quite creative in certain areas of the curriculum and can be good at technology, art and drama and lateral thinking.

Typical characteristics of a dyslexic child are:

- literacy and numeracy levels are well below their chronological age
- spelling levels are well below their chronological age
- bizarre spellings
- poor phonological awareness
- frequent loss of place when reading
- complaints of distorted or blurred word shapes
- confusion of high frequency words
- poor sequencing of letters, reversal of letters/numbers

- substitution of words in speech
- difficulty in organizing themselves and their belongings
- inability to remember simple sequences; such as days of the week, months of the year
- problems following oral instructions
- poor sense of time and direction
- errors when copying from the board or other pieces of paper
- co-ordination difficulties
- secondary emotional or behavioural difficulties due to low self-esteem and lack of motivation.

Dyslexia tends to be resistant to conventional teaching methods, but appropriately targeted specific interventions, the application of information technology (IT) and supportive counselling have all been found to be helpful in mitigating the effects of dyslexia.

Dysgraphia

Dysgraphia is defined as a difficulty in automatically remembering and mastering the sequence of muscle motor movements needed in writing letters or numbers. It is not linked to the child's intelligence or type of teaching. It exists in varying degrees, ranging from mild to moderate. It can be diagnosed and it can be overcome if appropriate remedial strategies are taught well and conscientiously carried out. Whilst it may occasionally exist alone, it is most commonly related to other learning problems.

Dysgraphia:

- is a processing problem
- causes writing fatigue
- interferes with communication of ideas in writing
- contributes to poor organization on the line and on the page.

Dyscalculia

Dyscalculia is defined as a difficulty with calculations and with rapid processing of maths.

Disabilities with mathematical areas are as complex as those associated with reading. They may also be dependent on reading abilities. A difficulty with mathematics may be due to an individual's ability to process language, or may be related to visual spatial confusion.

Dyscalculic learners lack an intuitive grasp of numbers and even if they produce a correct answer or use a correct method, they may do so mechanically without confidence.

Dyspraxia or developmental co-ordination disorder

Dyspraxia is also referred to as a specific learning difficulty. Children with dyspraxia have problems with motor co-ordination and can appear clumsy when moving around the classroom or playground. They will have perceptual motor problems and find writing and using scissors difficult. Children may suffer from oral or motor dyspraxia. In oral dyspraxia, they may also have pronunciation difficulties caused by problems in controlling oral movements and the tongue. Developmental dyspraxia is suspected when it is obvious that the difficulties are not due to a medical condition. Most diagnoses are made by paediatricians or other healthcare professionals, such as occupational therapists.

Depending on their age, children with dyspraxia may demonstrate:

- clumsy behaviour, e.g. bumping into objects or falling over
- very high levels of motor activity, including feet swinging and tapping, hand clapping and inability to sit still
- high levels of excitability
- avoidance of constructional toys, such as jigsaws or bricks
- poor fine motor skills; immature drawings
- difficulty in judging distances, so they find ball games hard and may bump into other children
- slowness when dressing, e.g. inability to tie shoe-laces, do buttons
- difficulties when changing speed and direction without tripping over
- no sense of danger
- general lack of co-ordination
- difficulty in riding a bike
- immature use of writing equipment
- uncertain hand dominance
- difficulty in producing some speech sounds and inability to communicate their ideas easily (oral dyspraxia)
- difficulty with organizational skills
- limited concentration; tasks left unfinished
- aggressiveness or rough play because they have difficulty controlling their movements
- poor social interactions and difficulties making friends
- sensitivity to sensory stimulation, including high level of noise, tactile defensiveness, wearing new clothes.

Cognition and learning will be a focus for most teachers when teaching children with a variety of special educational needs. In some of the more well-researched syndromes, there will be known patterns of learning needs which can be planned for and addressed. Some of the learning difficulties associated with the more well-known conditions are given below as examples. This is by no means an exhaustive list.

AUTISTIC SPECTRUM DISORDER (ASD)

Children on the autistic spectrum who display the triad of impairments, also display underlying patterns of cognitive or learning difficulties such as:

- inflexibility of thinking/rigidity
- poor imagination
- lack of generalization
- showing isolated skills (islets of ability which do not represent pockets of normal development but are often, themselves, the product of a deficit)
- problems processing information
- thinking skills which do not follow a hierarchical pattern
- problems understanding cause and effect learning
- classifying and storing learnt factual information in a manner that cannot be retrieved in a new situation
- random idiosyncratic learning patterns
- lack of choosing between options.

DOWN'S SYNDROME

Children with Down's syndrome may:

- be strong visual learners but poor auditory learners
- have difficulties with short-term auditory memory and auditory processing
- have problems with consolidation, retention, generalization and transfer of skills
- have a tendency to avoidance strategies.

FRAGILE X SYNDROME

Children with Fragile X syndrome may:

- repeat words and phrases, or the last words in a sentence, over and over

- fail to respond to direct questions
- give answers not obviously related to the question
- speak in rapid bursts
- have poor fine and gross motor co-ordination
- dislike work based on writing
- find large, noisy, unstructured group times distressing
- find it easier to learn in the morning, after a settling-in period
- become distressed by eye contact, touch, questioning in front of others
- react badly to pressures of time
- be oversensitive to relatively minor upsets and/or have disruptive outbursts
- prefer practical, physical activities
- have slight motor co-ordination problems
- enjoy repetitive tasks, which may have a calming effect.

CEREBRAL PALSY

Cerebral palsy (CP) simply means that there has been some injury to the brain during development which has resulted in difficulty transmitting the necessary impulses from the brain to the muscles for co-ordinated movement. Many children born prematurely will develop some movement difficulties relating to early neurological injury. Most mild motor abnormalities noticeable during the first few months of life will improve and may completely resolve with time. When motor impairment persists, a diagnosis of cerebral palsy may be considered. For a diagnosis of cerebral palsy, the following are necessary:

- movement of muscles has to be adversely affected
- the motor impairment has to be due to a neurological injury
- the injury or lesion must be static (not getting worse, but no longer resolving)
- the injury has to occur whilst the motor system is still developing (usually before, during or immediately after birth)
- the impairment in movement does not resolve with time.

Cerebral palsy comes in a variety of different forms and with a continuum of severity. It can be so mild that it is only noticeable when the individual is stressed or is involved in certain activities, but it can be so severe as to limit most voluntary movement. It may take several years for the full impact of a child's cerebral palsy to become apparent. The motor impairment from a neurological cause is often associated with later learning difficulties. The most likely reason for this association is that early motor signs are indications that there has been early neurological damage to the part of the brain that is involved in movement and where there is such damage, there is greater likelihood of additional damage that may go undetected in the early years. Cerebral palsy is one aspect of neurological damage which may occur in many other conditions.

The types of cognition and learning difficulties associated with cerebral palsy which may be seen in the classroom are problems with executive functioning. This is a term used to describe a set of mental processes that helps to connect past experience with present action. Executive functions are higher order processes that enable individuals to plan, sequence, initiate and sustain their behaviour towards some goal, incorporating feedback and making adjustments along the way. Executive functioning is also particularly associated with neuro-behavioural conditions such as attention deficit hyperactivity disorder (ADHD), obsessive compulsive disorder (OCD) and depression.

In summary, whatever the cause, whether through general delay or as a result of more specific difficulties, known syndromes or behavioural conditions, the child's special educational needs will impact significantly on their cognition and learning and, consequently, their ability to access a school curriculum.

CHAPTER 4

Behaviour, Emotional and Social Development

Children should be recorded as having a behaviour, emotional and social difficulty (BESD) if it is their primary or secondary special educational need and they are at School Action Plus or have a Statement. (Until recently the term emotional and behavioural difficulties – EBD – was widely used.) BESD covers the full range of ability, and encompasses a number of diagnostic categories. These children's behaviours and emotions may present barriers to learning, despite effective school behavioural policies and management, in an otherwise effective pastoral and social curriculum. Children may be withdrawn or isolated, destructive or disturbing, hyperactive or lack concentration. They may have immature social skills or present with challenging behaviours. Children may be diagnosed with conduct disorders, such as oppositional defiant disorder (ODD), attention deficit hyperactivity disorder (ADHD or ADD), syndromes such as Tourette's syndrome, eating disorders, depression or attachment disorders. There is obviously a crossover between these groups of children and others, particularly with children on the autistic spectrum whose behaviour can also be challenging because of emotional and behavioural difficulties.

It is known that children with identified special educational needs are more than nine times as likely to be permanently excluded from schools than other children and they are more than three times as likely to be persistently absent. Many children with special educational needs fail in school due to a lack of understanding which could result in them being labelled as 'badly behaved'.

The category of BESD is probably the most relative and interactional of all the special educational needs categories identified. It may be difficult to define the severity as behaviour may vary in different environments and with respect to individuals. In most situations, the behaviour is a result of stress perceived by the child. The child will often exhibit a 'fight or flight' response, either becoming fearful, withdrawn or exhibiting aggressive, anti-social and disruptive behaviour. Children are usually identified as having BESD if their behaviour:

- is not age appropriate
- results in isolation from peers
- negatively affects the classroom/learning environment
- places unreasonable demands on teaching staff
- leads to negative self-concept and low self-esteem
- restricts learning opportunities (both for the child concerned and others in the class/school)
- creates dangerous situations.

Many strategies will already have been tried, but, for whatever reason, have failed to reduce or eliminate the behaviour and, in some cases, inadvertently, the strategies may even have exacerbated the behaviour. In some cases, the environment, itself, may be causing the stress in the first place, perhaps because it cannot offer calm or stress-free surroundings. Sometimes, it is the interaction between the child and the environment that is a problem, perhaps because inappropriate or excessive demands are being made. A change of teaching arrangements and/or teaching environment may be necessary.

The concept of 'emotional intelligence' is now frequently seen in psychological reports and there are now some standardized tests that yield an emotional intelligence (EQ) score. Emotional intelligence is a person's ability to manage in the following domains:

1. knowing one's emotions – self-awareness and recognizing a feeling as it happens (this is a keystone to EQ)
2. managing emotions and handling feelings
3. motivating oneself and emotional self-control
4. recognizing relationships – social competence and incompetence which include specific skills involved which will underpin popularity, leadership and interpersonal effectiveness; all necessary qualities for interacting with groups in school.

Emotional intelligence will have a profound impact on both children and teachers who are managing classrooms. Emotional literacy which is the ability to identify and communicate feelings is the starting point for many of the interventions for children with BESD. These approaches have their roots in therapeutic interventions which often provide the necessary supportive framework within schools.

CHAPTER 5

Sensory and Physical Needs

HEARING IMPAIRMENT

Hearing impairment is the preferred educational term. 'The term "deaf" means all types and levels of deafness, including unilateral deafness and temporary deafness such as glue ear' (National Deaf Children's Society).

- Mild deafness – This can cause difficulty following speech, mainly in noisy situations. The quietest sounds that can be heard are 25 to 39 decibels.

- Moderate deafness – Children with moderate deafness may have difficulties following speech without a hearing aid. The quietest sounds they can hear are 40 to 60 decibels.

- Severe deafness – Children with severe deafness rely heavily on lip-reading, even with a hearing aid. The quietest sounds they can hear are 70–94 decibels. British Sign Language (BSL) may be their first, or preferred, language and they may prefer to describe themselves as deaf to emphasize their deaf identity as they consider themselves as part of the deaf community.

- Profound deafness – The quieter sounds that profoundly deaf children can hear average 95 decibels or more and BSL may also be their first or preferred language, together with lip-reading.

Definitions courtesy of Royal National Institute for the Deaf (RNID).

There are also children described as deafblind, who may have some hearing and vision, whilst others may be totally deaf and totally blind. There are other ear problems which may have an effect on schooling, including glue ear, perforated ear drums and tinnitus. Whilst these, in themselves, would not be a reason for a Statement of special educational needs, they may add to an already complex picture and so should be mentioned.

Hearing loss is assessed in terms of the average threshold over three frequencies for the better ear.

There are two types of hearing loss. The most common is a *conductive hearing loss* which is caused by anything which impedes the passage of sounds down the canal to the tympanum and mechanical transmissions by the oscicles across to the inner ear. In its most minor and transient form it can be caused by a build up of wax, which is easily syringed out; a heavy cold may block the ear or even a change in altitude. Mild hearing losses include glue ear. *Sensorineural hearing loss* is caused by damage to the nerves in the inner ear or damage to some other part of the auditory pathway, possibly in the brain itself, so-called central deafness. Childhood illnesses, of which the most common is meningitis, can cause this hearing loss. Other causes include birth complications or infections during pregnancy, such as mumps or measles (rubella). Some children who can detect sound normally cannot make sense of what they hear.

Most types of conductive loss can be treated, but the same is not true of sensorineural hearing loss, although cochlear implants may now be used. Sometimes the hearing loss is made up of two components, part conductive and part sensorineural and this is referred to as mixed hearing loss. Conductive hearing loss is never greater than 60 decibels, whilst sensorineural loss can range from slight to virtually total loss. In order to give some sort of idea of loudness of sound, the following table can be used:

0 decibels	Quietest sound heard by a young adult
30 decibels	Barely audible speech
65 decibels	Normal conversation at 1 metre
80 decibels	Shouting or orchestra playing
90 decibels	Damagingly loud
100 decibels	Very loud disco
120 decibels	Aeroplane at close quarters

Reproduced by permission of the National Deaf Children's Society (NDCS).

VISUAL IMPAIRMENT

Visual impairment is the preferred educational term, as it refers to all degrees of reduction in vision. However, the terms blind, partially-sighted, educationally blind and low vision are also used. Surprisingly, there is no agreed definition of sight problems amongst children. Terms such as 'sight problem' and 'visual disability' have been used to mean different things in different studies and contexts. Local Authority data from visual impairment advisory services also vary and individual services have their own criteria for deciding whether or not a child with sight difficulties will be included on their case load. This means the definition of a child as visually impaired, i.e. receiving support from a specialist teacher of the visually impaired, may be more prevalent in some authorities than others. In addition, some teachers are not keen to use rigid criteria, because individual children vary so much in their visual functioning. Proportionately, more children with severe sight problems and blindness now have additional, often very complex, disabilities and very premature and low birth-weight babies are at particular risk of severe sight problems and blindness.

A person is legally blind (sometimes called 20/200) when, with the best correction of vision, they can see at 6.096 metres (20 feet) what a normally sighted person can see at 60.96 metres (200 feet). A person is described as 'partially-sighted' or having 'low vision' if they have enough vision to read large print. Judgements are made according to performance on sight tests and can be described in the following three categories:

- Very low visual acuity, where a person cannot see things clearly or cannot see details.

- Severely restricted visual field, because the person does not have a full range of sight, e.g. there may be severely reduced side-vision and the person cannot see without moving their head.

- A combination of loss of both visual acuity and field.

A child who, though not necessarily without sight, but who needs to be primarily educated by non-sighted methods, using tactile and auditory means, or a child who uses Braille, is often described as 'educationally blind' (sometimes described as functionally blind), although this term is often used for adults rather than children where there is a preference for the term visually impaired.

Low vision can be described as severely impaired vision, which, nevertheless, allows vision to be used as a channel for receiving information. A child with low vision may be able to use it effectively in the near environment with appropriate lighting, position and low vision aids, such as magnifiers. They may also use Braille.

Although there is no statutory definition of partial sight, these are children who, nevertheless, have problems learning by the virtue of their visual impairment and require special provision during education. Within the educational context, partial sightedness is generally used to mean children who have vision useful for all school tasks but who require adaptations to teaching methods and materials, e.g. producing worksheets in larger fonts.

There are other forms of blindness, such as cortical blindness, which refers to a brain condition, not an eye condition, but which results from damage to the visual systems in the brain that deals with processing and integrating visual information. Cortical blindness can be a temporary or a permanent impairment and can range from severe visual impairment to total blindness. Because cortical blindness is a neurological impairment, vision is more severely reduced than can be explained by an eye examination. Cortical blindness is also referred to as cortical visual impairment, cerebral blindness, central visual disturbance and cerebral visual impairment.

PHYSICAL IMPAIRMENT

There are many physical difficulties, the main one being cerebral palsy, which has already been mentioned. In addition the following conditions may be included in this category:

1. Juvenile chronic arthritis has an unknown cause but it is thought that the inflammation of the joints and sometimes other parts of the body is caused by abnormal antibodies in the blood.

2. Brittle bones is usually an inherited condition, resulting from an abnormality in the protein structure of the bones which causes them to break easily.

3. Muscular dystrophy is a progressive weakness of all the muscles due to muscle fibre being replaced by fat and fibrous tissue. This degenerative change is technically known as dystrophy.

4. Duchenne muscular dystrophy only affects boys and most will be in a wheelchair before their teens with limited life expectancy.

5. Spina bifida affects the spinal cord and the physical consequences will depend on the spinal level of the lesion and the amount of damage to the spinal cord. This may involve paralysis of the trunk and lower limbs, partial paralysis, loss of sensation and incontinence.

6. Hydrocephalus often occurs in conjunction with spina bifida and, as such, the child will have more learning difficulties than if spina bifida occurs alone. This is where circulation of cerebral-spinal fluid through the brain is hindered by the malformation at the base of the brain. The ventricles from within the brain become distended and would eventually compress cells and nerve fibres. The result, if not corrected quickly after birth, is mental disability and sometimes spastic paralysis of the lower limbs and epilepsy. It is possible to drain off the excess fluid into the blood stream by inserting a 'shunt', but there are lots of problems associated with the actual shunt itself.

7. Spinal injuries consisting of damage to the spine can occur as a result of a trauma, e.g. a road accident or a sports injury and also an infection.

8. Associated with motor impairments are often hidden difficulties which may also impact on educational progress. These include asthma, diabetes, epilepsy, heart conditions, hearing impairment, speech and language difficulties and visual difficulties.

The types of movement disorders range from:

1. **Spasticity** meaning 'stiff'. This is where the limb muscle is tight and with sudden movements or stretching, the muscle strongly contracts. This can result in deformities of the limbs, pelvis and spine as the child grows. The child has to work hard to walk and move.

2. **Athetosis** is where the limbs make involuntary purposeless movements because the muscle tone changes rapidly from floppy and loose to tense and still in a way the child cannot control, but the muscles are normal and not spastic.

3. **Ataxia** is a loss of voluntary muscle control, resulting in a lack of balance and co-ordination in the whole body. It will also affect spatial awareness and the judgement of the body position relative to other things around the child.

4. **Tremor** is a shakiness in the limb involved which is increased when an attempt is made to use that limb.

5. **Mixed** movement disorders are when children have all four limbs affected and have both spasticity and athetosis.

Limb involvements

1. Monoplegia: one limb.

2. Hemiplegia: upper and lower limb of the same side.

3. Paraplegia: lower limbs only.

4. Diplegia: major involvement of lower limbs; upper limbs less involved.

5. Triplegia: three limbs involved, one upper and both lower.

6. Quadriplegia: major involvement of all four limbs.

CHAPTER 6

Complex Needs

Complex needs (sometimes used interchangeably with the description of multiple needs) usually defines a group of children with multiple needs (more than one) that are inter-related or inter-connected. Needs may vary from profound to moderate, but the defining feature is that the end presentation will transcend several different areas of need providing quite a challenge to an educator. Children with complex needs will have to negotiate a number of different issues in their life, and each child will have a unique interaction of strengths and weaknesses, requiring a personalized and individualized response from different educational, therapeutic and social services. Thus, in addition to looking at the complexity of special educational needs, children who fall into this category of having complex needs are those who span different departments in a Local Authority because of their social and emotional needs. The Common Assessment Framework, which was introduced as part of the Every Child Matters Programme, was intended to co-ordinate early assessments of children with less significant needs who would benefit from short-term targeted intervention in a preventative fashion, but whose difficulties would fall short of thresholds of specialist services. However, children with complex special educational needs, frequently with their health needs arising from clinical diagnoses, are still falling through the net because of the lack of integrated services, although some Local Authorities are moving towards the development of integrated assessment frameworks to address this problem.

There are a number of genetic syndromes that will come under the heading of complex needs. The following are examples to highlight the complexity of difficulty which may be encountered in schools today.

RETT SYNDROME

Rett syndrome was first identified in 1966 but Dr Andreas Rett. The condition went largely unnoticed until 1983. This condition is complex and challenging and, so far, has only been diagnosed in girls. The cause is currently thought to be an unpredicted development of a fault in a gene in the X chromosome. The girl usually reaches broadly typical milestones of development for about the first year of life until reaching a sudden stop. A period of regression follows, during which she appears to lose many of her previously acquired skills. After this period of regression, which may last for a few days or many months, the girl exhibits profound and multiple learning difficulties which will remain throughout her life. Stereotypical hand movements develop, such as hand clapping, patting or wringing and physical difficulties will emerge which will become evident as she grows. Some girls may walk with a broad-based gait, others may never walk and others may develop scoliosis and some suffer from epilepsy. A child like this will have needs in many different areas, such as sensory perceptual difficulties and/or physical difficulties and will require a range of therapeutic intervention. Girls with Rett syndrome are an example of a child with complex needs (for more details, refer to the Rett Syndrome Association UK website).

WILLIAMS SYNDROME

Williams syndrome was first recognized as a distinct entity in 1961. It is present at birth and affects males and females equally. It can occur in all ethnic groups and has been identified in countries throughout the world. It is a rare genetic condition (estimated to occur in 1 in 7500 births) which cause medical and developmental problems. Children with Williams syndrome share similar facial features which can become more apparent with age. The majority have some type of heart or blood vessel problem and some have elevations in their blood calcium level. Adult stature is slightly smaller than average and there is a slow weight gain. Many young children have feeding problems, although these tend to resolve as the child grows older. Children have sensitive hearing and often have low muscle tone and lax joints. Children with Williams syndrome have a very social personality, perhaps excessively so, and have a unique strength in their expressive language skills, compared to developmental delayed milestones in other areas. Distractibility is a common problem (for more details, refer to the Williams Syndrome Association UK website).

PRADER–WILLI SYNDROME

Prader–Willi syndrome is a complex genetic disorder present from birth. The main characteristics are excessive appetite, low muscle tone, emotional instability, immature physical development and learning disabilities which can sometimes be very mild. Children with Prader–Willi syndrome are complex children who present a challenge in school and, in particular, with respect to their overeating behaviour which can lead to behavioural difficulties and psychological needs. The complex medical, nutritional, psychological, educational, social and therapeutic needs of children with Prader–Willi syndrome require an integrated approach (for more details, refer to the Prader–Willi Syndrome Association UK website).

ANGELMAN SYNDROME

Angelman syndrome was described by Dr Harry Angelman in 1965, based on three children with characteristics now known as Angelman syndrome. Angelman syndrome is not usually recognized at birth or in infancy as developmental problems are non-specific during this time. The most common age of diagnosis is between 3 and 7 years, when the behaviours and features become most evident. All children with Angelman syndrome have developmental delay which is functionally severe. They will have no or minimal use of words with receptive and non-verbal communication skills higher than verbal ones. Usually the child has a movement or balance disorder, ataxia of gait and tremulous movement of limbs. The child with Angelman syndrome has behavioural uniqueness, consisting of any combination of frequent laughter/smiling, an apparent happy demeanour, easily excitable personality often with hand-flapping movements, hypermotoric behaviour and short attention span (these behaviours are the reason that this syndrome has been termed the Happy Puppet Syndrome). There are other clinical features associated with Angelman syndrome, including distinct facial features and seizures. Again, the medical and development problems, coupled with hyperactivity and personality traits make this syndrome complex in terms of meeting needs (for more details, refer to the Angelman Syndrome Support Education and Research Trust (ASSERT) website).

These are only examples of the types of complex needs which are found in children. There are many others which make schooling a very challenging area.

CHAPTER 7

Medical Needs
and School Trips

The Code of Practice, paragraphs 7:64–7:66, sets out that a medical diagnosis or disability does not necessarily imply special educational needs. However, some children may have medical conditions which, if not properly managed, could limit their access to education. Medical conditions may have a significant impact on a child's education and, in particular, the way they function in school, e.g. medical conditions may affect the child's cognitive or physical abilities, behavioural or emotional state. There may also be an indirect impact, perhaps through missing school as a result of treatments in hospital or through chronic illness. In addition, the effects of a medical condition may be intermittent, but the impact of this may also affect access to the curriculum. Changes in the individual child and changes in the peer group; such as the onset of puberty, may also necessitate the school looking at curricular demands.

For some children with medical needs, support will be required so they can attend school regularly and participate in school activities. Other children may be unable to attend school because of their medical condition, and where this occurs, arrangements should be put in place by Local Authorities to ensure continuation of their education.

There is no legal duty which requires school staff to administer medication. This is a voluntary role, but clearly, staff who do volunteer to administer medication require support from the head teacher and parents. They require access to information and training and reassurance about their legal liability. Guidance has been issued by the Department for Children, Schools and Families, so that schools can draw up policies on managing medication and supporting individual children with medical needs.

Whereas in a maintained school, the Local Authority is responsible for all health and safety matters, this may be more of a grey area in a non-maintained school, and it would be worthwhile finding out who has the ultimate responsibility or authority if things go wrong.

The school should have a policy for ensuring that children with medical needs receive proper care and support. A copy of the policy should be available on request. It should set out whether the head accepts responsibility, circumstances in which children may take non-prescription medication, the school's policy of assisting children with long-term or complex medical needs, the need for a prior written agreement from parents for any medication prescribed, or non-prescription drugs to be given to a child, the policy on children carrying and taking their medication themselves, staff training, record keeping, storage and access to medication and the school's emergency procedures. A healthcare plan should be drawn up jointly by the school, parents, health professionals and, if possible, the child. It may be necessary to carry out a risk assessment for first aid provision and the management of medical conditions.

COMMON MEDICAL CONDITIONS

The most common medical conditions which cause concerns in schools are listed.

Asthma

Children with asthma have airways which narrow as a reaction to various triggers. The triggers may vary and children will be aware of their own triggers. Exercise and stress can precipitate asthma attacks and the narrowing or obstruction of the airways causes difficulty in breathing and can be alleviated with treatment. About 1 in 11 children has asthma diagnosed at some time, and, on average, there are two children in every classroom in the UK with asthma. Most children with asthma will relieve their symptoms with medication using an inhaler and most will have charge of their own inhaler from an early age. In a few severe cases, children may use an electrically-powered nebulizer to deliver their asthma medication. Children with asthma must have immediate access to their inhalers when they need them. Every 16 minutes, a child is admitted to hospital in the UK because of their asthma. Parents must ask that children be allowed to carry their inhalers with them, and if the child is too young or immature to take personal responsibility, staff should ensure that it is stored in a safe but accessible place and marked with the child's name. Inhalers must also be available during PE, sports activities and school trips. Parents should provide schools with a spare inhaler in case the inhaler is accidentally left at home or runs out.

A child's healthcare plan should identify the severity of their asthma, individual symptoms, any particular triggers; such as exercise or cold air, and their treatment.

QUESTIONS TO ASK ABOUT ASTHMA

1. How will the child access their inhaler? A total of 43 per cent of children with asthma have stated that within the last month, their asthma prevented them from doing everyday activities.

2. Where will it be kept?

3. How will the inhaler be available during PE, sports and school trips?

4. Is the school aware of potential triggers for asthma; such as the use of chemicals, keeping furry animals, etc.? Is there a place for the child to go if the room is full of fumes, e.g. in science or art?

5. Is the healthcare plan updated regularly and are triggers and treatment identified?

6. Does the school have a policy on the use of inhalers?

7. Is the school aware of the school policy guidelines published by Asthma UK?

8. Is the school aware that one in ten children with asthma state that they have been bullied because of their asthma?

Information courtesy of Asthma UK. Correct as of May 2009.

Epilepsy

Around 1 in 130 children in the UK has epilepsy and about 80 per cent of them attend mainstream schools. Not all children with epilepsy experience major seizures (also known as fits). The nature, frequency and severity of seizures will vary greatly from child to child. Some children can exhibit strange or confused behaviour, experience strange sensations, e.g. a funny taste, jerking (convulsions) and/or loss of consciousness. Parents need to inform the school what type of seizures their child has and the manifestations. Seizures are described by which part(s) of the brain the epileptic activity starts in. There are two main types:

1. Partial seizures

   • Partial seizures involve epileptic activity in just part of the brain. In simple partial seizures, the child is fully conscious and is aware of their surroundings, whilst in complex partial seizures the child partly loses consciousness and is not aware of what they are doing. They may not remember the seizure.

   • Secondary generalized seizures (sometimes a partial seizure can spread to the rest of the brain, and become generalized).

2. General seizures
   - Generalized seizures involve epileptic activity in both halves of the brain and can happen without warning. The child loses consciousness during a seizure.
   - Absence seizures are also a type of general seizure. These are hard to spot so some further information on this type is given below.

ABSENCE SEIZURES

Absence seizures mainly occur in childhood. During an absence, the child gives the appearance of daydreaming or shutting off. The child loses consciousness, usually for less than 10 seconds, and is unaware of what is happening around them. As most children tend to daydream at times, absences can be very hard to spot, especially in classrooms. However, some children can be having hundreds of absences a day. These children are missing out on tiny pieces of information, e.g. they might hear the first part of a sentence but not the end. They may hear the instructions to go out and play, but not when to come back. In some cases, if they do not do what is expected of them, this can be mistaken for bad behaviour. Parents and teachers may lose patience with children if they don't realize that they are, in fact, having a seizure. If such seizures are suspected, it is important to keep some kind of diary, if possible, to monitor the frequency. About one-third of all children with absence seizures has problems with learning or behaviour.

The symptoms of epilepsy for most children are well controlled with medication, but sometimes this causes drowsiness. For some children, triggers can be stress, over-excitement, boredom or lack of sleep. Others have to avoid flashing or flickering lights or video games with certain computer graphics, geometric shapes or patterns. Parents need to inform the school what are the likely triggers so that action can be taken to minimize them, e.g. using different methods of lighting.

Epilepsy occurs in a number of syndromes, such as Angelman syndrome. It is also a defining feature in rare conditions; such as Landau–Kleffner syndrome (LKS), which is an age-related epilepsy syndrome of childhood, characterized by a loss of speech and language skills with seizures. It has an overlap with a rare condition called electrical status epilepticus of slow wave sleep.

Some children have severe forms of epilepsy, which are difficult to control with drugs and they continue to have seizures. These children may well be in specialist schools or residential placements. They may have identified syndromes which will raise complex issues to do with learning and communication as well as the epilepsy.

QUESTIONS TO ASK ABOUT EPILEPSY

1. Has the school had any previous experience of children with epilepsy? Has the school received any awareness training? Does the school have a written policy on epilepsy (the school nurse will be able to help with this and, perhaps, produce one if there isn't one)? There should be a healthcare plan drawn up.

2. Does the teacher feel confident in their knowledge of epilepsy? If not, training should be updated about epilepsy in general and the specific aspects of the child's epilepsy.

3. Who will administer emergency medication, if relevant, such as rectal diazepam? Are they properly trained and willing to give the drug? If a seizure diary needs to be kept, who will do this?

4. Epilepsy can cause problems with memory, communication, learning and behaviour. The anti-epileptic drugs taken to help control seizures can also affect behaviour and may have side-effects; such as dizziness or drowsiness. Ask whether there is a facility for a suitable rest period, if necessary.

5. Ask how other children are educated about epilepsy. This will avoid bullying and also make sure that the child is looked out for, particularly if they are not good at recognizing their own symptoms.

6. Most children with epilepsy can participate in the same activities as other children. However, epilepsy is a condition that is covered by the Disability Discrimination Act, even if a child's seizures are controlled with medication. Therefore, the school must make every effort to ensure full access to education including extra-curricular activities. Ask how that will occur.

7. The swimming teacher and life guard must have a full understanding of the child's epilepsy so they can quickly identify if the child needs help in the water. Does the school use the 'buddy system' which pairs children up so that everyone has someone to look out for them in the water? This could help the child with epilepsy feel they are not being over-protected and increase everyone's safety.

8. Certain lessons may have safety issues for all children, but some children with epilepsy may require additional safety measures. Ask, particularly, about equipment in the following areas:

   - science
   - food technology
   - design and technology
   - sports and PE
   - contact sport (it may not be advisable for the child to play contact sports if their epilepsy was originally the consequence of a head injury)

- swimming
- water sports
- cycling
- horse-riding
- climbing and hiking (heights may be a danger to children with epilepsy and climbing may be dangerous to a child whose seizures are not controlled).

9. If there are out-of-school activities and visits, there may be extra considerations and adjustments to make. Ask how risk assessments are carried out and what action would be taken in an emergency. If a member of staff, trained in first-aid or administering medication, is not available for an out-of-school visit, the school must make alternative arrangements. This may mean training extra members of staff or including other people on the trips; such as the school nurse or a parent.

10. If the child has transport to and from school, e.g. on a school bus, does the Local Authority provide properly trained drivers and escorts? This may mean an escort will need to receive training in first-aid for seizures or how to give emergency medicine.

11. Residential visits. Some children with epilepsy have seizures at night. Excitement, fatigue and irregular eating or sleeping patterns may trigger a seizure. Medicines normally taken outside school hours may need to be administered. Ask how a residential trip will be managed.

12. Around 5 per cent of children with epilepsy are photo-sensitive and may be affected by flickering lights or patterns. Flashing lights or strobes, as in a disco or in some theatre shows or films, may trigger a seizure. Schools will need to check to see if the theatre/cinema/disco will use flashing light effects beforehand. Ask what plans are in place to ensure this will occur.

13. Many children with epilepsy are likely also to have special educational needs. Ask how teachers will try to make the most use of 'good periods' if the child has frequent absence seizures in school.

14. If the child has absence seizures, which may result in difficulty in keeping track of activities or instructions in the classroom, ask if teachers can provide written instructions to fill in the gaps or ask how a teaching assistant will be used to help the child in the classroom.

15. Problems with short-term and long-term memory may result in homework being forgotten. Ask the teacher how homework is going to be provided (perhaps by emailing parents).

Diabetes

Diabetes is a condition where the child's normal hormonal mechanisms do not control their blood sugar levels. About 1 in 700 school-age children has diabetes. Children with diabetes normally need to have daily insulin injections to monitor their blood glucose level and to eat regularly.

QUESTIONS TO ASK ABOUT DIABETES

1. If the child can give their own injections, they will need supervision and also a suitable private place to carry this out. Ask how this will be made available.

2. The child will need to monitor their blood glucose levels, using a testing machine, at regular intervals. They may need to do this during the lunch-break or more regularly if their insulin needs adjusting. Again, can the school provide a suitable place?

3. Children with diabetes must be allowed to eat regularly during the day; this may include eating snacks during class time or prior to exercise. What arrangements are needed, particularly if the school has staggered lunch-times? If a meal or a snack is missed, or after strenuous activity, the child may experience a hypoglycaemic episode (hypo) during which the blood sugar levels fall to too low levels. How will the PE/games teachers be made aware of the need for the child with diabetes to have glucose tablets or a sugary drink to hand?

4. The school must be aware of the symptoms that could be indicators of a 'hypo' in the child, which could include hunger, sweating, drowsiness, pallor, glazed eyes, shaking, lack of concentration, headache, irritability or mood changes such as angry or aggressive behaviour. The school must know what to administer immediately and also after recovery and to know whether to call an ambulance. Who will be responsible for ensuring this occurs? Does the child have a diabetes record card? Is there a healthcare plan drawn up?

5. Children may have a greater than usual need to go to the toilet or have a drink. Schools should watch for these symptoms, including tiredness and weight-loss which may indicate poor diabetic control and alert parents of these signs. Who will do this?

6. If there are residential trips, what arrangements will be made to ensure the child can take part?

Anaphylaxis*

Anaphylaxis is an extreme allergic reaction requiring urgent medical treatment. Children with such severe allergies are aware of them from a very early age and know what they can/cannot eat and drink. The most common cause is food; in particular nuts, fish and dairy products, but wasp and bee stings can also cause allergic reactions. The condition can be life-threatening, but it can be treated with medication. For further information, refer to the Anaphylaxis Campaign website (www.anaphylaxis.org.uk) which contains guidelines for schools.

QUESTIONS TO ASK ABOUT ANAPHYLAXIS

1. Children are normally prescribed a device for injecting adrenalin – which looks like a fountain pen (called an EpiPen) and is pre-loaded with the correct dose of adrenalin. Ask who would be trained to give the injections.

2. The timing of the injection may be crucial. Is this clear in the healthcare plan? Are suitable procedures in place, so that swift action can be taken in an emergency? Has training of staff taken place (this must occur before the child enters the school)?

3. Is there a suitable safe, yet accessible, place for storage and how will all staff be aware of the condition and who will be responsible for administering the emergency treatment?

4. Many schools are now nut-free zones and are aware of the importance of ensuring that a child does not come into contact with the allergen. This should be discussed with the school and parents should bear in mind the risk at break and lunch-times, cookery, food technology and science lessons and outdoor activities or school trips. What arrangements will be in place during breaktime and lesson time to avoid contact?

5. What are the arrangements for day and residential trips?

These medical conditions, of course, do not cover the whole range found in mainstream or special schools, but are a flavour of those most commonly found in schools.

---

* Information provided by The Anaphylaxis Campaign, the only UK charity to exclusively meet the needs of the growing numbers of people at risk from severe allergic reactions (anaphylaxis) by providing information and support relating to foods and other triggers such as latex, drugs and insect stings. The Campaign provides a wealth of freely available information and also offers tailored services for individual and corporate members. Visit the website www.anaphylaxis.org.uk.

GENERAL MEDICAL QUESTIONS TO ASK IN A MAINSTREAM OR SPECIAL SCHOOL

1. Has the school drawn up an individual healthcare plan for the child? Who has contributed to it? If the child has to attend hospital appointments on a regular basis, special arrangements may need to be made and this should be discussed with the school in conjunction with drawing up a healthcare plan. It may be necessary to check how the child can access those appointments and the role the school might play.

2. What are the necessary safety measures that need to be put in place and how can the school ensure that the child and others are not put at risk?

3. Does the school have a full-time nurse on the premises? How frequently does a school doctor visit?

4. What are the links between the child's GP or paediatrician, as appropriate?

5. What information does the parent need to supply to the school about the child's medical condition and treatment, and who should this be supplied to?

6. How will the school respect the child's cultural and religious views with regard to healthcare, where relevant?

7. What will the school do in a medical emergency and how will they communicate with the parents?

8. If the child requires complex medical assistance, does the school have someone already in post with the special training needed, if not, how soon will they be able to recruit someone? What training has there been, or what training will be given?

9. If a child has a potentially life-threatening condition, how does the teacher feel about having the child in class and what back-up cover is there available should an emergency occur and necessitate immediate action?

10. At times of the school day, where other staff may be responsible for the child, e.g. playground assistants, how will they know about the healthcare plan and what training and advice will they get? If an emergency arises at these times, how quickly can they summon help from a more senior member of staff?

11. Does the school link into any voluntary organizations specializing in particular medical conditions who may be able to offer advice or school packs?

12. It is deemed to be good practice to allow children who can be trusted to do so, to manage their own medication from a relatively early age

and the school should encourage this. Staff may then only need to supervise a child taking their medication themselves. If this is the case with the child in question, ask the school whether the child can carry and administer their own medication? A parental consent form will need to be signed. If the medication has to be taken at certain times and the child has to leave the classroom to do this, what reminders can be put in place and how will the risk to disrupted education be minimized when the child misses time, e.g. it may be preferable instead of the child finding the medical room a long way from the classroom, that the school nurse attends the classroom and the medication is taken outside the door? (This would need to be done with the child's consent because of confidentiality and to protect their own feelings about being different.)

13. What will happen if the child refuses to take medication?

14. What records are kept? Although there is no legal requirement for schools to keep records of medicines given to children and which staff are involved, it is good practice to do so. Parents need to ask the school what records they do keep.

15. Ask how the child can participate in extra-curricular sport or in the PE curriculum, depending on their needs. If there are restrictions on a child's ability to participate in PE, then this should be included in their individual healthcare plan and questions should be asked about what strategies will be used. How might the school involve an occupational therapist or physiotherapist in drawing up a PE timetable to ensure the child can access this part of the curriculum?

16. Ask if teachers supervising sporting activities are aware of any relevant medical conditions and emergency procedures. Some children may need to take precautionary measures before or during exercise, and/or need to be allowed immediate access to their medication if necessary, e.g. asthmatics.

17. If the child requires supervision on school transport, ask who will be providing this and what training the supervisors will have and who will give this.

18. How will the school ensure privacy and dignity is given to the child? Will same-sex helpers be available for personal needs?

19. How will medical information be kept confidential and who should have access to records and other information about the child? If the child has the capacity of understanding, then will the school want to involve the child in this decision?

20. Some staff may be, understandably, reluctant to volunteer to administer intimate or invasive treatment because of the nature of the treatment or fears about accusations of abuse. Health Authorities will have a

'named professional' to whom schools can refer to for advice. It may be necessary for the school to arrange for two adults; one the same gender as the child, to be present for the administration of intimate or invasive treatment and this will need to be discussed in terms of resourcing, before the child arrives. If this affects the child in question, ask about this aspect.

SCHOOL TRIPS

The child has a right to go on any school trip that is part of the curriculum. If it is an extra-curricular activity, then the school may have a right to refuse the child, but would have to show what 'reasonable adjustments' they have considered before saying no.

QUESTIONS TO ASK ABOUT SCHOOL TRIPS

1. What are the reasons for the activity/visit and how appropriate is it for the child, e.g. if the trip focuses on physical tasks, such as climbing, what are the options if the child has a physical difficulty and cannot participate in this?

2. How will the school make 'reasonable adjustments' to ensure that the child can participate? Discuss the sort of issues that might arise and give suggestions how the school might be able to deal with them, e.g. if an autistic child has aversions to particular sounds or animals, it may be possible for a parent to accompany them on the visit or avoid the part of the visit which could cause behavioural issues.

3. What is the venue like? Has anyone done a site visit or spoken to someone who has been there? Depending on the child's difficulties, various issues may need to be considered; such as suitable toilet facilities and ramps. Demonstrators may need to be told about a child with a short attention span or problems with understanding complex language. If the venue is nearby, it may be preferable for a parent and/or a teacher to make a visit and consider its suitability and then make suggestions, either to the staff on the site and/or the teacher organizing the trip, so that risks can be minimized. Ask if the site carries out individual risk assessments to ensure that the specific needs of the child can be addressed.

4. Will the child be briefed so that they know where and when they are going and what will happen when they get there? The school may need to draw up a visual timetable and talk the child through behavioural expectations. This will be particularly important for autistic children. The school may be able to show photographs of the

venue, provide more detailed information about what will happen during the visit and make sure that appropriate communication cards are available for the day.

5. How will the staff and helpers be briefed, both in advance and on the day? Will a briefing sheet be available? Every member of staff and every parent/carer/helper should be aware of the child's difficulties and it may be necessary on some visits to make one adult responsible for a named child to ensure the visit is successful.

6. If it is a residential trip, ask about any specific arrangements for the evenings and nights; particularly if the child requires specific bedtime routines, additional care or waking night staff.

7. Will a higher than usual staff–child ratio be needed to help the child cope, including possible 1:1 support?

8. Will there be a need to administer medication and what is the likelihood of having to deal with a medical emergency?

9. What are the chances of the child getting lost or running away? (Most venues will be less secure than the average school.)

10. How will being in a different setting affect the child's behaviour? (Be prepared in advance.)

11. Is there a need for an adult of the same sex to accompany the child to the toilet?

Reprinted with the kind permission of The Advisory Centre for Education (ACE).

PROFESSIONALS WHO MAY BE INVOLVED WITH THE CHILD WHO HAS MEDICAL NEEDS

School nurses

School nurses have two key responsibilities:

- To assess, protect and promote the health and well-being of school-aged children and young people.
- To offer advice, care and treatment to individuals and groups of children, young people and the adults who care for them.

School nurses can offer services in three areas:

- As the first point of contact for children and parents needing health advice or information. This involves assessing individual needs, offering care and treatment and referring on to other services as necessary. Many school nurses provide 'drop-in' sessions in schools for this purpose.

- Supporting children with ongoing or specific health needs. This may include children with complex health needs or a learning and/or physical disability. Activities could include direct care and treatment, promotion of self-care, supporting parents, referral to other specialists and co-ordination of a range of services.

- Initiating and supporting activities for promoting health across the school and community. These public health activities include contributing to personal, social and health education (PSHE) delivery, working with the school to achieve the Healthy School Standard or advising on whole-school programmes to address particular issues, e.g. sexual health and healthy eating.

QUESTIONS TO ASK ABOUT THE SCHOOL NURSE/DOCTOR

1. Is there a full-time nurse or doctor on the premises? If a residential school, is the cover for 24 hours? (Some independent schools have their own doctors.)

2. Will the school nurse/doctor help with the individual healthcare plan?

3. Will the school nurse/doctor advise on training for school staff willing to administer medication or other aspects of support?

4. Will the school nurse/doctor be available at open days or parents' evenings?

5. How does the school nurse/doctor liaise with the child's GP?

6. Is there a room set aside for children who may need times to lie down during the school day and how is this furnished? Is it supervised?

7. What are the roles that the school nurse undertakes (sometimes this may involve some counselling)? If so, what are their qualifications and experience in delivering this service?

General practitioner (GP)

GPs are part of the Primary Healthcare team and have a duty of confidentiality to patients. Any exchange of information between GPs and schools about a child's medical condition should be with the consent of the child, if they have the capacity, or, otherwise, that of the parent(s).

QUESTIONS TO ASK ABOUT THE GP

1. A parent should speak to their GP and find out whether they should be involved with a child's school and whether they advise teachers directly about a child's condition, or work through the school nurse.

2. Ask how the GP liaises with the school health service.

3. A parent should ask whether the GP is willing or able to write letters in support of a particular child or range of treatment or, even, with respect to schooling. The GP is often the one person who may know the family and child over a number of years and be aware of the difficulties that a family is having in managing a child with severe difficulties in the home situation. The GP may be willing to set out their view in a letter to the Local Authority with respect to what they have observed and, for example, their views on residential schooling or the provision of further social services input.

Other health professionals

1. The community paediatrician is a specialist with an interest in disability, chronic illness and the impact of ill health on children. They may give advice to the school on individual children or health problems generally. Some community paediatricians hold regular surgeries in special schools and will consult with staff and parents and attend annual reviews or other multi-disciplinary meetings.

2. There may be involvement from neurologists, neuro-developmental paediatricians or other hospital-based consultants who have had long-term involvement with the child. It is very important that communication takes place with the school.

3. There may be a number of other therapists who work within the school who may have involvement with the child. All therapists should be registered with the health professions council and registration should be checked.

4. There are many other interventions which are currently being trialled in school, including nurture groups at primary and secondary levels which may impact on children with medical needs.

For many special schools, working on a daily basis with health professionals, will be part and parcel of the day's work. For mainstream schools, it may be a new experience which will require much more support, perhaps through in-service training and supervision of staff and the child may be a 'guinea pig'. Ask what the existing arrangements are, what potentially can be put in place and, in particular, look at how the school, therapists and parents will work together and evaluate outcomes.

CHAPTER 8

The Current Law on Special Educational Needs

Deborah Hay★

This chapter deals with the main areas of law that might concern parents, setting out, in outline form, some considerations when choosing a school for their child with special educational needs. It is not meant to be definitive and cannot be relied on for legal advice.

SPECIAL EDUCATIONAL NEEDS (SEN)

The main legal framework, in relation to children with special educational needs and disability discrimination is contained in Part 4 of the Education Act 1996 and Disability Discrimination Act 2001.

The Education Act 1996 requires the Secretary of State for Children, Schools and Families to issue a Code of Practice, providing guidance for special educational needs to which everyone involved with children with special educational needs must have statutory regard including the Special Educational Needs and Disability (SEND) Tribunal. The SEN Code of Practice sets the framework and ethos within which Local Authorities make decisions and it has to be taken seriously by Local Authorities and Tribunals hearing cases about children with special educational needs. The SEN Code of Practice sets out guidance through all the stages of the legal framework, including:

- school action and school action plus
- statutory assessment

★ Deborah Hay is a barrister specializing in Education, Community Care and Administrative Law. Deborah regularly speaks and lectures at conferences and seminars, is a member of the Disability Rights Commission Panel on Education Law, and a member of the Law Education Practitioners Group Management Committee. She has been closely involved in the committee considering and evaluating the form of the new SEND Tribunal rules and their implementation.

- statementing
- annual reviews
- decisions to cease to maintain statements.

Reference to the Code of Practice and the legal definition of what constitutes a special educational need has been discussed in other chapters.

EXPRESSING A PREFERENCE FOR A SCHOOL

Parents have the same right to express a preference for the school they wish their child with special educational needs to attend in the same way as parents of children without special educational needs, subject to the school being able to meet their child's needs, the placement not being incompatible with the delivery of efficient education to other children or with the efficient use of public resources (schedule 27, paragraph 3, Education Act 1996).

Where parents wish their child to attend an independent school, they can rely on the general principle that children should be educated in accordance with the wishes of their parents, subject to that incurring no unreasonable public expenditure and being compatible with meeting their child's needs (Section 9, Education Act 1996). This general principle has to be taken into account, but is not overriding.

For many parents, the choice of school is paramount and it is for this reason that many appeals are taken to the SEND Tribunal.

THE SEND TRIBUNAL

The SEND Tribunal resolves disputes between parents/carers and Local Authorities and/or schools regarding the way in which the SEN framework is being put into practice, together with disability discrimination claims concerning admissions and exclusions from schools, or allegations of discriminatory treatment within schools. The SEND Tribunal has jurisdiction to consider appeals regarding:

- refusal of a Local Authority to carry out a statutory assessment or a reassessment of a child's special educational needs following a request by a parent or by the child's school
- refusal to make a Statement of the child's special educational needs, after a statutory assessment
- refusal to change the school named in the child's Statement
- decision not to maintain (deciding to cancel) a child's Statement
- decision not to change or amend the Statement following reassessment

- the content of Parts 2, 3 and 4 of a Statement.

It is important to be aware that there are issues the Tribunal cannot deal with and reference should be made to the SEND Tribunal website.

The SEND Tribunal has recently undergone a radical transformation and is now operating under a new set of rules which are intended to streamline and speed up the process. The process for Local Authorities and parents should now take an appeal from start to finish in 22 weeks. The appeal process, which now includes 'case management', to ensure that all the necessary information is ready and available to reach the decision on the day of a Hearing is set out, in detail, on the SEND Tribunal website. It is quite a complex process and the Local Authority should offer parents details of groups they may be able to get advice from, such as:

- voluntary organizations which help parents through the process
- parents' groups
- an independent parental supporter
- a parent partnership advisor.

Parents may also seek independent private advice from solicitors who are experienced in education law through the Law Society or voluntary organizations. Some public funding is available, but not for representation at the Hearing and further advice from a legal representative should be sought on this aspect.

A child can attend the Hearing and give evidence, but it is unlikely that they will stay for the full Hearing and so parents must organize childcare for them. Parents and Local Authorities will bring along witnesses to the Hearing to provide expert evidence and it is, therefore, necessary to think ahead as to whom would be the most appropriate person to bring in this situation (which could be someone from the child's school). However, it is likely that parents will need independent expert reports to deal with differences of opinion with the Local Authority regarding their child's needs (including speech and language therapy, physiotherapy and occupational therapy).

SPECIFIC ISSUES IN STATEMENTS

Therapies

Many of the arguments between parents and Local Authorities arise from the perceived need for therapy provision to be specified and quantified in a Statement of Special Educational Needs. The requirement for specificity within Statements has its starting point in paragraph 8:36 of the Code of Practice 'A Statement should specify clearly the provision necessary to meet the needs of the child. It should detail appropriate provision to meet each identified need...'. Paragraph 8:37 states that Local Authorities must not 'in any circumstances, have blanket policies not to quantify provision'. When considering specification and quantification, however, parents do need to consider how practical their requirements are. If a child is within a mainstream school, the amount of time a child will spend out of the classroom must be considered, particularly if significant amounts of therapy are requested, which may affect their entitlement to access the National Curriculum, and if the requirements of therapy lead to resources not usually available in a mainstream school, such as a large room for sensory integration therapy. This will depend on the age of the child and the flexibility of the curriculum at that particular stage.

The delivery of therapies is subject to case law which makes it clear that speech and language therapy will be an educational provision in the vast majority of cases and so where the provision is specified, the Local Authority will be under an obligation to provide and fund the therapy input either through the NHS, or, crucially, from a private provider if it is not possible for the NHS to provide what is required. Over time, this has been extended to occupational therapy in most cases and also physiotherapy. Where any therapies are identified as special educational provision the Local Authority is obliged to arrange that provision and has ultimate responsibility for ensuring the provision is made for the child.

If a Local Authority is arguing that occupational therapy/physiotherapy and/or therapies are not educational needs, the parent has to prove that the provision directly relates to a child's learning difficulties and they will, therefore, need evidence to support this.

If it is demonstrated that the child's difficulty is not an educational need, it should not be put into Part 2 of the Statement, e.g. if a child has difficulty in sleeping, it must be proven that this impacts directly on their education and access to the curriculum and therefore can be described as an educational need. If the special need is placed in Part 2, then there must be provision to meet that need in Part 3 of the Statement. This provision must then be clearly set out and quantified. It is often argued that a special school, which is delivering therapies all the time to its children, does not need to specify the provision of therapy to an individual child. This is, however, not the case, and even if the child attends a special school, Parts 2 and 3 should be very clear on this subject.

Inclusion

Parents have an absolute right to choose a mainstream school for their child if they wish and if no Statement is maintained for a child, then they must be educated within a mainstream school. If a Statement is maintained for a child, then they must be educated within a mainstream school unless their parents want them to be educated in a special school, or education in a mainstream school would not be compatible with the provision of efficient education for other children.

The underlying philosophy is that children should be able to have their needs met in mainstream schools amongst their peers, both with and without special educational needs. If the Local Authority wishes to rely on the exception to the mandatory duty to educate children in a mainstream school, then it must demonstrate that there are no reasonable steps that can be taken to overcome the difficulties with the provision of efficient education for other children.

If parental choice is for a special provision and the Local Authority maintains that the child's needs can be met in a mainstream school, this is likely to lead to an appeal to the SEND Tribunal.

Home education

Home education is known as 'Education Otherwise' than in school and parents have an absolute right to make their own non-school-based arrangements for their children's education. However, the Local Authority does have a duty to satisfy itself that those arrangements are suitable and can take enforcement action if it feels the arrangements are not adequate. This is particularly the case with children with special educational needs and home educators must ensure that all the child's needs are being addressed. Further details on this are set out in Chapter 33 on 'Home Education'.

In England, when a parent wants to remove a child from the school roll in order to home educate, they need to go through a deregistration process which involves writing to the head teacher or proprietor of the school. There is no requirement for the parents to obtain the school's and Local Authority's agreement to educate their children at home and it is not necessary for parents to give reasons for their decision.

Deregistration does not apply to children who have been placed by the Local Authority in special schools. In this situation, a child cannot be deregistered without the Local Authority's consent and this restriction is meant to protect the interests of more vulnerable children by ensuring that their special educational needs are met. However, the parental right to educate otherwise than in school does extend to children with special educational needs.

DO PARENTS NEED LEGAL ADVICE?

There is no doubt that parents are increasingly willing to seek legal advice where they feel their child's education is not being properly addressed by schools and/or Local Authorities. The system is becoming more complex and there are more rigid statutory time limits, which does put pressure on parents and Local Authorities to reach agreement. However, even with good intentions on both sides, despite negotiating and trying to compromise, it is not always possible to reach agreement.

The SEND Tribunal process can be rather daunting and there may be areas in which advice and support from a solicitor is helpful, both in terms of procedure and also process. The other main reason for seeking legal representation is for the presentation of a case at a final Hearing.

Other areas which may require legal involvement are admissions to schools, exclusions from schools and disability discrimination, all of which are complex subjects in their own right.

QUESTIONS TO ASK IF A PARENT OR LOCAL AUTHORITY WANT TO SEEK LEGAL ADVICE

1. Does the solicitor specialise in education law and, if so, in what specific areas?

2. How many cases has the solicitor taken in the last year in the area in which advice is sought?

3. What is their success rate?

4. What is the fee structure for work undertaken?

5. What is the level of experience within the department as a whole in case back up is needed?

6. Does the solicitor provide links to experts who have experience and expertise in the area where advice is needed?

7. If a case cannot be settled, what advice does the solicitor provide for the Hearing itself and is an advocate used?

8. What experience does the solicitor have in working together with a particular Local Authority and are there good working relationships which may help the course of negotiations, perhaps leading to a successful outcome prior to a Hearing?

There is complex case law in the area of special educational needs and many parents do feel a little like a 'David fighting a Goliath' when the Local Authority has access to a legal department with all the experience that this entails. Parents who seek legal advice should not feel that this will necessarily provoke an adversarial exchange. On the contrary, it may take the heat out of a tricky situation, allowing representatives on both sides to be less emotionally involved, settling things in the best interests of the child.

PART 2

UNDERSTANDING the BACKGROUND

CHAPTER 9

Understanding the Child's Needs and the Role of Assessment by a Psychologist

At the outset, it is very important to differentiate between psychological assessment and psychological testing.

Psychological assessment is an over-arching term which will not necessarily follow a pre-conceived format, but the psychologist will ascertain what needs to be done based on documentation, presentation of the child at the time and also what else needs to be discovered. There should be hypothesis raising on behalf of the psychologist and then the psychologist will decide on the form of assessment which may or may not involve formal or informal testing to consider various possibilities. Standard psychological tests are not accessible to some children and, in these cases, there are other forms of assessment which are possible, including dynamic assessment, developmental questionnaires and, of course, clinical observation, which should form the underpinning of any assessment undertaken.

Psychological tests fall into several categories, but this does not mean that all categories of tests will be used with every child and the choice of test will very much depend on the age, stage of development, cognitive ability and, clearly, what tests have already been administered by others.

---

* Information in this chapter has been quoted by kind permission of Raymond Lloyd Richmond, *Guide to Psychology and its Practice*. www.guidetopsychology.com.

TYPES OF PSYCHOLOGICAL TESTS

1. **Intelligence tests** aim to measure intelligence. There is a big debate about the definition of *intelligence*. It should be a measure of potential not a measure of what has been learnt (as in an attainment test) and so it is supposed to be culture-free. To design and administer a test that is really culture-free is very difficult and so most intelligence tests fail to satisfy this objective.

    This is not the place to engage in a debate on the concept of intelligence, but it is important for parents and teachers to understand that intelligence quotient (IQ) is the expression of the ratio of mental age to chronological age, e.g. a 6-year-old child with a mental age of 6 would have an IQ of 100 (average IQ score), whilst a 6-year-old child with a mental age of 9 would have an IQ of 150 and a 6-year-old child with a mental age of 3 would have an IQ of 50.

2. **Dynamic assessment** is a process of assessment which does not use standardized tests; it is an interactive method of assessing learning potential. Rather than just accepting a response to a question as in most standardized intelligence tests, the psychologist works with the child on a series of tasks to observe what can be achieved with guidance and structure using a test–intervene–test format.

3. **Achievement or attainment tests** attempt to measure how much a child knows about a certain topic, i.e. the knowledge they have attained, such as in maths or science. Again, scores will be age-related with standardized norms with 100 being the average. Most tests also give percentile scores so that a child scoring at the 45th percentile will mean that 55 per cent of children would score above this level.

4. **Neuro-psychological tests** attempt to measure deficits in cognitive functioning, i.e. the ability to think, speak, reason, etc., and cover such areas as executive functioning which includes the ability to plan or organize. This can be affected by various types of brain damage, including milder forms, such as dyspraxia as well as the more serious forms of brain injury. These tests can be given by a neuro-psychologist but, increasingly, educational and clinical psychologists have also been trained in administration of these tests.

5. **Personality tests** attempt to measure basic aspects of personality, but will include areas such as self-esteem, academic self-concept and clinical tests, such as measures of levels of anxiety, aggression or depression.

Psychological tests are administered and interpreted by a psychologist and in the case of children in school, this will usually be an educational or clinical psychologist. Some psychologists have additional, specialist, training in certain areas such as autism, and most hold chartered status which reflects that they undertake further continuous professional development to keep up to date with new research and findings. However, teachers are increasingly undertaking some aspects of testing, e.g. for access arrangements (where children with special educational needs obtain the necessary time or support to be judged on equal terms in external examinations). It is therefore important that when the psychologist undertakes an assessment, they are clear what has already been done in schools. Psychological tests are usually closed tests, which can only be administered by trained psychologists. Tests are copyrighted by the publishers and, for professional reasons, the security of the tests must be maintained so that children cannot practise the tests. It is, therefore, important to differentiate between tests that can only be given by psychologists and other tests that can be given by teachers.

There are clinical tests also used by a psychiatrist who might look at checklists of symptoms in order to diagnose certain clinical conditions. Whilst some of these diagnoses will be in the province of psychiatrists alone, e.g. diagnosis of obsessive compulsive disorder, other diagnoses may well stray into the areas also undertaken by psychologists, such as the diagnosis of Asperger's syndrome, attention deficit hyperactivity disorder (ADHD) or other areas of functioning.

Standardized psychological tests are used for three reasons:

1. The information from tests should be more consistent than the information from a clinical interview. In other words if two psychologists were administering the same test, in theory the results should be quite similar. This would be important in legal disputes or if a diagnosis is essential. In reality, this is sometimes not the case as the child may react differently to different people or in different environments and it is always important to understand that if results are very inconsistent then the psychologist should be challenged to explain the reasons why this may be the case.

2. It is often easier to get information from tests rather than from a clinical interview alone. This is because, sometimes, children feel intimidated in a clinical interview and do not reveal their actual wishes, feelings or, indeed, function as they normally would. Also the interviewer may not be as experienced in getting the information as one might hope.

3. When a psychologist has administered a test over a number of years, and is very competent at giving the test, it is far easier to notice the subtleties of performance in a child, which may be the key to their functioning.

However, there are many difficulties with psychological tests, which include aspects of validity and reliability. Validity is known as the accuracy or usefulness of a test, e.g. if you wanted to develop a test to determine whether a child would be good at maths, it may not be sufficient merely to give them a page of sums involving the four operations of addition, subtraction, multiplication and division, as that would not test other areas of mathematical reasoning. Similarly a test may not be reliable, e.g. in a personality test, a child may answer according to how they feel at the moment and yet say something different when they are at home or in school. No psychological test is ever completely valid or reliable because a human being is just too complicated for another person to know everything there is to know with full confidence. Thus, even after extensive testing, there may be uncertainty and remaining questions to ask.

Some Local Authorities will have assessment policies and these are often based on professional Codes of Practice issued by the British Psychological Society and Association of Educational Psychologists. They will need to be consistent with statutory assessment procedures and the Special Educational Needs (SEN) Code of Practice.

WHAT IS AN EDUCATIONAL PSYCHOLOGIST?

Educational psychologists will work alongside, or together with, schools. Until recent changes to the profession, educational psychologists also had to be qualified teachers as well as educational psychologists. Now, educational psychologists follow a three-year doctorate course and so many more will have the title of doctor in their qualification. However, there are also clinical psychologists who will undertake assessments, usually in clinic or hospital settings, but who may also visit schools if required. Most educational psychologists will contribute to statutory assessments, rather than clinical psychologists. It may be helpful to ask why one type of psychologist is being used in preference to another. Some local health teams; such as the Child and Adolescent Mental Health Service (CAMHS), will use clinical psychologists and if, for example, a child is seen through that route, they may find themselves assessed by a clinical rather than an educational psychologist.

Psychologists are guided by a Code of Practice which can be found on the British Psychological Society website. From July 2009 all practitioner psychologists must be registered under the Health Professions Council (HPC). Educational psychologists are involved with all kinds of problems encountered by children in education, including, social, emotional, behavioural and learning difficulties. The majority of educational psychologists are employed by Local Authorities, while a growing number work as independent or private practitioners.

Clinical psychologists work largely in health and social care settings, including hospitals and health centres as part of a CAMHS team or social services. Most clinical psychologists are employed by the NHS, but some work in private practice.

WHAT HAPPENS IN A PSYCHOLOGICAL ASSESSMENT?

Psychological assessments can take many forms, including pencil and paper tasks, puzzles, drawings and games. One of the most important features of the assessment is the dialogue between the psychologist and the child and the clinical observation of the child's behaviour and test response. Psychological assessments are usually individually carried out, but not always. A parent has the right to be present during an assessment which may be extremely helpful in some circumstances. However, it is important to consider what is in the best interest of the child and sometimes children will react differently if parents are in the room and this should be discussed with the psychologist before the assessment begins. It is difficult to state how long an assessment will take as this can vary, depending on what assessment tools are used and how the child responds. It may, in fact, be necessary to carry out assessments over more than one session. The tests may look like work given in school or may look like nothing the child has seen before. Many different skill areas are covered, depending on who is undertaking the assessment, but most assessments will include measures or opinions on:

- general intellectual (cognitive) or developmental level
- language and communication
- memory and learning
- problem solving
- planning and organization
- fine motor skills
- visual spatial skills
- academic skills
- behaviour and emotions
- social skills and interaction.

There will be many children who require more in-depth assessments in the areas of speech and language and communication (from a speech and language therapist), fine and gross motor skills (from an occupational therapist or physiotherapist) and behaviour/emotions (from a clinical psychologist or child psychiatrist), although all these areas are covered by educational psychologists in some part.

Most psychological reports will include sections which contain a summary of other reports, the child's response to assessment, observation, the assessment results, views of the parents and teachers and the wishes and views of the child. Clearly, depending on the age and stage of development, some children will be able to express their views quite clearly, whilst others may not. In the latter circumstances, sometimes children are able to identify their feelings with the use of pictures or symbols.

It may not be immediately obvious to a parent or teacher how different environments will impact on a child. The child should, therefore, be viewed as part of the following contexts:

- school
- family
- community.

There will be factors in all of these environments which will interface with the child's own knowledge and skills. Past experience will also have a part to play as this will have affected a child's development and progress and may help to explain some of the features of presentation. The child's view of the world is the way in which the child makes sense of the world and of events that have occurred. Sometimes this may be different to the way in which teachers or parents perceive an event and so it is important to be able to put oneself in the child's shoes as well. Assessments ideally should look at all these different features.

At the end of an assessment, there is usually a feedback meeting with parents and/or teachers to discuss the results, although this may not take place immediately. This can sometimes involve the child if appropriate to their age and developmental maturity. A written report will be completed outlining the results of the assessment and the recommendations for intervention. A parent should receive a copy of this report and it will be important to ascertain who else receives the report which should remain confidential and only available to those people who are directly involved in any decision making with regard to the child.

WHY IS AN ASSESSMENT IMPORTANT?

When considering a school placement, it is very important that an assessment has been carried out prior to determining whether a school is suitable. The assessment should bring some in-depth clarity to the child's needs and that will help to formulate the kind of provision that is being looked for. The assessment may, for example, give some clues as to whether a child works well with a more challenging peer group and whether they would be better placed in a peer group where they may be top of the class, rather than at the bottom.

A full psychological assessment will establish a child's strengths and weaknesses and will help to answer some questions about a child's special educational needs. However, a psychological assessment carried out at a certain point in time may be limited in its usefulness, particularly if a child is going through a transition between different stages of education. What was helpful at age 3 years may not be so helpful at age 11 years. It is important to ensure that as far as possible, psychological assessments are updated and the child is reviewed so that the latest reports do really reflect the current position at the time.

These reports usually become a permanent part of a child's record and are likely to follow them throughout life. It is, therefore, essential that the reports are read carefully, and if a parent or teacher does not agree with any aspect of the report, this should be raised with the psychologist at the time and concerns or queries can be put in writing. It may be helpful if these queries accompany the report. Although most psychologists will agree to amend or change their report if they are wrong on a factual point, changing an opinion is a different matter and there would need to be clear evidence as to why an opinion which has been formulated may be questionable. Psychologists acknowledge that they are not always correct, particularly if new information, not previously available, is forthcoming.

Once a report has been agreed, it can become a powerful instrument in determining what provision is required and, ultimately, placement. This is why an assessment is essential before choosing a school and it can direct a parent or other professional to draw up a suitable shortlist of possible schools.

CHAPTER 10

How to Draw Up a List of Schools

TYPES OF SCHOOL

At the time of writing, schools fall into the following categories.

Schools maintained by the Local Authority

1. **Community schools** used to be called county schools. The Local Authority is responsible for school admissions and decides how children are admitted.

2. **Voluntary controlled schools** are schools that are maintained by the Local Authority. Originally, most of these were church schools, but they are now run like community schools. Although these schools have close links with the church authorities, only some of the governing body are appointed by the religious foundation. The Local Authority is responsible for school admissions and decides how children are admitted.

3. **Voluntary aided schools** are maintained by the Local Authority but are strongly supported by the respective religious authority. Most of these schools were set up by churches or other faiths and a few by charities. The school's governing body decides the admissions criteria and offers places to children and at many faith schools most, or all, children will be given a place at the school, depending on their religion.

4. **Foundation schools** used to be grant maintained schools. The school's governing body decides the admissions criteria and offers places to children.

5. **Trust schools** are a new type of state-funded schools, which are similar to voluntary aided and foundation schools, and set their own admission rules. Parents, voluntary groups and businesses can set up these schools and appoint a majority of governors and the governing body is the admission authority.

6. **Academies and city technology colleges** are funded by the government and private companies. They operate as independent schools, but do not charge fees and admit children of secondary age on a similar basis to other state schools. The governing body is the admission authority. They are not recognized as independent schools in the full sense of that term.

7. **Comprehensive schools** are open to all children at secondary level. At banded comprehensive schools, children are assessed and are admitted to certain bands so there is a balance of ability across the school.

8. **Fully selective schools** are generally secondary grammar schools and children are assessed for a place by taking tests organized by the admission authority. These are not necessarily independent schools.

9. **Partially selective schools** or schools which give priority to aptitude are secondary schools where a certain number of children (about 10%) are assessed for a place under rules decided by the admission authority where priority is given to a certain aptitude.

10. **Specialist schools** – most state secondary schools now offer a curriculum speciality and a few partially select children on the basis of aptitude for that speciality, e.g. music.

Independent schools

These schools are also known as private or fee-paying schools. A list of independent schools can be obtained by contacting the Independent Schools Council Information Service (ISC), or the Department for Children, Schools and Families (DCSF). The definition of an independent school, under the Education Act 2002, is defined as 'any school that provides full-time education for five or more pupils of compulsory school age or one or more pupils with a Statement of Special Educational Needs or who is in public care and is not maintained by a Local Authority or a non-maintained special school'. An independent school is not dependent on government or Local Authority finance and has freedom of choice in selection of children and setting its own curriculum.

Whilst there is no legal definition of an *independent special school*, the DCSF considers that any independent school where at least half of the children have SEN and at least 25 per cent have Statements, should be considered as a school catering wholly or mainly for children with SEN. There are currently over 200 independent schools designated as catering wholly or mainly for children with SEN.

In order for a child with special educational needs to be educated at an independent school, the school needs:

1. to be approved by the Secretary of State as suitable for the admission of a child for whom a Statement is maintained and

2. the Secretary of State consents to the child being educated there.

When a Local Authority wishes to name an independent school in Part 4 of a Statement of Special Educational Needs and has obtained the school's agreement to accept the child and a place is available, then consent must be sought from the Secretary of State.

When parents are appealing to a SEND Tribunal, and wish the Tribunal to order the Local Authority to name an independent school in Part 4, then 'enabling consent' must be sought, but in this case, consent is valid for a specific Tribunal hearing only and if the Tribunal is not found in the parents' favour, then the consent lapses. Unless the school has offered a place to the child, Tribunals will not order a Local Authority to name an independent school in Part 4 of their Statement.

Full lists of approved special schools including independent schools should be available from the Local Authority.

Special schools, centres or units

Special schools make special educational provision for children with Statements of Special Educational Needs, whose needs cannot be fully met from within mainstream provision. Special schools are part of a spectrum of provision and most are maintained. There are three main types:

- **Maintained special schools** are either community or foundation schools (as defined by the Education Act 1998). These are funded by the Local Authority and are broadly subject to the same legislative procedures as other schools.

- **Non-maintained special schools** are not maintained by the Local Authority and are approved as special schools under Section 342 of the Education Act 1996. These are non-profit-making schools run by charitable trusts and funded primarily through child fees charged to the Local Authority which places children there. The underlying principle is that these schools should be treated broadly the same way as maintained schools and they have to demonstrate that they operate to a level at least to an equivalent of a state-maintained special school and their day-to-day running is controlled by a governing body, with the articles and instruments agreed by the Secretary of State. To keep non-maintained special school status, schools must comply with the non-maintained school regulations. Non-maintained special schools cater for children with extreme and/or low incidence difficulties and provide very specialist schooling.

- **Independent special schools** are approved by the Secretary of State under Section 347 of the Education Act 1996 as suitable for admission of children with Statements of Special Educational Needs. These schools are wholly funded by child fees and can be run on a profit-making basis. Most children are placed by Local Authorities but parents can also fund privately (as mentioned above).

The Local Authority will maintain a number of special schools, centres or units within its own area. They will usually provide information to parents on these. In addition to maintained special schools at one end of the continuum, there will be a range of provision available including:

1. **Pupil Referral Units (PRU)** are a type of school providing education for children of compulsory school age who may otherwise not receive suitable education. The focus of the units is usually to get children back into a mainstream school and may include teenage mothers, children who have been excluded from school, school-phobics or children who may be in the assessment phase of a Statement. Pupil Referral Units should have a management committee but Local Authorities have overall responsibility. Regulations for a PRU are not the same as other schools. There is now a move to replace PRUs with alternative models of provision.

2. **Local Authority secure units** are run by Local Authorities and the Youth Justice Board who purchases beds from them. There is a general requirement to provide education and training for 30 hours a week for 38 weeks of the year and the educational provision will vary between units. These are different to the secure training units which have been set up under private finance initiatives and are operated by private providers, managed by the Home Office. Children aged between 10 to 17 years in the secure training units are provided with formal education for 25 hours a week 52 weeks per year and children have the opportunity to gain mainstream qualifications.

3. **Beacon schools** are schools that have been identified as amongst the best performing in the country and represent a model of successful practice in order to spread effective practice to others. The Beacon Schools Initiative is designed to raise standards through good practice and it is anticipated that they will work in partnership

with other schools, pass on their particular area of expertise and, by doing so, encourage others to reach the same high standards.

Beacon schools can offer advice on a wide range of areas, which includes special educational needs. Beacon schools can assist with resources, including visits, in-service training, mentoring, consultancy, workshops and providing networks for professional support and improvement.

Specialist schools (not to be confused with special schools)

Any maintained secondary school can be designated as a specialist school in any one of ten specialist areas, or they may combine any two specialisms.

The schools meet full National Curriculum requirements but have a special focus on the chosen specialisms.

Residential schools, centres or units

Most mainstream schools offer the opportunity for children to take part in a residential experience, which can be very powerful in developing independence and self-organization and in building relationships between children and teachers. If a child with special educational needs attends a mainstream school, they should be able to access the range of residential experiences offered, despite their learning difficulty or disability. This may take quite a bit of planning and it is important to establish, very early on, what residential experiences will be available to ensure full access to the curriculum.

In the case of children with special educational needs, residential schools (sometimes referred to as boarding schools) can provide for specialist residential school placements for varying numbers of weeks in the year, usually between 38 and 52 weeks. There are a number of reasons for residential placements being granted, but usually it is around the need for a waking day or 24-hour curriculum. This usually translates to meaning that the child's individual education plan is followed through to the evening so that help with areas of their development is given out of school hours, from experienced staff and with an appropriate peer group which can continue to build on their learning and provide them with more opportunities for development throughout the 'waking hours'. It should be mentioned that a waking-day curriculum can be provided without residential provision, usually through an extended curriculum provided by a combination of Local Authority services, including social services and respite care. It should not be assumed that if a child requires a waking-day curriculum on a Statement of Special Educational Needs, that this always necessitates residential schooling.

STAFFING WITHIN SCHOOL

In order to draw up a list of schools it will be necessary to consider what staff should be part of the school team and whether they should be at the school full time, part time, or off-site but used in a consultative capacity. It will be necessary to consult other chapters in this book for the necessary information on qualifications and experience in a cross-referencing exercise. Typical staff groups in maintained or special schools may include all or some of the following personnel:

- Head teacher.
- Other teaching staff (it is always helpful to know who is on the senior management team as that offers information about the importance of a certain role, e.g. is the SENCo or head of a specialist unit in a mainstream school on the Senior Management Team?).
- Special Educational Needs Co-ordinator (SENCo) or Inclusion Co-ordinator – is this a full- or part-time position?
- Head of care and residential staff (if applicable).
- Teachers (qualifications may be very important, particularly specialist qualifications).
- Learning support assistants, also called teaching assistants, or inclusion assistants (qualifications and experience may be very important and some close questioning may be needed here as these are often the least trained individuals in a school spending the most amount of time with the most complex children).
- School nurse.
- Mobility officer (if relevant).
- Physiotherapists and physiotherapy assistants.
- Occupational therapists and occupational therapy assistants.
- Speech and language therapists and speech and language therapy assistants.
- Social care workers.
- Ancillary staff.
- Family services co-ordinator (if relevant).
- Counsellors (qualifications will be important).
- Psychotherapist.
- Art therapist.
- Music therapist.
- Drama therapist.

- Specialist teachers for sensory needs (such as teachers for the visually impaired/teachers of the hearing impaired).
- Other specialist teachers who may attend from advisory services of the Local Authority, such as specialist teachers for autism or dyslexia.
- Clinical psychologist.
- Educational psychologist.
- Child psychiatrist.
- Paediatrician.

HOW TO DRAW UP A LIST OF SCHOOLS

1. There must be clarity with regard to the child's special educational needs. This is where assessment is critical.
2. Is mainstream inclusion the way forward and the parental choice?
3. It will be necessary to try and establish either the child's primary need or, in the case of very complex needs, the provision which can meet all the various needs.
4. In some cases, choice of a type of school may not be initially obvious, e.g. even if a child has severe autism, it may still be possible to consider a mainstream school rather than a specialist autistic provision or a more generic special school may be preferable to ensure that the child has appropriate role models.
5. Although it should be self-evident, it is necessary to clarify whether the school should be a nursery, infant, primary, secondary or post-16 establishment. This may also depend at what point in the school year the search for a school begins. For a child, for example, who has already started Year 6, it will be sensible to consider secondary provision as well as primary provision.
6. Consider distance and whether this is important or not.
7. Consider day or residential placement and, again, whether this is important or not.
8. Refer to the different types of schools set out in this chapter and consider whether a specific type of school would be more acceptable to the family values, e.g. a faith school. Perhaps the child has strengths in music and would prefer to attend a specialist school?
9. Consider whether it is important for the child to attend a school which has post-16 or a sixth form as that may mean fewer moves.
10. Is the preference for a single-sex or co-educational school?

Once having considered these preliminary questions, the next step would be to request a list of schools from the Local Authority which they should be able to provide. There are many internet sites which can provide a full list of maintained and non-maintained schools, mainstream and special schools, day and residential schools. A complete list of schools, including independent schools, is available on EduBase, also known as School Lookup, which is maintained by the DCSF.

The Office for Advice, Assistance, Support and Information on Special Needs (OAASIS) has compiled lists of independent special schools/colleges for children with ADHD, Asperger's syndrome, autism, behaviour, emotional and social difficulties (BESD), dyspraxia or Tourette's syndrome. It also has helpful information sheets on this topic.

However, it is always important to consider the possibilities of full-time or part-time mainstream inclusion.

At this point, finding a school can be very daunting, even for professionals, but first steps are:

1. Contact with the Local Authority.

2. Use a public library.

3. Try to find a choice advisor who provides independent advice to parents; in particular to help those who might find the admissions process from primary to secondary school difficult (this service should be available from the Local Authority).

4. Information online; such as EduBase, OAASIS or other organizations for parents of children with different types of special educational needs.

5. Draw up a shortlist, thinking about the child's special educational needs and personality. Also consider the family's needs and practical arrangements for getting the child to school. There really should be no more than three or four schools on the shortlist or it will not be possible to assimilate the necessary information. This list may include both mainstream and special schools.

6. Trying to find a school from a huge database is frequently unsuccessful, unless the name is already known. If a type of school is being looked for, such as a specialist school for dyslexic children, then it might be better accessing information through a web-search engine, a voluntary organization, a parent group or through word of mouth. With a list of schools, it will be possible to apply a geographical location search and any other variations to them before shortlisting them. Once a shortlist of schools is drawn up, the specific questions in this book will become pertinent.

7. Use the chapters in this book to look at specific areas of need, types of provision and for specific models of school. It will inevitably involve cross-referencing and even some doubling up on information, but the end result will be that a much more informed decision on the choice of school will be possible.

CHAPTER 11

Getting the Right Documents

After drawing up a shortlist of schools, it is helpful to look at as much documentation as possible, as, ultimately, this may help to decide which schools should remain on a shortlist and which schools can be dropped at this point. Although it may sound obvious, the first 'port of call' should be the website of the Local Authority where the school is situated, which will then direct the user to the school website. In the case of non-maintained schools, it will, of course, be necessary to go directly to the school's own website. These websites can be confusing, but perseverance will often turn up what is needed. However, a recent survey of Local Authority websites revealed that many were still not putting the necessary information up and so one must go beyond the site. It must also be remembered that even if a website is excellent, it may not have been updated for some time.

I would recommend that the following documents should be consulted, although some may be more easily available than others.

THE SCHOOL PROSPECTUS

By law, the school prospectus must include information about admissions of children with special educational needs and disabilities.

From 1 September 2005, the regulations for the school prospectus changed and there is much more flexibility over what is included. As a result, it must be remembered that a prospectus is a marketing tool and not an objective reflection of the school. School prospectuses must be published in the school year immediately preceding the admissions' school year, i.e. prospectuses published in 2006/07 will be for admissions in 2007/08 and they must be available at least six weeks before the deadline for applications or the date when parents have to express a preference for a school (whichever is the earlier). School prospectuses should be made available by the governing bodies in languages other than English or in alternative formats, e.g. Braille.

The only obligatory content of the school prospectus is information about special educational needs and disability provision. The required information is:

- Arrangements for the admission of children with disabilities.

- Details of steps to prevent disabled children being treated less favourably than other children.

- Details of existing facilities to assist access to the school by children with disabilities.

- The access ability plan (required under the Disability Discrimination Act 1995) covering future policies for increasing access to the school by children with disabilities.

- Information about the implementation of the governing body's policy on children with special educational needs and any changes to the policy during the last year.

A prospectus must be available at the school for reference or copies must be provided free of charge to parents, including prospective parents, on request. Many prospectuses are now available to print off from a school's website.

SCHOOL PROFILE

The school profile is published online and is designed for schools to communicate with parents about the school's progress, priorities and performance. Hard copies should also be available for parents without internet access.

Although all maintained schools, except nurseries, need to publish a school profile, non-maintained schools, independent schools and academies are not required to complete a school profile. So, these schools will have to be contacted directly for this information.

The school profile contains the following information:

- Data provided and updated by the Department for Children, Schools and Families (DCSF) on an annual basis.

- Summary of the latest Ofsted Report.

- Narrative sections written by the school, updated at least once every academic year.

The narrative sections include the following headings:

- What have been our successes this year?

- What are we trying to improve?

- How have our results changed over time?

- How are we making sure that every child receives teaching to meet their individual needs?

- How do we make sure our children are healthy, safe and well supported?

- What have we done in response to our Ofsted report?
- How are we working with parents and the community?

Schools with sixth forms and those schools with alternative provision for their children complete a further series of questions. Alternative provision refers to education commissioned from external providers by schools for some of their children. This can include full- or part-time placements in PRUs, further education colleges, hospital schools, tuition centres, e-learning centres and a range of alternative projects provided by the voluntary or private sector. The school should include these provisions and report to parents about the education these children receive.

SCHOOL MAGAZINE

Most schools produce a school magazine and it can be an interesting insight and guide to life at the school. Typical sections will include recent drama productions or sports achievements, as well as merits for achievements both academic and socially. Many magazines reflect the children's work (although bear in mind that this may be heavily selected) and should also reflect the range of children within the school and, in particular, what the children with special educational needs contribute in their own way.

SPECIAL EDUCATIONAL NEEDS POLICY

All schools must have a policy. It will be specific to the school and reflect the needs of the school population. A typical format for a special educational needs policy in schools should include the following headings:

- Introduction.
- Objectives.
- Roles and responsibilities.
- Admissions and inclusion.
- Specialist provision.
- Allocation of resources.
- Identification, assessment, provision and review.
- Access to the curriculum.
- Access to the wider curriculum.
- Monitoring and evaluating the success of the education provided for children and young people with SEN.
- Arrangements for dealing with complaints from parents.
- Arrangements for in-service training.

Parent information

The SEN Code of Practice believes that all parents of children with SEN should be treated as equal partners. The school should have positive, user-friendly information and help parents to access advice. Parents, in turn, should make their views known. Many schools also produce a leaflet for parents and make reference to the local parent partnership service. Parents should be fully consulted before the involvement of Local Authority support agencies and be invited to attend any formal review meetings at all stages.

COMPLAINTS PROCEDURE

All maintained schools and maintained nursery schools are expected to have in place a procedure to deal with complaints relating to the school and to any community facility or service that the school provides. Reference should be made to the individual school's procedure, but the underlying principle is that concerns ought to be handled, if at all possible, without the need for formal procedures.

BEHAVIOUR POLICY

Every school must have a behaviour policy, including disciplinary measures, determined by the head teacher in the light of principles set by the governing body. The policy must be designed to promote good behaviour and deter adverse behaviour, including all forms of bullying. The policy must be publicized to school staff, children and parents.

Following the establishment of a statement of general principles of behaviour and discipline drawn up by the governing body, the head teacher has the legal duty to establish the more detailed measures (rules, rewards, sanctions and behaviour management strategies) on behaviour and discipline that forms the school's behaviour policy.

It is important that measures are taken to prevent all forms of bullying, including bullying related to race, religion and culture; homophobic bullying; bullying of children with SEN or disabilities; sexist or sexual bullying and cyber-bullying (an increasingly prevalent form of bullying). As far as is reasonable, the rules determined by the head teacher can also include measures to regulate behaviour outside school premises, when children are not in the charge or control of members of staff. In taking into account SEN, disability and the circumstances of vulnerable children, the school is guided by the Disability Discrimination Act 1995 and the SEN duties in the Education Act 1996, together with the Disability Discrimination Act 2005, which provides the statutory framework that emphasizes equality of opportunity for children with SEN or disabilities in accessing school education. There is clearly a significant overlap between those who have a disability and those who have

SEN, but there will be some children who fall into one category and not the other. It is recommended that parents and teachers consult the latest guidance which sets out the reasonable adjustments that might be expected for individual children. The key points are that schools:

- must make reasonable adjustments in the application of their behaviour policy to disabled children
- must make special educational provision for children whose behaviour-related learning difficulties call for the provision to be made
- should be alert to the potentially disproportionate impact of the school's disciplinary framework on vulnerable children
- should identify at-risk children in advance
- should proactively plan how the school's disciplinary framework should be applied for each of these children
- should ensure that all those in contact with the child know what has been agreed
- should make sure that every vulnerable child has a key person in school who knows them well, has good links with the home and can act as a reference point for staff when they are unsure about how to apply the disciplinary framework
- should ensure that all staff are aware of appropriate referral procedures.

Parents and professionals who are already aware of potential difficulties, as a result of either challenging behaviour or behaviour related to the child's condition, which will present as challenging, e.g. not being able to sit still or pushing into a line, should consult the individual school's discipline and behaviour policy and raise specific questions with the school, if necessary.

THE OFSTED REPORT

The Office for Standards in Education, Children's Services and Skills (Ofsted) was set up on 1 April 2007 in order to inspect and regulate care for children and young people and inspect education and training for children of all ages. Ofsted carry out hundreds of inspections and regulatory visits each week and publish their findings on their website.

Following an inspection, all schools have to prepare an Action Plan and the weaknesses identified by Ofsted must be addressed if the school is to improve the quality of education it provides for its children. The main areas that need to be improved are organized in the Inspection Report, under the heading 'What the school should do to improve further'.

It is important that the Ofsted Report is read and understood and the Action Plan is requested if there are any issues that need to be addressed.

These Action Plans can be quite detailed and should have the dates which the school is working towards or when the outcomes have been achieved.

Ofsted Inspections are carried out under Section 5 of the Education Act 2005. They involve a process of evidence gathering in order to provide an assessment of how well a school is performing. This results in a written report, indicating one of four grades – Grade 1: outstanding; Grade 2: good; Grade 3: satisfactory; Grade 4: inadequate – used for grading areas of learning, leadership and management, overall effectiveness and for teaching and learning sessions observed. There is a three-year cycle for the inspection of schools and the school, normally, receives two clear working days notice. If there are concerns about the safety or well-being of children in a school, Her Majesty's Chief Inspector has the power to authorize the inspection of a school without notice. If a school is causing concern, it can be placed in special measures or given a notice to improve as a result of a Section 5 Inspection. From September 2009, Ofsted have launched a revised schools inspections framework which requires more frequent inspections for schools which are graded 3 or 4 and a longer interval for schools which are graded 1.

If one does not have internet access, the governing body of a school must make a copy of the report available upon request to members of the public. They are entitled to charge for this; not exceeding the cost of reproduction.

All independent schools are also inspected by Ofsted on a regular cycle and these inspections lead to a published report. The main purpose of these inspections is to advise whether independent schools meet the prescribed standards for registration. The report will tell the school, parents and wider community, whether the requirements for registration are met and provide the school with an independent external view of its strengths and weaknesses. Independent schools catering wholly or mainly for children with special educational needs, and which are approved under Section 347 of the Education Act 1996 are also inspected. Schools that are in the membership of the Independent Schools Council are inspected by the Independent School's Inspectorate (ISI). A copy of the report is sent to the school and to Local Authorities which fund places for children who have a Statement of Special Educational Needs or who are in public care.

The Commission for Social Care Inspection (CSCI) was combined with Ofsted at its inception. Although the new organization retained the name of Ofsted, the CSCI inspectors brought their invaluable background in social care to Ofsted and the remit now includes inspections for categories which previously came under CSCI, namely:

- children's homes
- adoption and fostering agencies
- residential family centres

- schools and colleges which provide care for children and young people in boarding schools, residential further education colleges and residential special schools.

It is, therefore, very important that if a residential school is being considered, the Ofsted inspection report on social care is analysed. These reports are carried out under the Care Standards Act 2000.

ACHIEVEMENT IN ATTAINMENT TABLES (FORMERLY PERFORMANCE TABLES)

It is necessary to look at the current guidance on the DCFS website as regulations do change.

The school's achievement and attainment tables, which should include Key Stage 2 through to Key Stage 5 results, should be published. The results include information from the school and, in particular, the number and percentage of children with Statements of Special Educational Needs or who are supported at School Action Plus. They also include a contextual value added measure (CVA), a year-on-year comparison and absence rates. The CVA scores shows how well children have progressed since primary school, taking into account a range of individual circumstances, such as gender, age and deprivation. At Key Stage 4, GCSE or equivalent achievements are set out and at Key Stage 5, A Level or equivalent achievements are set out. It is necessary to know how to read the achievement and attainment tables as information about the general attainments within the school may be relevant for a child with SEN.

It is important to be clear what information can be obtained from these tables, as they only provide part of the picture of each school's overall achievements. Every Local Authority and school publishes achievement and attainment tables. The National Curriculum sets standards of achievement in each subject for children aged 5–14 years. More information can be sought from the QCA website as standards do change.

The P Scales are a set of descriptions which record the achievement of children with special educational needs who are working below Level 1 of the National Curriculum. There are eight different levels from P1 (lowest) to P8 (highest). P8 is the average level for a child in the reception year. From September 2007, all mainstream schools are required to submit data, using the P Scales, for children aged 5–16 years with special educational needs in English, mathematics and science. Previously, this data was recorded as W (working towards National Curriculum 1).

OTHER DOCUMENTS AVAILABLE FROM THE SCHOOL

In addition to the documents already referred to, the following could be requested (where relevant to a particular situation):

- sample of a home/school agreement
- accessibility plan
- sex education policy
- race equality policy
- work schemes and syllabuses
- health and safety policy and risk assessment
- religious education syllabus
- charging policy.

FURTHER USEFUL INFORMATION

Extended schools

Following the publication of *Every Child Matters: Change For Children* (DfES 2004), more than one in three schools now provide access to extended services. An extended school works with the Local Authority, local providers and other schools to provide access to a core offer of integrated services. These may include:

- A varied range of activities, including study support, sport and music clubs, combined with childcare in primary school.
- Parenting and family support.
- Swift and easy access to targeted and specialist services.
- Community access to facilities, including adult and family learning, ICT (information and communication technology) and sports grounds.

These will often be provided after the school day, but not necessarily by teachers or on the school site. Ofsted will report, during school inspections on how extended services are contributing to improved outcomes for children and young people. It may be helpful to know if a school is providing such a service and whether this is something that a specific child can access. It may also provide a framework for dialogue if a child requires an extended or waking day curriculum.

Local Authority policies and criteria

The Local Authority will have a policy on educating children with special needs. They may also provide criteria for Statements for children with SEN, but these may change so it is necessary to ensure the most up-to-date version has been consulted. These criteria are specific to the Local Authority and may be challenged during appeal proceedings.

National Performance Framework for SEN

The National Performance Framework gathers together a set of indicators to assist Local Authorities in the process of monitoring, self-review and self-improvement in order to improve their performance in meeting the needs of children with SEN. The indicators are split into four categories:

- contextual information
- inclusion data
- pupil outcome data
- service delivery data.

Ultimately, the information provides SEN data on each Local Authority which can be used to compare performance.

The information set out will include, for example, the number of appeals to the SEND (Special Educational Needs and Disability) Tribunal, children with new Statements placed in maintained special schools and many other useful pieces of information. However, it is necessary to be cautious when analysing these results, e.g. Local Authorities with high percentages of children with new Statements placed in maintained special schools are not necessarily non-inclusive. It may be that the needs of most children with SEN in mainstream schools are being met without a Statement. Similarly, Local Authority policies differ widely as to whether a pre-school child needs a Statement to access special provision. If a pre-school child does not have a Statement, it does not follow that they are not getting the necessary provision or early intervention.

It may also be of interest to find out about the management of SEN expenditure and the way in which resources are delegated by the Local Authority to schools.

There is a proliferation of documents and guidance for Local Authorities which cannot be the focus in this section. The essential point is that the Local Authority must be accountable for its effectiveness, and information should be available that is crystal clear to parents and professionals who request it.

In summary, there are many helpful documents available to read even before a school visit takes place. It is, however, essential that parents and professionals have in mind what their questions are and what information they need to find out, or the paperwork will be overwhelming. It is also necessary to think about what is really important and what is not and weigh that up when focusing on the individual child's needs. It may be positive to find out that a mainstream school has the best specialist unit in the Local Authority for autism, but not necessarily relevant if the child has severe dyslexia.

PART 3

SETTING UP a VISIT

CHAPTER 12

How to Set Up a Visit

It is important to consider not only what you, as a parent or professional, are hoping to get out of a school visit, but also to have some consideration for the school itself. Schools are normally large places which have busy schedules and timetables. They are also some of the most unforgiving places to visit because time moves on irrespective of whether visitors are late. In other words, if an appointment is scheduled, there may be no flexibility and if visitors are late, the school's timetable will move on without them and the visitor may not get to see or observe a particular class or session. Another obvious, but important point to remember, is that school days are punctuated by breaks and lunchtime and depending on the time of day that a visit is arranged, the visitor may or may not be able to see these aspects of school life as well as formal lessons. Sometimes arriving at the school at the beginning or end of the day will tell the visitor far more about the school than a formal interview. Watching children pile out of the school at the end of the day or boarding the transport, will give an idea of the type of child at the school and clues about general behaviour.

Some parts of the year, or school term, are busier than others. Visiting a school near Christmas or at the end of July will usually mean that the normal timetable is suspended, and whilst the visitor may get to see a nice play rehearsal, it will not convey anything about literacy or numeracy.

It will also be necessary to understand the structure of the school to make sure that the visit has been set up with the most appropriate person. Although it is right and proper to make the appointment with the head teacher, sometimes the head teacher is not the most appropriate person to meet with, particularly if it is a very large comprehensive school. It may be more helpful to meet with the Special Educational Needs Co-ordinator (SENCo) or the head of year. Sometimes in large comprehensives, there are two heads of year; one of whom deals with pastoral matters and the other with academic matters. Depending on the child's needs, it may not be necessary to meet with both. On some occasions, it may be beneficial to meet with specific subject teachers, e.g. if the child has a physical difficulty, but enjoys games or physical education, it would be helpful to see the PE specialist to discuss how the child will be able to access that particular part of the curriculum, whilst on other occasions, the class teacher or form tutor will suffice.

There are also several practical difficulties to overcome:

1. Be very clear about what year group the child is currently in and what year group they will be entering. Some children are not educated within their chronological age group, but it may be assumed when entering a new school that they will be placed back into their actual year group, e.g. a lot of Local Authorities do not allow children to be back-classed and prefer to put them back into their correct age group.

    However, some special schools educate children according to Key Stages rather than year groups, particularly if the classes are small and there would not be a viable class or if there are mixed needs and children are better placed in one class than another. This information needs to be clarified before a school visit, or it could result in discussing the completely wrong year group or meeting the wrong teachers.

2. Try and clarify the different positions and responsibilities within the school. The SENCo may have different responsibilities in an early years setting as opposed to a primary or secondary school. The SENCo usually has responsibility for the day-to-day operation of the school's SEN policy and for co-ordinating provision for children with SEN through the different graduated phases. However, the SENCo may be part time and so it is necessary to be informed whether they will be present on the day of the visit. In addition, in some schools, the role of SENCo is a shared role and in some small schools the head teacher can also be the SENCo. Most schools, however, stress that special educational needs is not the sole responsibility of the SENCo and that SEN in a school is the responsibility of all staff and it is the SENCo's role to manage this.

    It is, therefore, important, when making an appointment, to establish who ultimately will be the person responsible for the management of the child's special educational needs, and if this will be the SENCo, it would be advisable to meet with them during the visit.

    There are national standards for SENCos. Although SENCos must have a good knowledge of special educational needs, the national standards, in fact, focus on expertise in leadership and management as these are key skills when co-ordinating staff and programmes for children, particularly in mainstream schools.

There is currently a proposal for a nationally accredited training for teachers new to the role of Special Educational Needs Co-ordinator which should, come into being by 2011.

3. Be clear from the outset, and when organizing the appointment, what you hope will be gained from the visit as this will give the school an idea of how long the visit should be and over what time period. It can be very frustrating turning up for a visit which you believe will be three or four hours long and the school has put aside 15 minutes with a whirlwind tour. Many schools do include a general tour of the school, and this is very helpful as it gives a general context so that a visitor can see areas of the school which, perhaps, are not relevant now, but may be relevant in a few years time. Some schools suggest that children take visitors on these tours and that can be very enlightening and, perhaps, offer a different perspective than if the tour is carried out by an adult. If one is hoping to observe a class in action and ask specific questions, a school visit may take two to three hours.

4. The timing of a visit will almost determine what questions will be asked. If the child's needs have not been fully identified, the visit may not be as helpful compared to when a final Statement of Special Educational Needs has been issued and then more direct questions can be asked about provision. It may be necessary in fact to return to the school at a later stage to look again at the facilities when things become clarified over time. It is preferable to set aside a substantial amount of time to discuss the child's needs and the Statement, but also to make it clear before the visit that you would like to see (and observe) the class the child will be placed in, as this will give some idea of their peer group. Sometimes, this will be refused on the grounds of confidentially or, indeed, because of practical difficulties, e.g. the class may not physically exist if looking at a Year 7 class whilst the child in question is in Year 6. On other occasions, schools are reluctant to take visitors into classes for good reason, e.g. if the class has some autistic children whose behaviour will be affected by strangers in the room. However, the question should be asked *before you go into the school*, so that the school and class teacher are prepared for visitors should class visits be permitted.

5. It is always helpful, having made an appointment, to follow this up with written communication to confirm the date, time and who the meeting is taking place with. If this is done by email, then it may be necessary to check that the email has been received and noted in the school diary. Do not leave this to chance.

6. Take the name of the secretary (or administrator) who has made the appointment for later reference and out of politeness. It is also helpful

to check on parking facilities, often very difficult to find in a school, and it may take up some time if you are not pre-warned, making you late for an appointment.

7. There may be things that are very specific to the child which you want to observe or try to find out more about when you are in school, e.g. if the child has real issues about food or specific dietary requirements, it may be helpful to ask if you can have a meal with the children and teachers in the school whilst you are there. When looking at a residential school, it will certainly be necessary to visit the care/ residential accommodation, but rather than see empty spaces, it may be better to request a visit when the children come back from school to see how things are actually managed.

8. In addition to sitting in a formal lesson, ask to observe children in the playground or in an outdoor activity or, even, swimming, to see how dressing and undressing is taught, if that is a relevant concern. Again, this may not be possible due to confidentiality which should always be discussed with the school.

9. It may be helpful to meet the head of care, and if so, this needs to be specified before the visit takes place. If possible, talk to the children in the residential part as well, but it is preferable to ask permission beforehand so that everyone is comfortable with this request.

10. Before making an appointment, talk to other parents who have children in the school already. It may be less relevant for professionals to do this. If necessary, ask the school to make contact with such parents or find out the name of one of the governors who may be able to provide contacts. This will give an insight, but do remember that this is one person's experience, which may be quite different to another person's and the child's needs may be quite different to another child's.

11. If the child is going into a unit attached to a mainstream school, it will be very important to visit the specialist unit or class and also the mainstream class where inclusion will take place. This can sometimes be overlooked, particularly if it appears that the child is spending a lot of time in a specialist class or unit. Even if this is the case, it may be that playtimes and lunchtimes are still spent in the general school playground or the canteen/dining hall and so this aspect should be considered during the visit.

12. Once the meeting is set up and confirmed, then there is a need to obtain the necessary documents and make sure they have been read carefully beforehand so any questions can be raised. In addition to being clear about the child's needs, questions or concerns that have been raised through the documentation, e.g. in the Ofsted Report, should be discussed if they are going to be relevant to the child's

provision. There is nothing confidential about any of the documents listed in the previous chapter and the head teacher should be very willing to discuss the issues raised. The way in which questions are phrased will often determine the response given. This is a skill that needs to be practised on someone else before going on a school visit to make sure that, as a visitor, you don't come across as being critical or accusatory when, in reality, all you are trying to do is to find out the facts. Good will and good intentions on both sides is desirable. This is not an exercise to look for pitfalls or negative points, but to get an overall perspective of the school, its strengths and weaknesses and whether it can be an appropriate placement for a particular child. However, it is your visit and perhaps the only opportunity to ask the questions you want to ask.

Any outcomes or findings should not reflect in any way on the good education that the school may otherwise provide for other children at the school.

SHOULD THE CHILD BE TAKEN ON A SCHOOL VISIT?

The Code of Practice, in the chapter on child participation, quotes Articles 12 and 13 of the United Nations Convention on the Rights of the Child:

Children who are capable of forming views, have a right to receive and make known information, to express an opinion and to have that opinion, taken into account in any matters affecting them. The views of the child should be given due weight according to the age, maturity and capability of the child.

It is a fine balance between listening to a child and ensuring that their views are valued, whilst at the same time, needing to make informed decisions and not over-burden them with decision-making procedures, where their experience, knowledge and understanding is not yet sufficient to make appropriate judgements. Psychologists will try and present the child's views in or with the psychological report. At SEND proceedings, the views of the child concerning the issues raised will be asked for or the reasons why it has not been possible to ascertain these views. It is, therefore, important not to just ignore the child's voice.

When visiting schools, some parents take their children with them and, particularly at pre-school level, this may be the first time that the child is in a larger group environment and this may be an opportunity to see how they will cope. However, for other children, it can be quite a stressful experience, which will make a school visit more limited in what can be achieved or evaluated by the adult. If visiting several schools, this may also confuse the child or raise expectations, which cannot be realized, if they like a particular school but do not get offered a place. For older children, school visits may result in very helpful views or opinions being expressed, which could be a turning point for some parents.

It may be advisable for the child to attend a proposed school for an assessment or a visit once a place has been offered or before they begin, particularly if they will need a transition period.

For a residential placement, it is sometimes suggested that a child attends on an overnight basis, but this could be difficult as a child may become homesick on a short stay and attribute negative views about the school, where a slightly longer time would have ironed out some of these problems (or, indeed, vice-versa).

Parents will have to judge what to do, depending on the circumstances. They should also listen to advice from the school and/or other professionals advising them. Ultimately, the parents will need to decide the best way forward, based on their own knowledge of their child.

ISSUES OF CONFIDENTIALITY

Some schools have confidentiality policies, but most school communities understand that no one can offer absolute confidentiality. The definition of confidentiality is 'something which is spoken or given in private, entrusted with another's secret affairs'. The confider is asking for the content of the conversation to be kept secret. Anyone offering absolute confidentiality to someone else would be offering to keep their conversation completely secret and not discuss it with anyone.* In practice, there are few circumstances where absolute confidentiality is offered.

At the beginning of any conversation, it will be necessary to clarify that the conversation is not to be considered as confidential. There are, sometimes, assumptions made that 'throw away' or anecdotal remarks will not be noted. It should be made quite clear that any remarks or discussions may be disclosed. However, it is also important to consider other children and therefore other children should not be referred to by name or identified, e.g. during a discussion about other children's needs within the same class.

As a visitor to a school, it is essential to respect confidentiality within the classroom. The following points should be noted:

1. Personal questions about children, or their difficulties, are inappropriate in a classroom environment.

2. If questions need to be asked about a child's needs which may have a direct impact on the child under discussion, e.g. in a case of very

---

*   Bristol Healthy Schools Programme.

challenging behaviour that has been observed, it is important to depersonalize the discussion so that issues can be explored without personal information being disclosed.

3.   Staff should respect the presence of other people and children when they are having conversations and if they do not do this, this may alert you to a problem of confidentiality within the school.

Clearly, there are situations which relate to ensuring children's safety and well-being and sometimes, for this reason, schools are reluctant to allow other parents into a classroom.

Schools must abide by various laws which relate to confidentiality. In addition, parents and professionals should be aware of the following Acts:

- **The Human Rights Act 1998** gives everyone the right to 'respect for his private and family life, his home and his correspondence', unless this is overridden by the 'public interest', e.g. for reasons of child protection, for the protection of public safety, public order, health or morals or for the rights and freedoms of others.

- **The Data Protection Act 1998** applies to personal data of living, identifiable individuals, not anonymized data, manual and electronic records. Schools need to be clear, when collecting personal data, what purposes it will be used for and schools should have policies to clarify this to staff, children and parents.

- **The Freedom of Information Act 2000** amends the Data Protection Act and gives everyone the right to request any records of a public body including what schools hold about them. A school may withhold information if it is considered that the information may damage the recipient if disclosed. The school's data or record-keeping policy should also cover the requirements of this Act.

Under the new SEND regulations, maintained schools will be required to allow a professional, instructed by a parent, into the school to assess the child's functioning in the school setting. This was not the case previously, where schools could refuse entry. This may be part of an assessment of the child and also an evaluation of whether the school can meet the child's needs. The school may ask for a Criminal Records Bureau (CRB) check.

Within the context of confidentiality, parents should be aware of the Criminal Records Bureau, not only in relation to individuals working with vulnerable children, but also if they are considering private tutors, therapists, counsellors or other individuals. The CRB is run as an Executive Agency of the Home Office by civil servants and in partnership with the Department of Health and the Department for Children, Schools and Families (DCSF) for the provision of information that is held by them, of people considered unsuitable or banned from working with children and vulnerable adults.

Since May 2006, it has been mandatory for all maintained Pupil Referral Units (PRUs), schools and other employers in the education service to obtain a CRB check for new appointments. This also applies to independent schools.

Current legislation does not allow the self-employed or individuals to apply for a CRB check on themselves, as they cannot ask an exempted question of themselves. However, a self-employed person can apply for a CRB check by registering with an agency. It is also possible, as an individual, to make a 'subject access' request to their local police force under the provisions of the Data Protection Act 1998, which will provide up-to-date details of any criminal records in the UK.

It may be relevant to discuss the ways in which schools follow policies on confidentiality, e.g. this might be very important if there are discussions about contraceptive advice and pregnancy for a child with learning difficulties. However, it is mentioned in this chapter because it may be raised as an issue in terms of a visit to the school or whether permission can be given for observation within the classroom. This should be clarified prior to the visit, and then, if necessary, there would still be time to check the policy with the Local Authority, the Department for Children, Schools and Families or independent advisors; such as law firms specializing in education.

Chapter 13

Looking at the Physical School Environment in General

Children's learning can be greatly influenced by their surroundings, and good ventilation, lighting and fresh air are all conducive to learning. The layout of the school, architecture, décor and facilities can all shape the learning environment and also have a major impact, particularly on children with special educational needs. The school building, itself, can sometimes create fears and concerns for a child and the better it looks the more inviting it may be. Some schools are still located in Victorian buildings with, clearly, inadequate facilities both within the walls and outside. Even some more modern schools have not been built with children with special educational needs and disabilities in mind and huge changes are required; not only in the obvious places, such as stairs and corridors, but also in toilets and changing areas.

In addition, the use of information technology has changed the face of learning and the installation of equipment has also challenged the fabric of many buildings. Added to this, is the introduction of facilities for children with special educational needs, such as induction loop aids which may require structural changes to buildings in addition to health and safety regulations.

WHAT ASPECTS OF THE SCHOOL ENVIRONMENT CAN MAKE A DIFFERENCE?

Some basic aspects make significant differences for children with special educational needs. Decent lighting is most important for children with

---

* The source for some of the material in this chapter was *Family Guide to School Environments* (2008), published by BCSE and Morgan Ashurst.

visual impairments. For children with sensory needs there are a host of subtle difficulties which will impact on their concentration. Narrow, winding corridors will be almost impossible for wheelchair users or children with gross motor difficulties. There are behavioural issues which might also be created by environmental conditions, such as hidden corners being a haven for bullies.

Children with visual impairments will need different surface textures and clear signposting, whereas those with hearing impairments may need carpets and curtains to soften sound. Children with autism may require reduction of detail, good levels of light and natural ventilation and good quality acoustics. Noise can be a real issue for some children with autism or hearing impairment and noise reducing floor and ceiling coverings can prevent reverberating sound.

Environmental issues have been recognized as being quite critical and, indeed, a school, which went into special measures, has recently been heralded as a revitalized design icon following work by a multi-disciplinary team of architects, engineers, construction managers, performance artists, educational psychologists and researchers working on improvements to the school which had a significant impact on achievement, teaching and culture.

ARE SPACE AND COLOUR IMPORTANT?

The amount of space that children with autistic spectrum disorder (ASD) like to have between themselves and others (proxemics) can be quite critical and in residential accommodation, there should be enough circulation space. Some new schools have been built with curved walls which reduce the existence of harsh corners and provide some cues by which to lead the children from one area to another, compensating for any visio-spatial weaknesses.

For children with attention deficit hyperactivity disorder (ADHD) or challenging behaviour, high-level windows, which reduce risk may be a good idea. While open windows may aid good learning, it can increase traffic noise and also provide a focus for escape.

Changes in ambient colour can be used to signal a mood or atmosphere in a sensory room or during an interaction. The range of colours, therefore, is important, e.g. red appears to have an arousing effect and green to have a calming effect, although for some children prolonged exposure to any one strong colour produces discomfort.

Research evidence seems to show that shades of pink and purple have a positive effect on managing behavioural symptoms, and grey, which is a neutral and non-reflective colour, provokes no extremes of reaction and has also been widely used.

Not all children will be able to read signs, so research shows that making different areas of the school look different from each other, whether the difference is marked by colour or displays, helps children work out how to get from one place to another.

WHAT ABOUT OUTDOOR AREAS?

Many schools are beginning to appreciate that outdoor areas can be turned into stimulating spaces to study science and also create an outdoor classroom. Increasingly, new ideas to promote environmental issues are coming into schools and schools are beginning to recycle and are trying to reduce their carbon footprint. Whether this will have an impact on any children with special educational needs has yet to be seen, but creating a healthier environment may, for example, have an impact on children with asthma who can be affected by poor physical conditions in schools.

For many children, the playground can be a daunting place, particularly for children with special educational needs who may be integrating well into mainstream schools in classroom time, but the social arena of playtime is quite another challenge. The playground environment will often offer clues about the value that a school puts on helping children to integrate and the way in which thought has gone into different areas of the playground, allowing quiet areas for those children who might find it harder to play sport and the type of equipment that is provided. Some schools will provide sensory areas for children with PMLD.

Very vulnerable children, who fall over, need to have rubberized playground surfaces as well as, of course, proper supervision. Wheelchair users may need accessible playground equipment; such as lowered goals in football.

It is now a legal requirement, under the Disability Discrimination Act, that entrances and exits are accessible to disabled people. There should be ramps as well as steps. These benefit not only wheelchair users, but parents pushing buggies.

CAN SCHOOL EQUIPMENT AND FURNITURE MAKE A DIFFERENCE?

There may be issues for children who have difficulty in carrying text books, so personal lockers or other suitable storage facilities need to be visible and appropriately placed. A child who ends up having a teaching assistant to carry their books and equipment loses some of their vital independence.

Look at the size of chairs and desks to consider whether school furniture is appropriate for the need. Sitting posture is very important to avoid back pain and children who need sloping surfaces, e.g. with dyspraxia, need to adjust school desks or chairs accordingly, so furniture has to be flexible. Are computers accessible to all and is there enough space around them for children with mobility difficulties?

Horrible toilets mean children drink less during the day in order to avoid going. The resulting dehydration can cause constipation, headaches, fatigue and lack of concentration. Insecure doors in toilets can be a trigger for bad behaviour and a place where children often try to avoid.

Having established many different features that are important in the physical surroundings, there is a need to consider what type of environment will suit a child's needs. Whilst some of this information may be gained through written questions or information, much of it can be observed during the school visit.

QUESTIONS TO ASK ABOUT THE GENERAL PHYSICAL SCHOOL ENVIRONMENT

1. Will the physical environment be suitable for the child in question, e.g. will they be able to access all parts of the school and care environment? Are there different levels? Are there lifts? Is the outdoor environment suitable or are the paths/grass areas completely unsuitable? What is the furthest distance children need to walk between lessons? Do they need to?

2. What are the acoustics like for a child with a hearing impairment?

3. Is the layout of the school suitable for a child with a visual impairment and are there resources available to ensure that the child can be as independent as possible, e.g. handrails, different textures on flooring etc.?

4. For children with emotional and behavioural difficulties, is the environment calm and secure?

5. Is the environment a low arousal environment for children with sensory difficulties or autism? Is the lighting appropriate? Are classes warm enough/too warm?

6. Is it a suitable for using electric wheelchairs?

7. Does the care accommodation feel homely whilst, at the same time, is it appropriate for children with different needs and abilities?

8. Can a quiet and calm place be located for the child within the school grounds or play areas? Are there any parts of the school or playground that are unlit or unsupervised? Who supervises the use of play equipment? How many classes have break in a particular area at the same time?

9. Is the technology mobile or are all the computer facilities located in one room? Are they accessible for wheelchair users?

10. How do staff help children feel like members of smaller communities within the larger school environment?

This chapter has primarily dealt with the physical environment of the school, but the classroom environment is also crucial and similar questions will apply, e.g. is there sufficient space in the classroom itself?

There is no substitute for looking, watching and seeing what is in front of your eyes. Some schools may be set in impressive buildings or beautiful grounds, but what is more important is the fact that the school is cared for and thought has gone into how the setting is conducive for the children's learning and what potential the school has in adapting to new challenges. Some very simple changes, such as reducing the distance to walk between classrooms by timetabling rooms differently, will make the school day much easier for a child with physical needs.

CHAPTER 14

Looking at the Classroom Environment

It is important to try and spend some time, preferably, observing teachers working with the children in the classroom where the child will be placed, or, if this is not possible (perhaps because the class is not yet in existence), then to see a class in the potential year group, e.g. if the child is in Year 6 and transferring to secondary school, it would be preferable to observe a Year 7 class rather than a Year 10 class. The following questions are raised, but many may be more applicable for professionals, rather than parents, as judgement about what goes on in a classroom is a skilled task based on years of experience. Nevertheless, parents should also be aware of the kinds of things to look out for.

QUESTIONS TO ASK ABOUT THE CLASSROOM
ENVIRONMENT

1. When generally walking around the school, note how teachers speak to the children and, in particular, how they deal with behaviour. Are the staff calm and do they appear caring? If shouting is heard, ask questions about the circumstances, rather than making assumptions that this is representative.

2. Look at the accommodation, particularly if the child is to be withdrawn, and ascertain whether there is a specific classroom, or small room for this or whether it is an ad hoc arrangement. If teaching is to be delivered in a group, is the classroom big enough for separate groups; if not, where will the group teaching take place?

3. Try to observe children in the playground as well as in lesson time. Do the staff and children look happy? Look at how involved the staff are in children's play activities. What facilities are available and, in

particular, are there are places in the playground where it is hard for teachers to observe and children may become isolated and bullied?

4. If permitted (and permission should be asked), talk to the children about the school. This is particularly helpful when visiting special schools, as children may share their experiences prior to attendance at the school and the way in which the special school is different.

5. In the classroom, note the class sizes and how well the numbers fit into the accommodation provided. Is there physical space for additional resources, e.g. a work station or wheelchairs? Note the organization and the way in which lessons start and finish. Are the goals and objectives of the lesson clearly set out in a visual format and do the children understand them? Are different strategies used for children who cannot access the usual format?

6. Is the furniture appropriate? Can the height of the desks or chairs be altered? Can new furniture be ordered if necessary?

7. Note the teaching methods in use. Are they varied enough? Is there a good balance in the class between visual aids and activities involving listening and speaking? Are worksheets designed for different abilities? Look at the standard text books for the age group; what is the text difficulty and compare the readability age levels of the text with the child's reading ability, if known. How much reading, note-taking, copying and free-writing, if necessary, is there in the class? Would the child be able to access the work without a reader or scribe?

8. Ask to see copies of record sheets and individual education plans (IEPs) to give you some idea of how these are drawn up. Clearly, there are issues of confidentiality and no copies should be retained unless the names have been removed.

9. Look at the timetable and consider where withdrawal sessions might fit in. In a special school, where does the focus lie and what are the priority areas for the teacher? Listen to the way in which the teacher explains things. Is the language easy to follow; if not, is it backed up by visual aids? What is the pace of the lesson? Does it move too fast and what are the modifications put in place for children who need additional help to keep up? How much time does the teacher spend with individual children? Does the teacher circulate or stick to one group? If there are children already being supported in class, how frequently does the teacher bring them into the lesson? Does the learning support assistant (LSA) know in advance what the teacher will be doing? Ask the teacher and/or the LSA how they plan the content of the lesson. Is the child receiving most of the lesson via the LSA rather than the teacher? What is the adult-to-child ratio and is it sufficient for all the children with different needs in the classroom?

10. If there is a child with special educational needs already in the class, how involved is the child with other children? Do the adults in the class initiate social interactions if these are not spontaneously forthcoming from the children themselves? Is the classroom set up to facilitate social interactions so that children have face-to-face contact, e.g. round a group or horseshoe shaped table? How do the staff encourage children? For example, look at the way humour is used, whether words of encouragement are understood by all children; how prompting takes place and the ways in which confidence is boosted in general. Ask about the marking system. Is it appropriate for all the children? Has the teacher differentiated the marking system?

11. Is the language used culturally sensitive? When the teacher explains things, is the language clear? Will further differentiation be needed if the child has a severe language difficulty? Ask the teacher how the language of the classroom would be addressed on a day-to-day basis, particularly in a mainstream classroom.

12. How are questioning skills used to help children learn? Are questions open ended or structured? Is the teacher alert to the fact that some children need questions rephrased so they can answer?

13. Is there generally a good working atmosphere in the classroom? Do peers make fun of others behind their backs? Do teachers condone racism or bullying by turning a blind eye or offering dismissive remarks?

14. If work or behaviour is not appropriate, how does the teacher ensure that unfair comparisons are avoided and the child does not feel a sense of failure? What reward and sanction system is used in the class? Ask if teachers are observed by other teachers as part of the regular practice in the school. Find out if the Special Educational Needs Co-ordinator (SENCo) is regularly in the classroom or whether their role is a 'hands-off', sitting in their own room, approach?

15. Circulate and look at the children's work. Does the work reflect what is being taught and are the children learning as much as they are capable of doing? If children need help in class, how do they alert the teacher's attention? Do they queue up at the desk and waste lots of time, or do they sit wasting time at their desk whilst they wait for someone to come over? Look at the wall and noticeboards; can the children access the information? Are all the children's work displayed? Do the classroom displays reflect any specialist approaches used in the class or school, e.g. signs?

16. Do children help each other in the class and is this encouraged? Do the children generally seem to be enjoying themselves and, similarly, do teachers seem to be enjoying themselves? Look at the other children and consider whether these children could be the child's friends or

are there children who could pose a threat, e.g. is it appropriate to place a particularly frail or vulnerable child who is not mobile in a class of children with challenging behaviour? If a child will be in a minority, either in terms of their special educational need, gender, religion, culture or background, will the child fit into the class? If you have concerns, raise these with the teacher and ask how they would address them (it is not necessarily a bad thing to be the only child with special educational needs in a class, but the teacher needs to explain how the child will be included and socially integrated).

17. Do children behave well in lessons and around the school? Are they generally courteous and respectful? How do teachers give children choices and how do children make choices? Do children show initiative? Can they take responsibility and is responsibility offered to them? In a special school/provision, how is the teaching adapted to enable children to learn effectively, despite their difficulties, and does the teacher appear to do this spontaneously?

18. When looking around the classroom, are most of the children engaged in the lesson or is there a lot of time-wasting and avoidance?

19. Is information and communication technology (ICT) effectively used? Has the teacher prepared tasks so they are ready to go, or is there time-wasting, because things are not yet set up? Does the teacher know how to repair things, or do they have to call other people? Are signs and symbols used generally? Are there visual timetables in class?

20. What are the toilet facilities like and how easy are they for the child to access, particularly for young children or children on toileting programmes?

21. Are classes ever taught together? If so, for what lessons? Will this have a positive or negative impact?

22. Is the building open plan? Do classrooms open onto a general resource area? Does this affect noise levels? Will this be appropriate for a child with ASD, hearing impairment or sensory difficulties?

In summary, if there is something you observe and do not understand, ask the teacher at the end of the lesson so that you are clear as to the reasons why something occurred so you do not jump to the wrong conclusions. Any observations must be made in the context of a child with special educational needs, e.g. putting three classes together for an afternoon of teaching may be very beneficial for some children, but, perhaps, disadvantageous for a child with autism, where the level of noise may be unacceptable. This does not reflect bad practice within the school, but you do need some clarity as to what might occur if an autistic child, for example, attended there.

PARENTAL INVOLVEMENT

The Special Educational Needs Code of Practice includes a chapter entitled 'Working in Partnership with Parents'. Whilst one would always hope that relationships between parents and schools will be smooth and mutually beneficial, given the kinds of issues that may arise, both parties will need a lot of understanding and benefit of the doubt. The Code of Practice states 'All parents of children with special educational needs should be treated as partners' (para. 2:2). Parents should be supported and empowered to:

- recognize and fulfil their responsibilities as parents and play an active and valued role in their children's education
- have knowledge of their child's entitlement within the SEN framework
- make their views known about how their child is educated
- have access to information, advice and support during assessment and any related decision-making processes about special educational provision.

Professionals visiting schools will also want to ensure parental voices are heard.

QUESTIONS TO ASK ABOUT PARENTAL INVOLVEMENT IN SCHOOL

1. Does the school provide a leaflet for parents, setting out how they will ensure the Code of Practice is addressed and does it make reference to a parent partnership scheme?

2. How does the school generally keep parents informed about their child?

3. Is there a home/school diary; if so, is it sent home on a daily or weekly basis? Parents should find out if this is a diary openly read by children and, if so, what comments are expected. Is it just a list of activities or is it a conduit for notes between teachers and parents?

4. If a parent wanted to speak to a teacher or LSA, how do they make appointments? Is the teacher happy for informal chats at the school gate, or do they want to avoid this?

5. Are there parents who spend time in the classroom, either with their own child or with other children? Is there a way in which parents can watch teachers work with their child, e.g. through DVD/video presentations? This has been a very successful venture undertaken at some special schools, and can also work well the other way round, where parents take DVD/videos of their child at home so that the

teachers can see the different ways they behave or strategies that parents carry out.

6. How often are formal written reports issued? When are parents expected to attend IEP meetings either to set goals or review them? When are parents invited to formal reviews on their child? What is the format for annual reviews? Is there an opportunity to meet with other parents and, if so, are these formal or informal occasions and what types of discussions take place?

7. Can the child in question meet with any children before they begin school, and, if so, can the school provide a list of names? (Check confidentiality issues.)

8. When considering residential schools, there will be some very specific questions that parents and professionals may want to ask, as discussed in Chapter 32, 'Residential Schools'.

9. How does the school accept feedback of any concerns and would they be accepting of new ideas? If the school is a long way from home, what arrangements are in place to keep parents in touch and how will children see each other socially? If it is important to the parents, ask the school how they will be aware of the child's cultural and religious needs and what kinds of activities will take place to promote these.

10. How can parents become more involved with the school, if they want to? Can they contact the governing body?

11. Is the school able to inform parents of their rights without parents feeling that this will disrupt their relationship with the school?

12. Can parents offer their knowledge to the school by becoming mentors?

CHAPTER 15

Making a Record of the School Visit

It is always difficult to know what to record and how to record it. There is always an element of subjectivity and care must be taken that innuendos or implications are not misinterpreted. Factual evidence is most important, but sometimes things are not 'black or white'. When a public body, such as Ofsted, monitor evidence, they have set headings and use a table to fill in results. The Ofsted website sets out the Record Of Monitoring Evidence (ROME), for new independent school registrations (2008). As a framework, this type of information can be recorded about all schools.

INFORMATION ABOUT THE SCHOOL

- name of school
- address
- telephone number/email address
- head teacher
- date of visit
- type of school (for special, note principle disability group)
- number on roll
- age range
- number of boarders (if residential)
- gender split
- fees – day/residential.

Some, or most, of this information may be needed, but not necessarily all of it. It is necessary to establish whether the school is under- or over-subscribed, whether they have a waiting list and, obviously, if they have a place for the child and how long the place will be kept. This is particularly important if there is an appeal to the SEND Tribunal (Special Educational Needs and Disability Tribunal), as this can sometimes take months and there will need to be a place kept available during that time. It is advisable to get an offer of a place in writing and a date until which the place will be kept open. If an appeal is taking longer than anticipated, it may be necessary to update this confirmation.

STAFF

- number of teaching staff
- full-time QTS (qualified teaching staff)
- part-time QTS
- number of teaching assistants (full-time and part-time)
- number of care staff (full-time and part-time).

This information may be helpful if adult-to-child ratios are important. There is an assumption that all teachers are qualified, but this cannot be assumed and this may be important to know, particularly if the school is a private, part-time institution. It may also be helpful to know how many newly qualified teachers (NQT) are in the school and, specifically, if they will be the child's class teacher.

SPECIAL NEEDS

- number of children with Statements of Special Educational Needs
- number of statemented children paid for by a Local Authority (if the school is non-maintained)
- number of children on school's SEN Register.

The number of children paid for by a Local Authority is very useful to know. First, it demonstrates that the school has been established as a school that can meet a particular special educational need, as the Local Authority is obliged to satisfy itself of this fact before funding a place, and, second, it will provide some kind of history with regard to Local Authority funding, e.g. if the Local Authority has already funded three or four children this may offer some confidence, although it must be stressed, that with inclusive education now gaining force, some Local Authorities would not have funded those places if the climate was as it is now.

ETHNIC MINORITIES

Normally, questions about ethnic minorities would not be asked, unless, of course, it was relevant to a particular situation. It may be necessary to establish that the school is culturally diverse. It may be helpful to know the proportion of children who enter school speaking English as a second language (and this is highlighted on Ofsted Reports) and, as a result, whether specific support is provided for English as an Additional Language (EAL) and how many children are supported. Again, this may have some subtle implications, e.g. if there is an autistic child entering a mainstream class, where the majority of children do not speak English as a first language, it will be helpful to consider whether there will be adequate language and communication role models, and what impact this may have when trying to develop social skills and communication.

Ofsted then go into much more detail under the following categories:

- The quality of education provided by the school.
- The spiritual, moral, social and cultural development of children.
- The welfare, health and safety of the children.
- The suitability of the proprietor and staff.
- The suitability of the premises and accommodation.
- The provision of information.
- The effectiveness of the school's procedures for handling complaints.

This is the way in which a formal body, such as Ofsted, evaluates the school, but, clearly, it is not for parents or professionals to look at all of these aspects, but some may be very relevant. Further information on ROME is available on the Ofsted website.

Following the launch of Every Child Matters in 2003, many educational bodies now measure their effectiveness against the main aims for every child as set out in that document. These are that every child, whatever their background or their circumstances, should have the support they need to:

- **be healthy** – enjoy good physical and mental health and live a healthy lifestyle
- **stay safe** – be protected from harm and neglect
- **enjoy and achieve** – get the most out of life and develop skills for adulthood
- **make a positive contribution** – be involved with the community and society and not engage in anti-social or offending behaviour
- **achieve economic well-being** – not being prevented by economic disadvantage from achieving their full potential in life.

Each of these themes has a detailed outcomes framework attached to it, which can be explored on the ECM website.

Following this initiative, Children's Trusts were formed which bring together Local Authority's Education and Children's Social Services, some Children's Health Services, Connexions and it can include other services such as Youth Offending Teams. Children's Trusts will normally be part of the Local Authority and will report to local elected members. It was hoped that key services for children would be integrated under a Director of Children's Services, accountable for Local Authority Education and Children's Social Services. It is certainly worthwhile to read this report, as it does emphasize some key features, which all parents and professionals will, themselves, want for children, including earlier intervention and integrated services where children are assessed. It also discusses children in care and the transition of disabled young people, and those with learning difficulties, moving from school to adulthood. The report identifies how a Common Assessment Framework (CAF) across agencies can be advantageous. This not only looks at specialist educational support, but the assessment identifies all the child's needs, not just the educational ones which may require intervention.

Although it will not be possible for a parent visiting a school to directly evaluate how the five outcomes from Every Child Matters are adhered to on a daily basis, nevertheless, it is helpful to keep these principles in mind as these do provide the overall framework for children's services. However, if the visit is initiated by a parent or professional for a specific reason, they will have their own questions in mind and it will be necessary to identify priority areas.

MAKING A RECORD OF THE SCHOOL VISIT

1. Ensure you have sufficient paper and pens. There is nothing more infuriating than running out of ink or having the wrong sized paper. Although small notebooks are handy for carrying around, an A4 size notebook, with a margin, is much more useful as notes can be jotted down in the margin and if you return to areas already discussed, there is the room to add additional points.

2. Make it very clear from the outset that notes will be made. It is important not to trust anything to memory. Don't be afraid to ask someone to slow down so notes can be taken. There are occasions when you will be specifically asked not to make notes on something that is said. This is quite tricky, especially if the information that is being shared is important. My advice is to state, at the beginning, that nothing should be shared if the person is not happy for it to be noted.

3. If other chapters in this book have been followed, then a series of questions which need answering will already have been mapped out. Again, make sure that sufficient space is left under your questions to write an answer, or you will be flicking backwards and forwards between pages which can be very annoying.

4. It is always preferable to arrange questions under headings before the visit takes place, so that the questions are organized in your mind and it is also far easier for the person responding to know what specific issue is being addressed rather than making it appear confused, e.g. if there are specific questions about therapeutic input, then it is preferable to ask about all the therapies one after the other, rather than interrupting with another train of thought. It is not always possible to set a fixed agenda and, obviously, one has to be flexible because thoughts do become connected in people's minds and then this can lead into a very interesting, relevant but different direction. However, after this, it is better to return to the notes and bring the discussion back to the topic under discussion.

5. Important information can be relayed while on the move or in the playground. In theory, recording information may be helpful using a sound recorder; such as the MP3, but this may be a step too far and cause others to feel intimidated. This may be the way to go in the future as technological developments in recording become more practical.

6. If you already have a lot of up to date factual information, then this can be stated at the beginning and all you need is confirmation that it is correct. This can save a lot time. Bear in mind that the information may seem up to date on the latest website but schools change very rapidly. It is also very helpful to just ask whether the school has any building programmes or significant policy changes occurring in the next couple of years. Sometimes, specialist units are already being discussed for schools and this can have an impact on a child. If a large building programme is going to begin and last for the next three years, and the child has significant sensory or hearing difficulties, it may help to know this beforehand. This should all be noted.

7. It is essential to try and be as objective as possible, but, at the same time, an opinion may be expressed. Your opinion, although based on factual evidence, obviously can be subjective. It may be that everyone thinks that the school will be excellent for the child, but if as a parent/professional, you feel that is not the case and have very good and sound reasons for stating this, when taking notes, jot down your own views in the margin linked to what is being said and that will trigger your thoughts again later.

8. There may well be some very organized people who can think in boxes and tables or visualize things in diagrams or schematically. However, it is not usually possible to fit things neatly in such a format on a visit as discussions move very rapidly. Long-hand notes are probably preferable.

9. There are occasions when things occur at school, and it is not possible to jot notes down immediately, e.g. if a child comes up to speak to you wanting to share information about the school, or if behavioural disturbances are heard, such as bad language being used or shouting. These things should be written down as soon as you can if you feel they may be relevant to your situation. It is better to discuss what you hear and give the school the opportunity to explain whether these incidents occur frequently or not.

10. It is important to transcribe notes as soon as possible, or things will be forgotten. With the best will in the world, notes can sometimes end up being quite scrappy or handwriting cannot be read, and if you need to make sense of notes, it is important that as little distance and time as possible is put between note taking and the visit. Write up the notes neatly or type them, and then revisit them perhaps the next day to ensure the accuracy. This needs to be built into your time when you are thinking about how long a visit takes or there is a real risk that after arrival at home or back in the office, events will overtake you and the time-frame becomes extended.

11. Keep careful copies of your handwritten notes in a file with all your other documents, making sure that you have dated everything correctly. These contemporaneous notes constitute important evidence if, for example, you are arguing that a school is inappropriate, or, likewise, if you wish the child to attend a school. You need to have good reasons for establishing why the school is the only appropriate school to meet the child's needs.

12. These are your personal notes and thoughts, which you are not obliged to divulge to others. However, they will only be useful if shared. If they need to be sent to others or the school in question (to check for factual information), then you will need to send out the notes in good order. This means they should be factual and should not contain anything you would be unhappy to share with the school; notes should be in ink, dated and original (not copied from elsewhere). There are legal guidelines for keeping contemporaneous notes.

13. It is often the case that when trying to summarize a discussion, some points need to be checked. Obtain an email contact before leaving the school and ask any further questions as soon as possible after the visit. Schools are usually very helpful in providing this further information.

It is necessary to remember that however objective one tries to be, whether as a parent or a professional, you may not be impartial. This may result in forming what appears to you to be an objective opinion, but, in reality, it is a subjective opinion because of your partiality.

This is often the reason why a parent prefers to visit with a professional they trust and, indeed, this can work both ways. A professional can also learn much about a child by undertaking a school visit together with the parent.

PART 4

LOOKING at SPECIFIC PROVISION/ INTERVENTION

CHAPTER 16

Teaching for Specific Learning Difficulties

As already outlined in Chapter 3, 'Cognition and Learning', specific learning difficulties (SpLD) is an umbrella term which will include dyslexia, dyscalculia, dyspraxia and other associated problems. This chapter will focus on teaching for dyslexia and associated literacy and numeracy difficulties. Dyspraxia will be covered in the chapter on occupational therapy.

DYSLEXIA

> Dyslexia is a specific learning difficulty which mainly affects the development of literacy and language related skills. It is likely to be present at birth and to be lifelong in its effects. It is characterised by difficulties with phonological processing, rapid naming, working memory, processing speed and the automatic development of skills that may not match up to an individual's other cognitive abilities. It tends to be resistant to conventional teaching methods, but its effects can be mitigated by appropriately specific intervention, including the application of information technology and supportive counselling. (British Dyslexia Association 2009)

The British Psychological Society working party report on dyslexia (British Psychological Society 1999) suggested ten different hypotheses that could be associated with dyslexia. The working definition now used by psychologists is 'dyslexia is evident when accurate and fluent word reading and/or spelling develops very incompletely or with great difficulty' (p.18).

DYSCALCULIA

Dyscalculia is defined as:

> a condition that affects the ability to acquire arithmetical skills. Dyscalculic learners may have difficulty understanding simple number concepts, lack an intuitive grasp of numbers and have problems learning number facts and procedures. Even if they produce a correct answer or use a correct method, they may do so mechanically and without confidence. (*National Numeracy Strategy* DfES 2001)

WHAT QUALIFICATIONS SHOULD A SPECIALIST SpLD TEACHER HAVE?

The Professional Association of Teachers of Students with Specific Learning Difficulties (PATOSS) was formed in 1987 as an association representing teachers who had gained the RSA (now OCR) diploma in specific learning difficulties. Since that time, when it was fairly simple to identify those teachers who had taken a specialist route, many other training courses now exist and it is sometimes more difficult to identify the necessary professional qualifications. If one looks on the PATOSS website, there are a number of courses and institutions providing diploma and certificate courses, some of which are full time and others distance learning.

The British Dyslexia Association (BDA) recognizes the need to try and establish, nationally and internationally, recognized levels of proficiency. Although many teachers, LSAs or therapists may attend introductory courses on specific learning difficulties, the BDA awards Approved Teacher Status (ATS) for professionals following a course with a minimum of:

- 40 hours of lectures plus seminars, tutorials and study time
- 20 hours evaluated specialist teaching
- 1 hour of teaching to be observed and assessed by a tutor who holds an associate membership of the BDA (AMBDA).

An associate membership of the BDA (AMBDA) means the professional has followed an accredited course consisting of a minimum of:

- 90 hours of lectures, seminars and guided learning hours plus private study time, including 12 hours of devoted study to psychometric testing
- 30 hours of evaluated specialist teaching
- 3 hours of teaching to be observed and assessed by a course tutor who holds AMBDA
- 3 diagnostic assessment reports, one of which must be observed and assessed by a course tutor who holds AMBDA.

The ATS or AMBDA can be awarded to qualified teachers, speech and language therapists, occupational therapists, educational psychologists or other psychologists with appropriate professional qualifications and experience. It is possible to find out whether a course is BDA accredited or is a recognized course by consulting the BDA or PATOSS websites.

There are also courses for learning support assistants which are also BDA accredited dyslexia training courses. A typical course might be for a one-day per week attendance over ten weeks (50 hours), plus 40 hours work in schools (which many LSAs are probably doing at the same time) and 60 hours private study. With this kind of course, the LSA may get a Dyslexia Action Certificate for teaching assistants (see Dyslexia Action website for further details).

Although the BDA have established a qualification for teachers to support children with dyscalculia, whereas the AMBDA is recognized by the Joint Council for Qualifications as an accepted qualification for the provision of support evidence on behalf of examination candidates with learning difficulties, the AMBDA in numeracy is not recognized in the same way. The AMBDA in numeracy focuses on how dyslexia affects maths learning; the diagnostic appraisal of maths skills and teaching specifically focused on numeracy. There are clearly many more teachers with the AMBDA qualification in dyslexia compared to those who have done the course in numeracy, but it is certainly worthwhile to find out whether a teacher has pursued either or both qualifications, particularly if the child in question has a very specific problem with maths or numeracy.

From June 2008 onwards, in order to be qualified to assess for disabled students' allowance, a practising certificate from PATOSS or Dyslexia Action will be required for specialist teachers who need or want to carry out assessments for post-16 students in colleges, universities, workplace training establishments and local authority assessment centres.

QUESTIONS TO ASK ABOUT SpLD TEACHING QUALIFICATIONS

1. Does the teacher have a specialist dyslexia teaching qualification recognized by the BDA or PATOSS? What course have they followed and what accreditation have they gained at the end of the course (a diploma is higher than a certificate level)? If an LSA is involved in teaching, then the same questions would apply, bearing in mind that they would not have followed the qualified teaching route as a basis.

2. What experience does the teacher have in teaching dyslexic children? How many children have they previously taught?

3. Can the teacher provide a diary of further in-service training courses they have recently attended to ensure that they are updating their knowledge? Can they state what specialist organization they belong to, such as the BDA, Dyslexia Action or PATOSS?

4. If a school or parents are looking for a private teacher, make sure references are available, verify insurance policies and see if the teacher has a CRB check. Lists of private tutors are available from PATOSS.

WHAT DO SpLD TEACHERS DO?

The main thrust of SpLD teaching will be multi-sensory teaching methods. This is an approach which helps the child to learn through more than one of the senses. Teaching in schools is mainly done using either sight or hearing. A dyslexic child may experience difficulties with visual methods; such as looking at diagrams or pictures, reading information from books or the whiteboard. A dyslexic child may experience difficulties with auditory sensations, such as listening to what the teacher says. With dyslexia, the child's vision may be affected by difficulties with tracking, visual processing or they may say that the words appear fuzzy or move around. A dyslexic child's hearing may be fine on a hearing test, but auditory memory or auditory processing may be weak and this will affect how much information they can gain through auditory means. Multi-sensory teaching, in addition to using the visual and auditory approach, also makes use of other senses, especially the use of touch and movement (kinetic). This will enable the brain to have additional memory traces to hang on to which will aid memory.

Synthetic phonics is currently the recommended method for teaching children to read and spell and the UK government have made the teaching of synthetic phonics compulsory in every primary school. Synthetic phonics has been found to be especially helpful to children with dyslexia. Synthetic phonics concentrates on teaching children the sounds of letters (rather than the letter names) and how these sounds can be blended to run together to make short words. It is not uncommon to find learning support assistants in school teaching synthetic phonics but it is important to check that the assistant has been trained on synthetic phonics and there are synthetic phonics certificate courses available. Currently, the Reading Recovery Scheme, which incorporates synthetic phonics, is being piloted in England under the government's catch-up reading programme for Key Stage 1, Every Child is a Reader. If successful, it will be in schools nationally by 2011 (alongside Every Child Counts).

Most individualized programmes contain a highly structured phonetic instruction training together with drill and repetition to compensate for short-term auditory memory deficits and multi-sensory methods to promote non-language mental representations. This may be referred to as precision teaching.

Computer assisted software is commonly used, with or without synthesized speech and speech feedback, which can allow the child to work more independently in the classroom.

Reading and writing go hand-in-hand and it will be necessary to fit the two components together which will, of course, include spelling. Depending on the severity of dyslexia, some children will require daily 1:1 sessions within small classes, whilst, at the other end of the range, children will improve with small group catch-up schemes, individual reading and spelling practice and varied teaching strategies in mainstream dyslexia-friendly schools.

To receive a quality mark as a dyslexia-friendly school from the British Dyslexia Association, schools must have:

- specialist trained staff
- regular screening and assessment of children
- early intervention
- multi-sensory teaching methods
- social support, such as buddy initiatives.

The Council for the Registration of Schools Teaching Dyslexic Pupils (CReSTeD)* is supported by the British Dyslexia Association and the Dyslexia Institute, which established CReSTeD to produce an authoritative list of schools, both maintained and independent for parents who were looking for a school for dyslexic children. One of the criteria operated by CReSTeD is whether the majority of staff and all English and specialist language teachers are qualified in the teaching of dyslexic children or are undergoing training. It is thought that dyslexia affects 10 per cent of the population and most children with dyslexia or specific learning difficulties will attend mainstream schools. The following questions can be asked either of a mainstream or a specialist school when relevant:

QUESTIONS TO ASK WHEN CONSIDERING A SCHOOL FOR A DYSLEXIC CHILD

1. How many dyslexic children are there in the school? Does the school undertake screening for specific learning difficulties and, if so, what was the result?

2. How many of these children are at School Action, School Action Plus and have Statements?

---

* CReSTeD provides a list of schools which meet CReSTeD criteria for their SpLD (dyslexia) provision. Full information and a list of schools may be obtained by phoning 01242 604852, or e-mail: admin@crested.org.uk.

3. How many teachers, specially trained to work with SpLD children, are on the staff and, specifically, what are their qualifications, e.g. are they BDA Approved? Do the teachers hold an SpLD diploma or advanced (Level 7) certificate (such as OCR with AMBDA)?

4. If there are no specialists on staff, how does the school access the Local Authority services for dyslexia and how frequently do the dyslexia teachers attend the school?

    The current aims of PATOSS are to ensure that there is:

    • awareness and foundation training for all teachers and support staff

    • a lead teacher (certificate level) in every primary school

    • two teachers in every secondary school or pupil referral unit

    • one expert teacher (diploma level) to be shared between a small group of schools.

5. How do non-specialist teachers address the needs of dyslexic children in their classes, and what specific training have the non-specialist teachers had during the last year?

6. What are the arrangements for catch-up in training for absent staff or teachers who join during the year? Training of whole-school awareness is likely to take up to one day.

7. How is special teaching delivered, e.g. in class, withdrawal, individually or in small groups?

8. Does the teaching take place in a department and, if so, are there any specific resources or equipment available and how does the school address the fact that the child has to leave other lessons to attend a different department or unit?

9. What specific intervention programmes are carried out in school? (These may include specific programmes; such as Alpha to Omega, AcceleRead/AcceleWrite, Hickey, etc., or software programmes such as WordShark/NumberShark, Smart Phonics 1, 2, 3 and Clicker Phonics.) There are many resources available. It is possible to do some research using the internet, which does have critical evaluations of some programmes. There is no 'one size fits all' and the SpLD specialist and/or psychologist should advise on what is suitable for an individual child.

10. Do these specific intervention programmes focus on both literacy and numeracy and do they use structured multi-sensory teaching?

11. Who supervises the programmes (this is particularly important if the programmes are predominantly carried out by learning support assistants rather than specialist teachers)?

12. What access to and training for ICT do dyslexic children have over and beyond the usual facilities available for all children?

13. How rigid is the school in their policies with regard to following a foreign language or minimizing GCSEs which a typical dyslexic child may take?

14. In addition to support in subjects such as English, is there further additional support available for other subjects? Does the school have a Quality Mark registration from the BDA for a dyslexia-friendly school? Is the school registered with CReSTeD?

15. Ask to see how homework is given and supported (this will be particularly important if the child has difficulty in copying things down at speed from the whiteboard into a homework diary) and also ask to see a typical Individual Education Plan (IEP) for a dyslexic child at the school.

16. Dyslexic children often have difficulties with self-esteem, confidence, organizational skills, etc. How does the school address these aspects? Does the school feel that the resources, which are currently available, are adequate and if not, what else is required and where could these be obtained?

17. Is inclusion seen as a priority area and if so, how will the dyslexic child be included in all areas of the curriculum?

18. Who would a parent contact, in the first instance, to discuss any concerns?

19. What adjustments are currently being made for dyslexic children in the school and how is the curriculum being differentiated? It is always helpful to ask for specific examples, perhaps by identifying children (not by name) who are currently in the school. If a child has slow or poor written skills, what time allowances are made by teachers during lessons, homework and in examinations?

20. What further training is needed by the school and is this already organized?

21. How does the school ensure that there are adequate opportunities for dyslexic children to work with other children with similar cognitive ability or with an appropriate level of cognitive challenge, despite their literacy or numeracy problems?

22. What other evidence can the school provide to demonstrate that their inclusive practice is being effective and having a positive impact?

23. How does the marking and assessment policy ensure that the child is assessed on the basis of their knowledge (rather than poor spelling)?

24. How does the school measure its effectiveness with dyslexic children? Is there qualitative evidence, e.g. increase in self-esteem and also, quantitative evidence, e.g. reaching expectations through the different key stages?

If a mainstream school has a specialist unit, resource base or provision, in addition to general questions, it will be necessary to ascertain exactly how many lessons the child will be included in mainstream classes, what the balance of time between mainstream and the unit will be and how flexible that will be. This will probably change from year to year and depend on the curricular needs. It may be that the child will need to spend more or less time within their class group, depending on the year group, for example, it may be very difficult for a child to miss lessons for specialist tuition at Key Stage 4 if they are doing a GCSE subject at that time.

If a specialist school is being considered, many of the questions will still apply but it may be necessary to combine these questions with the level of therapeutic input and the way in which an integrated system works within the school. It should not be assumed that all teachers in a specialist school hold a specialist qualification in SpLD and it will be important to ascertain exactly who will be teaching the child and in what lessons. Although there may be an assumption that the school will be dyslexia aware, CReSTeD clearly highlights that specialist schools will vary in their level of specialism. Registration under the CReSTeD system does not mean that the learning environment is solely dedicated for dyslexic children.

CHAPTER 17

Intervention for Sensory Needs

Sensory impairments will include children with hearing impairments (HI), visual impairments (VI) and deafblindness or multi-sensory impairments (MSI). From September 2009, a mandatory qualification (MQ) for teachers of classes with sensory impairments has been introduced and teachers will be expected to hold an additional specialist qualification as well as having qualified teacher status. This will be known as a mandatory qualification for teachers of children with sensory impairments. There are three versions of the qualification, for teachers of HI, VI and MSI. Teachers who are employed to teach classes of children and young people with a sensory impairment, who do not already hold an appropriate MQ will be required to gain a qualification within their first three years in post. It is also strongly advised that qualified teachers in support and advisory roles, and those working with children and young people in the early years and post-16 settings, will also complete MQ training. Although the regulations refer to teachers employed in schools, and not specialist peripatetic teachers employed in Local Authority SEN support services, the expectation is that such teachers would also have the relevant MQs.

HEARING IMPAIRMENT*

Most deaf/hearing impaired children attend mainstream schools, some of which have resource bases or specialist units led by qualified teachers of the deaf. (The term 'deaf' is used to cover the whole range of hearing loss in this chapter, but hearing impairment is the term generally used in school.) Definitions of hearing loss are covered in Chapter 5, 'Sensory and Physical Needs'. A smaller number of children are taught in special schools, some of which offer residential provision. It is a requirement that children in these

---

* Information from the Royal National Institute for the Deaf (RNID) is gratefully acknowledged.

schools and resource bases are taught by appropriately qualified specialist teachers of the deaf and that they obtain this qualification within three years of beginning their work with deaf children.

Peripatetic, or advisory teachers of the deaf, work for Local Education Authority advisory and support services for deaf children. They support deaf children who are integrated in mainstream and special schools on an individual basis. An important part of their work is collaboration with mainstream classroom teachers who teach deaf children throughout the day and the management of support provided by teaching assistants or communication support workers who often accompany deaf children in lessons. Peripatetic teachers also visit parents of very young children at home to advise about development and to work with them as appropriate. They also support deaf children with other disabilities.

Teachers of the deaf may also work as part of a team in hospitals or health centres and children who have cochlear implants are supported by a team of professionals, including teachers of the deaf, speech and language therapists and audiological scientists.

QUALIFICATIONS OF SPECIALIST TEACHERS OF THE DEAF

In order to train as a teacher of deaf children, teachers must have qualified teacher status (QTS) and have had some classroom experience before undertaking a teacher of the deaf training course. All teachers of deaf children must have special training and qualifications.

Deaf children have an entitlement to be taught by teachers who are effective and competent. Qualified teachers of deaf children should have a diploma/certificate course in teaching deaf children and the only current full-time course available is at the University of Manchester, although there are part-time courses at other universities. The University of Manchester's full-time course awards the University Post-Graduate Diploma in Deaf Education. Other universities offer Post-Graduate Diplomas in Education (Special Education – Hearing Impairment), an MA in Deaf Education (teacher of the deaf qualification) and other similar qualifications.

In addition to being qualified as a teacher of the deaf, there are many other qualifications which can be extremely helpful to ensure access for deaf children. These may include using different ways to communicate, including augmentative or alternative communication.

British Sign Language

British Sign Language (BSL) is the preferred language of over 70,000 deaf people for whom English may be a second or third language. BSL is a visual/spatial language with its own grammar, hand movements and facial expressions to convey meaning. The grammatical rules of BSL are not the same as the rules of English and it is important for teachers to be aware if the child has ever been exposed to BSL (perhaps at an earlier time) as their written work may reflect the different rules of BSL compared to written English. Communication support workers (CSWs), communicators, educational interpreters, signers and signing teachers are all titles used for the support workers who facilitate access to the curriculum for profoundly deaf/first language British Sign Language users. Whether it is in a school for the deaf, mainstream school or college and whether the philosophy is total communication or sign bi-lingual, access to education is often through these communication support workers. The minimum requirements are as follows:

- BSL Stage 2 or equivalent functioning.
- GCSE English and maths at Grade C or above.
- (Preferably) BTec/EdExcel qualification in Communication Support.

The CSW will often act as an interpreter within the learning environment and, again, it is important to ascertain their exact qualifications and experience.

Singalong

Signalong is a sign supporting system, based on BSL, designed to help children and adults with communication difficulties, mostly associated with learning difficulties. Signalong requires the person to speak as they sign, using simplified language in a grammatical way. Signalong is a total communication system in which the signer gives every clue to the meaning which is relevant in the situation, using body language, facial expressions and voice tone to reinforce the message. Training courses in sign-supported communication are given by the Signalong Group and, again, can range from introductory courses from 4–8 hours in duration to foundation courses (15 hours) to an OCN intermediate level 2 (30 hours). The tutor training course is an intensive five-day programme for people who have experience of signing and understand the context of learning difficulties, autism or the particular field in which they need to use augmentative communication. The tutor course carries OCN Level 3. Signs do not conflict with BSL but are more geared to a client group who find BSL too difficult to communicate with for a variety of reasons.

Makaton®

Makaton® is a system of communication that uses a vocabulary of key words, manual signs and gestures to support speech, as well as graphic symbols to support the written word. The signed vocabulary is taken from the local deaf sign language and begins with a core list of important words. However, the grammar generally follows spoken language rather than sign language and is used by people who have communication, language or learning difficulties and was specifically developed to aid functional communication for everyday use for children who were both deaf and had significant learning difficulties.

Cued speech

Cued speech is a simple sound-based system consisting of eight hand shapes used in four positions near the mouth, in conjunction with lip patterns, to make all the sounds in spoken language fully understood by deaf people. Mainstream teachers can learn cued speech in about 20 hours, so it is a very accessible method of helping a deaf child in a mainstream classroom to access speech.

Cochlear implant

A cochlear implant is a small complex electronic device that can help to provide a sense of sound to a child who is profoundly deaf or who has severe hearing impairment. The implant consists of an external portion that sits behind the ear and a second portion that is surgically placed under the skin. The implant has a microphone which picks up sound from the environment; a speech processor, which selects and arranges sounds picked up by the microphone; a transmitter and receiver/stimulator, which receives signals from the speech processor and converts them into electric impulses; and an electrode array, which is a group of electrodes that collects the impulses from the stimulator and sends them to the different regions of the auditory nerve.

An implant does not restore normal hearing, but can give a deaf child a useful representation of sounds in the environment and helps the child to understand speech. There are an increasing number of children in schools now with cochlear implants and because some of these children may have excellent speech, it is even more important for teachers to recognize some practical difficulties they may have in school, as well as the types of problems that could be encountered within the classroom.

WHAT DO TEACHERS OF THE DEAF DO?

A teacher of the deaf, as well as teaching speech and dealing with communication problems, also teaches the usual school subjects. This involves different techniques from ordinary teaching. The aims are to provide some means by which a child can live and function in a hearing world as normally as possible. The teacher will support children in mainstream classes, units or special schools and emphasize oral methods of communication, if this is at all possible. The teacher will be proficient in methods of signing to support language development and use a total communication approach. In addition to knowledge of language and communication, the teacher will understand and have experience of acoustics, use of hearing aids, auditory training and technology necessary to teach children with a hearing impairment. They will also have knowledge of cochlear implants.

QUESTIONS TO ASK ABOUT HEARING IMPAIRMENT IN SCHOOLS

1. In a mainstream school, ask how many hearing impaired children are in the school and how many have been in the school in the last three years? How have they progressed and what have been the outcomes?

2. In a mainstream school, are there any qualified teachers of the deaf in school or learning support assistants who have worked with the deaf? What are their qualifications and range of experience?

3. Has the school had any experience with cochlear implants?

4. Do teaching areas have good acoustics (sound quality)? Do they give off reverberations, echoes or let in too much noise from outside? An architect and acoustic specialist can advise on how best to absorb and control sound in a new or existing building. Ceilings, floors and walls can all be modified to create better acoustics. The best way to control reverberations in a room is to put fibre-board tiles or lightweight panels on the ceiling and use underlay on floors and line walls with fibre-board panels.

5. What adjustments could the school make to provide additional aids or services, such as equipment or to remove/alter a physical feature of a building? This may include fitting electronic display boards or permanent induction loops and could apply to classrooms, general facilities (such as gymnasiums or dining halls) and also residential accommodation.

6. What is the input from the local advisory service for hearing impaired children and how will they be able to advise on the latest developments and technology? Examples may be a conference folder (for use in small groups or on placements); alerting equipment (e.g. fire alarms, particularly in residential accommodation – these are usually flashing light systems or commercial paging systems); loop systems (including portable loops and infrared systems); mobile phones; radio microphone systems (some of these also work with cochlear implants); soundfield systems (this provides low level amplification of the teacher's voice via a microphone and evenly distributes it around the room from speakers mounted above head height). Soundfield systems help both hearing and deaf learners by cutting down distracting background noise and improving reception of the key speaker. Also ask about the ease of access to subtitled videos/DVDs, text communications and videophones.

7. If the child communicates by sign language, are there other signers in the school and are there possibilities of teaching members of staff and/or children how to sign to make the school an inclusive placement?

8. There are good pedagogic reasons for asking questions in the classroom. It would be helpful to establish whether mainstream teachers actually involve the children with hearing impairment by questioning or explaining directly. This can be ascertained through classroom observation which may reveal whether these children can become involved with question and answer sessions with the rest of the class, or whether this is done only through a communication worker or a teacher of the deaf. Is a sub-class environment being created with the teacher of the deaf and deaf children with the teacher of the deaf taking on the sole responsibility for supervising and teaching the deaf children, particularly when there is more than one integrating into a mainstream class? Are the teachers aware of the limitations of inappropriate seating location with poor field vision which can cause interference with the learning process?

9. How does the mainstream teacher ensure that the deaf child is involved in a group discussion with a number of speakers? If the child is lip-reading, is this happening directly, i.e. lip-reading the mainstream teacher or via the support worker? What does the mainstream teacher need to do to change their practice to facilitate direct lip-reading?

10. If a special school, what are the links with mainstream schools and how will the child receive normal language role models?

11. Are mainstream teachers aware that they should avoid standing with their back to the window as this casts their face in shadow and makes lip-reading impossible?

12. Does the mainstream teacher supply written materials to support spoken lessons?

13. In some cases, hearing impairment can lead to social isolation in a mainstream school and it may be helpful to ask if the child will be assured access to at least two other deaf children of a similar age and with a similar communication method, with opportunities to meet deaf children of other ages within the school. Where this is impossible, can the school provide the deaf child with an opportunity to meet other deaf children, either through regular video or telephone access to deaf children and other schools or with linking with other provisions?

14. In mainstream schools, investigate if deaf learners will have the support modifications they need to undertake a work experience placement in Key Stage 4.

15. If the school has a special unit or resource provision, how much time will the child spend in there? How will the child's needs be met in mainstream classes? What training have the teachers had in mainstream classes for teaching the deaf? If there is a communication worker, how will they liaise with the teacher of the deaf and mainstream teachers? What are the arrangements for linking with the speech therapy service?

16. What arrangements will be made to access outside activities within the curriculum, break and extra-curricular activities where the normal soundfield or loop systems cannot be used?

VISUAL IMPAIRMENT*

Increasingly, there are more children with visual impairment entering mainstream schools. Up to 40 per cent of children with visual impairment may have additional learning difficulties which may also need to be taken into consideration. This is an area of learning need which requires skill and expertise with a need to focus on functional vision and the impact that the visual impairment will have on access to the curriculum. (Definitions of visual impairment are covered in Chapter 5, 'Sensory and Physical Needs'.) It may be necessary to consider mobility and independence training, alternative methods of communication and, of course, resources for the visually impaired. Assessments will need to be ongoing and take place over time as the child's needs and stages of development changes. These assessments generally will be carried out by a qualified teacher of the visually impaired or a teacher undergoing specialist training to become a qualified teacher of the visually impaired (QTVI) under supervision. A QTVI's role will include offering a range of support available from the VI Support Service within the Local Authority. This will include:

- individual teaching
- in-class support
- teaching in specialist curriculum areas – e.g. Braille, mobility, keyboard skills and ICT, daily living skills
- planning with the SENCo/class teacher/subject teacher/learning support assistant
- supporting the work of the class to ensure full curriculum access
- advice on adapted materials and resources in the appropriate medium

---

* Information reproduced by kind permission of The Royal National Institute for the Blind (RNIB).

- provision of specialist equipment, where necessary and training given in its use to children and staff
- team teaching where appropriate
- awareness raising for peers
- training and information for school governors or administrative staff, as necessary.

It is particularly important that LSAs who are assigned to work with children with a visual impairment, receive induction and ongoing training in specialist aspects of the role, including the need to encourage independence. As the QTVI may not be available on a daily basis, communication channels must be effective. Specialist equipment, such as low-vision aids, closed-circuit televisions, adaptive information and information technology, are only helpful if teachers know how to use and repair them and the children are trained to use them independently.

For older children, a QTVI will need to support the school in the planning and monitoring of work experience placements.

QUALIFICATIONS OF SPECIALIST TEACHERS OF THE VISUALLY IMPAIRED

Every Local Authority has a visual impairment support service (often grouped with services for children with other sensory needs; such as the hearing impaired). This will include at least one qualified teacher of the visually impaired, and these are teachers who have undertaken specialist post-graduate training in working with children who are blind and partially-sighted.

From September 2009, with the introduction of mandatory qualification courses (MQ), it will be expected that teachers of classes of children and young people with visual impairments will be required to hold an additional specialist qualification in addition to qualified teacher status.

TEACHING ASSISTANTS FOR CHILDREN WITH VISUAL IMPAIRMENTS

There are courses intended for LSAs working with children whose visual impairment is their main or only disability, as well as for those working with children with visual impairment and complex needs. A customized BTec Level 3 advanced certificate in 'working with learners with visual impairment in educational settings' is one of the courses which is recognized by the Royal National Institute for the Blind (RNIB) and suitable for those working in mainstream schools or settings. The course has six units, each of which involves about 30 hours of study, including work which can be incorporated into the normal day in school. Courses look at aspects such as:

- provision roles and responsibilities
- vision and visual impairment
- effective practice
- curriculum access
- communication skills in a learning environment
- independence and social inclusion.

Courses are available throughout the UK and led by an experienced RNIB tutor.

LEARNING BRAILLE

Braille is a system used by blind people to read and write. It is made of a 6-dot cell with raised dots which are read by the fingers. The certificate in Grade 2 English Braille course teaches participants how to read and write in Braille. This is essential for anyone working alongside a child using Braille in an educational context. The course is open to teachers, LSAs, parents and support workers and leads to a Level 3 BTec advanced certificate. Again, it is certainly worthwhile to check if this has been obtained. Although Braille is commonly used, younger people are now exploring more portable communication methods, such as specific software programs which can also be accessed by their sighted friends.

QUESTIONS TO ASK ABOUT VISUAL IMPAIRMENT IN SCHOOLS

Fifty per cent of children, between 5 and 16 years, with sight problems are educated in mainstream schools or mainstream schools which are additionally resourced for blind and partially sighted children. Some children will, however, require a specialist placement. Only a very small proportion of children with visual problems attend special schools for the blind and partially-sighted (5%). A much larger group, approximately 32 per cent, attend other types of special schools, because they have complex needs, so it is important that when looking at a special school that very careful questions are asked about the provision for vision as well as other aspects.

1. Are there, or have there been, any other children in the school with a visual impairment? If so, what level of severity? How many children?

2. How have these children progressed at the school and what have been the outcomes?

3. What are the links between mainstream and specialist schools?

4. If the child has to be withdrawn from certain lessons for additional help or therapy, how will they catch up?

5. How will the child be included in PE and team games?

6. Will the child be able to access all areas of the curriculum, particularly at secondary school, given that there may be specific difficulties and special challenges?

7. Have all school staff (mainstream staff) attended courses in visual impairment and, if so, what kind of courses have they attended? How frequently? How recently?

8. How will the QTVI Service support the child and does the receiving school have experience and training to carry through their recommendations?

9. Will the child be supported by a Mobility Officer and, if so, how frequently?

10. What are the links between the teaching assistant and the QTVI? How will this work and when will the parents be involved?

11. If there are support staff who are designated for children with sight problems, have they undertaken any specialist courses or do they have an accredited qualification?

12. How will the support staff encourage the child's independence?

13. Is there a school nurse?

14. How will the teacher of the visually impaired liaise with other therapists who may be involved with the child, e.g. SaLT, OT, physiotherapist, etc.?

15. What is the range of ICT equipment that the child could access?

16. Does the school have a facility to enlarge printed material, or the means to produce tactile material if appropriate?

17. Does the school library have resources, such as large print books, audio or multi-sensory material?

18. Is there any special equipment to use in specific subjects; such as food technology, maths, science, PE, etc.?

19. Do the teaching areas have adequate sockets to enable electrical equipment or task lighting to be used and will this enable the child to sit together with the other children or will it involve sitting apart from them?

20. Can Braille or tactile reading systems be taught in the school?

21. If the child needs to use a communication system other than speech, what system will be used? How many other children in the school use this? Are the staff knowledgeable enough? Can the child access extra-curricular activities?

22. What is the lighting like in classrooms, corridors, hall, dining areas, on stairs, etc.?

23. Are there blinds or curtains that can control glare?

24. Is there good colour contrast throughout the school?

25. Do the edges of steps and stairs have good contrast?

26. Are classroom teaching areas free of clutter in circulations areas?

27. Are there accessible storage areas where the child's special equipment can be safely stored?

28. Does the school provide a generally quiet teaching environment in which it is easy to hear?

29. Are signs easy to read and is there the potential for tactile signage?

30. Are there separate play areas for ball games outside?

31. Are pathways and edges outside clearly defined?

32. Are there seats or benches in areas of shade?

33. Are vehicles well separated from pedestrians?

34. How will teachers anticipate the barriers to learning and plan ahead, so that participation in lessons is a positive one? Discuss strategies such as the teacher calling the child by name before speaking to them and see if the teacher feels this is workable.

35. How will the teacher allocate time to discuss planning with the QTVI and LSA? When will materials be adapted and will the time that this takes be additional to the number of support hours with the child?

These questions have been adapted from the RNIB website, with kind permission (www.rnib.org.uk).

There may be specific questions to ask about technology and equipment in schools as these change all the time, e.g. the child may not be able to access the whiteboard, which is commonly used in classrooms. The speed and manner which teachers use the whiteboard can result in exclusion within the lesson. It is necessary to ask how teachers would ensure the child is being included, which will involve some technical know-how on the part of the teacher as there are hardware solutions, wall-mounted options and laptop solutions which can be utilized.

MULTI-SENSORY IMPAIRMENT

Children with multi-sensory impairment have a combination of visual and hearing difficulties. They are sometimes referred to as deafblind, but these children may have some residual sight and/or hearing. Many of these children have additional disabilities and because of their complex cocktail of needs, it may be difficult to ascertain their intellectual abilities and also the primary need. Children with multi-sensory impairments have much greater difficulties accessing the curriculum and the environment, compared to those with single sensory impairments, and their incidental learning is very limited. The area of communicating with a deafblind child is highly specialist and will involve a number of decisions with regard to communication modes and aids which has to take into account the child, their multi-sensory impairment and the environment. Therapists who have experience with working with deafblind children will need to be consulted. Most of these children will be educated in specialist schools, but it is possible that with inclusive practice increasing, mainstream or dual placements could be an option.

QUESTIONS TO ASK ABOUT MULTI-SENSORY IMPAIRMENT IN SCHOOLS

1. Is there a good level of even light, including in toilets and changing areas? Can the school avoid sudden changes between bright and dim light or give the child time to adjust?

2. Are contrasting (light and dark) colours used to distinguish differences, e.g. doors from walls?

3. Are curtains or blinds used at the windows to avoid glare from reflected light and are matt rather than shiny surfaces used?

4. Is clutter avoided as it is dangerous for mobile children and distracting? Patterns on clothes and busy wall displays can be visually distracting – are there a lot of these?

5. Do teachers know not to move furniture around without telling children?

6. Are teachers aware that adults and/or children moving around unnecessarily can be highly distracting?

7. Can background noise be avoided as far as possible as it is more difficult for children to use residual hearing?

8. Can echoes be deadened with carpets and wallboards? Children with hearing impairment may suffer in noisy, echoing spaces such as dining halls.

9. Is there sufficient space to position furniture to make clear routes around the room and can larger open spaces be avoided without landmarks?

10. In the classroom, are there different textures on toys and are textures used to mark positions and places, on walls and underfoot?

11. Smells and air currents can be used which may help children recognize places and activities – are these recognized?

12. Could the environment be adapted to provide clear mobility routes, both between settings and within much used rooms?

13. Can the furniture be arranged so children can move from one solid object to another, rather than having big spaces?

14. Are there landmarks which are key points along a route that will inform a child where they have got to, either through touch, e.g. a corner of a wall or a draught from an always open door; sight, e.g. a picture; hearing, e.g. a string of bells fixed to a door; or smell, e.g. the photocopier room? Landmarks need to be safe and consistently available, e.g. smells may only be available at certain times, like lunchtime.

15. Are surfaces that children trail their hands along constantly checked for safety and comfort, e.g. no staples sticking out or head-height obstacles? It may help to explore the environment wearing earplugs and a blindfold or goggles (ask someone to watch you and keep you safe).

16. It will be necessary to ascertain the previous experience of the school and their work with children who have multi-sensory impairment. This will involve finding out the links with other services for the visually and hearing impaired, as well as the therapeutic services.

QUALIFICATIONS OF SPECIALIST TEACHERS OF THE MULTI-SENSORY IMPAIRED

Teachers of children who are multi-sensory impaired will need to gain a mandatory qualification in the education of children who are multi-sensory impaired within three years of beginning to work in this field.

Mandatory qualification status usually requires the completion of a two-year diploma course in the education of multi-sensory impaired children, an assessed teaching placement and some additional study. At the current time, there are two course providers.

A child who has multi-sensory impairment is likely to need the curriculum modified on an individual basis because each child's combination of hearing impairment, visual impairment and other difficulties will be different. What is common is that there will be a need to generalize learning, because deafblindness prevents children learning incidentally by watching others. Most children will require a 1:1 assistant or an intervenor (the intervenor acts as an enabler, working on a 1:1 basis, following an individually designed programme) and this assistant will need to have specialist training in multi-sensory impairment. According to Sense (the organization for deafblind people), there are six key approaches for professionals who work with children who are deafblind and questions will need to be asked as to how these approaches are implemented.

QUESTIONS TO ASK ABOUT MULTI-SENSORY IMPAIRMENT

1. Building trust – how many adults will work with the child and how will the relationship develop? It may be necessary to limit the number of different people to ensure the child can identify a particular personality.

2. Be consistent – as deafblind children receive little information from the world around them, events need to happen very consistently so they can make sense of them. How are particular routines carried out at school, e.g. dressing, getting ready for lunch, saying goodbye, etc.? How will furniture be kept in the same place so their independence and exploration can continue?

3. Help understanding – what cues will be used, what communication modes will be used?

4. Take time – as deafblind children will need to take much longer to receive, process and respond to information, they could miss out on other activities and how will this be incorporated into the daily routine?

5. Follow the child – how will choices be offered and how will control be given to the child wherever possible?

6. Be supportive – multi-sensory impairment frequently causes isolation, confusion and fear. Withdrawal or apparent regression can be a reasonable response to a crowded environment, someone approaching too suddenly or too many changes. How will all these aspects be controlled in the environment? How will opportunities be given to relax, particularly offering frequent breaks?

7. What resources are there in the school to provide a sensory environment?

8. How will therapeutic advice and input be integrated into the classroom and the residential side (if relevant)?

Reproduced (adapted) with kind permission of Sense, the organization for deafblind people.

CHAPTER 18

Autistic Provision

About 1 in a 100 people in the UK has an autistic spectrum disorder (ASD). The term ASD covers a range of children, from those who are low functioning and non-verbal (Kanner autism), to those who are high functioning (pervasive developmental disorder – PDD; or high functioning autism – HFA), possibly even with 'savant' skills or special abilities. It covers children with Asperger's syndrome, atypical autism or pervasive developmental disorder not otherwise specified (PPD–NOS).

QUALIFICATIONS OF TEACHERS WORKING WITH AUTISTIC CHILDREN

There are several courses at post-graduate level, designed for teachers who already have relevant teaching experiences, and other courses at certificate level for people who do not have teaching or similar academic qualifications.

The majority of courses are part time, designed for teachers who are working during the day. If there is concern or an interest about whether someone is specifically qualified to teach autistic children, it would be worth looking up the course they have been on and the specific content.

Courses vary greatly in levels and expectations, and accepting information from a school that teachers or learning support assistants 'have been on a course', can mean different things to different people. For example, the University of Hull offers a Level 4 University Foundation Award, where the entrance requirements are open to classroom assistants, teachers and parents with no formal entry requirements, whereas at the other end of the range, the University of Birmingham offers a Master of Education in Autism open to those who have a degree, or degree-equivalent in teaching, social care or health-related profession, with at least two years post-qualification experience and some experience of working with or living with children with ASD.

COURSES FOR TEACHING ASSISTANTS

There do not appear to be any formal qualifications necessary for teaching assistants working with autistic children, although, clearly, good practice will dictate that assistants should be supported by their Local Authorities or their employers by attendance on relevant courses. It will be important to check what course the assistants have been on and the content of the course as these vary widely. Many LSAs have been on courses; such as TEACCH (Treatment and Education of Autistic and related Communication-handicapped CHildren) and PECS (Picture Exchange Communication System – which is further described in Chapter 21, 'Speech and Language Therapy') whilst others will derive this knowledge through a cascade training effect which may dilute the contents unless, of course, it is constantly monitored and used. Some Authorities do employ PECS workers, specifically for that purpose. The National Autistic Society sets out the courses on offer to parents and professionals and details are given on the course content and length. If a course is provided in-house or by the Local Authority, information should be sought about the course content, length and what follow-up is provided for attendees.

QUESTIONS TO ASK ABOUT PROVISION FOR AUTISTIC CHILDREN IN SCHOOLS

1. How many children diagnosed with autistic spectrum disorder are currently in the school? It may be necessary to differentiate between the various diagnoses, e.g. classic autism or Asperger's syndrome in terms of provision, as the needs of these different populations will vary greatly.

2. If a mainstream school, has there been a whole-school ASD awareness training, and if so, how does the school ensure that this is updated on a regular basis? What did the awareness training consist of and who gave it?

3. Has the school been accredited by the National Autistic Society (NAS)? This is an autism-specific quality assurance programme. Criteria are applied to each area of the school reviewed, based on evidence of reaching specific Autism Accreditation Standards. Are staff aware of SPELL? (Structure, Positive – approaches and expectations – Empathy, Low arousal, Links. See NAS for further details.)

4. Does the school know about the National Autism Plan (NAP) for autism-friendly schools? Does it follow the recommendation from the NAP to have whole-school ASD awareness training at least once every three years.

5. In a special school, do staff have a recognized qualification, not just short-term attendance at courses? How many of the staff have this qualification and how many do not?

6. What courses have LSAs been on and what access do they have to specialist ASD staff?

7. What is the input from therapists? This should include looking at SaLT and OT, advisory teachers for autism (usually available in mainstream, rather than special schools), educational psychologists, clinical psychologists and behavioural specialists. How does appropriate liaison take place with staff and how are these times resourced (often Statements do not cover these liaison times, which are crucial to consistency)? Are there any arrangements for managed integration opportunities, either with mainstream schools (if child is in a special school) or with special schools (if child is in a mainstream school)? How is expertise shared across settings? If the child is in a dual placement, what are the integration and inclusion opportunities and how does the child maintain consistency in both placements?

8. Can the school demonstrate flexibility in the arrangements that can adapt to individual needs, e.g. behavioural policies which may be inappropriate for ASD children, particular arrangements of space and the environment, additional time for transitions, management of participation in assemblies, unstructured times (such as playtimes), etc.?

9. Is there provision for an escape route, such as a 'time out' room or quiet space? How will the school develop social interactional skills and emotional understanding? Does the school already use programmes; such as social stories and cartoons?

10. In the playground, does the school operate circle of friends/buddy systems to ensure all children are included? (Circle of friends is a strategy to promote inclusion into mainstream schools by facilitating groups of volunteer 'friends' and a focus child.) If the child has problems with communication, how will staff communicate with the child within the regular classroom?

11. How will the teacher ensure that there are visual forms of instruction in preference to verbal instruction; such as visual timetables or worksheets, and who will be developing these?

12. How will the use of computers help to teach the child?

13. How does the school work in conjunction with parents to ensure close home/school liaison on a daily basis and also consistency of routines?

14. How will the school manage changes, such as cancelled activities or changes in the environment?

15. How will the school provide a low-arousal environment so that lessons are held in calm settings, free from disruption or noise, which may cause anxiety? What other methods does the school use to reduce stimulation, e.g. relaxation, massage, music, snoezelen and sensory diet?

16. Does the school practice the TEACCH programme and, if so, in what way does it practise it? (Treatment and Education of Autistic and related Communication-handicapped CHildren. See NAS website for further details.)

17. How will the school ensure safety for a child who has little or no awareness of danger? Is the school site safe and away from the road? Look to see if there are locks or high handles on cupboards and doors and what the entrances and exits are like in the school – this is particularly important in a mainstream school.

18. Is the school able to adjust lighting to make the environment more sensitive to children with ASD? If the child is particularly hyper-sensitive, ask how the school will filter out background noise. Look at furnishings and carpets and whether patterns will be confusing. Similarly, smells may also be an issue.

19. Look at the layout of the room. In a mainstream school, it may be possible to create a sensory corner if there is no sensory room available. This may be a solution for some children who can then retreat to this when necessary. Even if one does not exist, it is helpful to look at the classroom to see if this could be provided.

20. Are the toilet facilities nearby and who will be able to access them with the child, if necessary?

21. It is helpful to be familiar with the various approaches used for children with autism and ask how these approaches are used, e.g. how frequently is PECS used in the classroom if the child uses PECS? Is PECS used throughout the school day, or is its use limited to times with food? In a school where there is a specialist autistic unit, is PECS also used in mainstream classes as well? If, for example, the child is using intensive interaction (further described in Chapter 21, 'Speech and Language Therapy'), are staff familiar with this approach and how many of them are trained to use it? If the child has been on an ABA (Applied Behavioural Analysis) Programme, is there anyone in the school trained or knowledgeable about this approach? Can it be utilized in school or what is the school's attitude, particularly, if parents or professionals have been positive about its use?

22. If the child has been on a home education programme, how will the school value and use what has been learnt and how will transition be managed?

23. If the child has Asperger's syndrome, are there any specific strategies that are used or programmes that the school have found to be beneficial?

24. How does the school monitor the progress of children with ASD, whether in a mainstream school or specialist placement? What are the outcomes of children with this diagnosis over the last five years? Where do the children go after transition, whether at secondary level or post-16? How is success monitored?

25. In a special school, how many children with autism are reintegrated back into mainstream school and how successful has this been?

26. What will the peer group be and how can the child interact either on an equal footing, or how will the child learn from the opportunities available within the classroom? Will the peer group provide appropriate role models in language and behaviour and, if so, how much time will the child be spending with them?

27. What importance does the school place on the ability of the child to generalize skills or behaviours and how viable are the links made with home to ensure that this takes place? How will teachers record behaviour and, in particular, stressful situations in order to act on them?

28. How are computers and information technology used for children and what ideas are there for ensuring accessibility and also minimizing over-use of computers for children who may become obsessed with them?

29. If a mainstream school, how are other children trained and educated to work with their ASD peers? Are there 'buddy schemes'?

30. What extra-curricular activities are there and how will the child access them, particularly if they are after school hours, i.e. will the LSA be available?

31. How will homework tasks be clarified and will there be opportunities for the child to do homework during the school day if necessary?

32. What support systems are in place to deliver life skills, if necessary, and will these take place in the community?

33. How will the school develop the individual child's special interests, e.g. in animals, etc.?

34. What special arrangements are in place for National Curriculum tests and public examinations, if the child has high anxiety levels?

35. Can the child access therapeutic or psychological help to alleviate anxiety either through 1:1 intervention or anxiety management groups? Who will offer these? How will sessions be included in the daily timetable?

CHAPTER 19

Art Therapy, Music Therapy, Drama Therapy, Play Therapy and Psychotherapy

Children with behavioural, emotional and social difficulties (BESD) cover the full range of ability and their difficulties may cause a barrier to learning. Equally a learning difficulty may lead to or exacerbate behavioural and emotional difficulties, but not all children with BESD will have a learning difficulty that calls for special educational provision, i.e. a special educational need. Children with BESD attract varying diagnoses and may include children with conduct disorders, hyperkinetic disorders, anxiety, social phobia, depression, oppositional and avoidance syndromes, etc. There may not be a firm medical diagnosis and children may also have a disability under the Disability Discrimination Act. A range of support, within a variety of settings, addresses the needs of these children and the various settings will be described in other chapters when looking at different types of schools which may include residential schools.

There is clearly an overlap with mental health difficulties in this category, although mental health professionals will obviously be involved with many children who exhibit other difficulties as well, such as ASD. The National Institute for Health and Clinical Excellence (NICE) has issued guidelines to address depression in children and young people as well as other related clinical guidelines on interventions with eating disorders, self-harm, anxiety and post-traumatic stress disorder amongst others. It is important to establish what the specific professional roles will be, as there could be a risk that the more people involved; the more information will drop through the net, unless communication is very clear. Schools should identify a key worker, or link person, for this purpose.

Within the school, the child could be supported by the SENCo, LSA, class teacher, pastoral staff, learning mentor, school counsellor, home–school link worker (if available) and personal advisors introduced as part of the Connexions Service. There may also be a range of therapists available within school, especially in a special school.

Outside of school, the child could be supported by:

- A range of therapeutic services; such as those described later in this chapter.
- Child and Adolescent Mental Health Services – CAMHS. This service may include clinical psychologists, psychiatrists, educational psychologists and community psychiatric nurses. In many areas CAMHS has been organized into four different tiers and it will be important to establish what, specifically, each of these tiers can offer to a child or school.
- Educational psychologists.
- Some schools have primary mental health workers available. The family could also be linked with health visitors, GP practice nurses and GPs, community paediatricians and speech therapists.
- Behavioural advisory teachers.
- Educational social workers.
- Health professionals – some school nurses carry out screening and early intervention.
- Social services staff with a remit to support children in need. Children may have additional problems which can bring them, and their families, to the attention of the social services department. Schools need to be aware that social workers have a remit for children and may also be part of the range of professionals working with families.

THERAPEUTIC SERVICES WHICH MAY BE OFFERED IN SCHOOLS
Art therapy

The British Association of Art Therapists (BAAT) describes art therapy as a form of psychotherapy that uses art media as its primary mode of communication, with a three-way relationship between the child, the therapist and the image or artefact. A trained art therapist will usually have a first degree in art, some experience of working in an area of health, education or social care, and a masters degree completed over two years, full time, or three years, part time. In order to work as an art therapist in the NHS and social services, it is mandatory to possess the post-graduate MA/MSc in art therapy or art psychotherapy. They should be a member of the BAAT, which is the professional organization of art therapists in the UK and has its own code of ethics of professional practice. It maintains a comprehensive directory of qualified art therapists in the UK. Art therapists are regulated by the Health Professions Council (HPC).

There are also art therapy assistants and assistant practitioners, who work with registered art therapists, usually with a group of clients, or, perhaps, alongside the qualified therapist or on their own. No academic qualifications are needed, and it will be important to be reassured that a qualified art therapist is involved in the supervision of the work of these assistants. Art therapy is especially beneficial for emotional and psychological disorders, as it provides a means of communication to express feelings that are too difficult to verbalize.

Music therapy

There are now eight music therapy training courses in the UK. Each is a post-graduate course requiring a high level of musicianship. Students are normally accepted only if they have three years of musical training, leading to a diploma or graduation from a college of music or a degree from a university. Occasionally, students who hold qualifications in subjects other than music, e.g. education or psychology, may be accepted if they have achieved a high standard of musical performance. The student usually completes a course which is an MA or MSc in music therapy. As in art and drama therapy, there are also musical therapy assistants and assistant practitioners. Music therapists are regulated by the HPC.

The British Society for Music Therapy (BSMT)* is open to anyone interested in music therapy. Music therapy stresses the development of a relationship between a child and the therapist. Music making forms the basis for communication in this relationship, as it is recognized that the ability to appreciate and respond to music is an in-born quality in human beings and usually remains unimpaired by disability, injury or illness and is not dependent on music training. For children who have little or no verbal communication, music therapy offers a safe, secure, space for the release of feelings and a form of self-expression. As a general rule, both child and therapist take an active part in the sessions by playing, singing and listening. The therapist does not teach the child to sing or play an instrument; rather the child is encouraged to use percussion and ethnic instruments and their own voices to explore the world of sound and create a musical language of their own. Whatever form the therapy takes, the therapist aims to facilitate positive changes in behaviour and emotional well-being.

Drama therapy

Drama therapy is a diverse profession and it is important to ensure that those who practise it are maintaining the standards of the professional body, The

---

* Information quoted here by kind permission of BSMT, www.bsmt.org.

British Association of Dramatherapists (BADth), and its Code of Practice. There are currently four post-graduate training courses in Drama Therapy in the UK that lead to a qualification approved by the HPC, accredited by the BADth and recognized by the Department of Health. To become a full BADth member, proof of registration with the HPC is needed.

Entry criteria to the drama therapy course would normally include a bachelors degree in drama or a psychological health-related subject or an appropriate professional qualification/degree, equivalent of one year's full-time experience working, paid or voluntary, with adults or children with special needs, e.g. mental health, learning disabilities, experience in practical drama work and good interpersonal skills. Students would usually have an MA in drama therapy or drama and movement therapy.

There are drama therapy assistants. Assistants working in a support role at a more advanced level may be called an assistant practitioner.

BADth* state that: 'Drama therapy is a form of psychological therapy in which all of the performance arts are utilized within the therapeutic relationship. Drama therapists are described as both artists and clinicians and draw on their training to create methods to engage children in effecting psychological, emotional and social changes.' They use a number of mediums and artistic interventions which will enable the child to explore difficult and painful life experiences through an indirect approach.

Play therapy

Courses are accredited by the British Association of Play Therapists. It is usual for students to hold a first qualification in either teaching, social work, occupational therapy or other related fields and to have extensive experience of working with children. Personal therapy and supervised practice are essential elements of the training. There are currently four courses accredited by the British Association of Play Therapists (BAPT)** which provide full membership and a qualification to practise. Students must have a post-graduate diploma in play therapy or an MA in play therapy.

BAPT describes the aims of play therapy as:

> An effective therapy that helps children modify their behaviours, clarify their self-concept and build healthy relationships. In play therapy, children enter into a dynamic relationship with the therapist that enables them to express, explore and make sense of their difficult and painful experiences. Play therapy helps children find healthier ways of communicating, de-velop fulfilling relationships, increase resiliency and facilitate emotional literacy. Children use play as a form of communication. So often children

---

* By kind permission of BADth, www.badth.org.uk.

** The information here is reproduced by kind permission of the British Association of Play Therapists (BAPT). Website: www.bapt.info.

referred to play therapy do not have the words to describe their thoughts, feelings and perceptions of their internal and external world.

Play therapists work with children aged between 3 and 11 years of age and, occasionally, adolescents who are suffering from a range of psychological difficulties and complex life experiences. Psychological difficulties may include depression, anxiety, aggression, learning difficulties and ADHD. Difficult life experiences may include abuse, grief, family breakdown, domestic violence and trauma. Play therapists work closely with a child's parents/carers throughout the play therapy intervention and occasionally undertake parent/child relationship intervention. There are various forms of play therapy, including a non-directive play therapy approach. The process of play therapy is currently defined by the BAPT as:

> The dynamic process between child and play therapist in which the child explores at his or her own pace and with his or her own agenda those issues, past and current, conscious and unconscious, that are affecting the child's life in the present. The child's inner resources are enabled by the therapeutic alliance to bring about growth and change. Play therapy is child-centred, in which play is the primary medium and speech is the secondary medium.

The BAPT regulates practice and conduct and registered play therapists agree to abide by the ethical basis for good practice in play therapy as a condition of their registration.

Child psychotherapy

Psychotherapy is a way of helping individuals to overcome stress, emotional problems, relationship problems or troublesome habits. Different approaches can be used, but what is common is that they are all treatments based on talking to another person and sometimes doing things together. Increasingly, these approaches are known as talking therapies. The terms cognitive psychotherapists, behavioural psychotherapists, cognitive behavioural psychotherapists or rational emotive behavioural therapists are all used and these therapists use the approach commonly referred to as cognitive behavioural therapy. This is where children and therapists work together to identify and understand problems in terms of the relationship between thoughts, feelings and behaviour. The approach usually focuses on difficulties in the here and now and can be short term. Other approaches use psychoanalytic therapy, and some use systemic theories.

A child and adolescent psychotherapist will usually work in specialist Child and Adolescent Mental Health Services (CAMHS) as part of a multidisciplinary team for children with mental health problems. The Association of Child Psychotherapists (ACP)* is the professional organization for psychoanalytic child and adolescent psychotherapy in the UK. It recognizes and monitors seven training courses in child and adolescent psychotherapy. Child and adolescent psychotherapists who have qualified on one of those training courses are eligible for full membership of the Association. Child psychotherapy is a graduate entry profession. Before commencing clinical training, students must have completed a two-year course of observational psycho-analytic studies, leading to a post-graduate diploma/MA or equivalent qualification. Trainees are required to have substantial experience of working with children and adolescents of varying ages in a number of settings. Trainees are expected to undergo a minimum of 12 months personal analysis. The clinical training, which takes place in a multi-disciplinary CAMHS team, or equivalent setting, usually takes at least four years.

OTHER THERAPEUTIC PROJECTS IN SCHOOLS

In addition to contact with a trained therapist, there are a number of projects within schools that may be relevant to the child with BESD. These projects also employ trained therapists, including child and adolescent psychotherapists.

The Young Minds Schools Outreach Service helps raise awareness of children and adolescent mental health issues in schools and community organizations. Awareness workshops or assemblies may help staff and young people gain an insight into mental health issues and there is a parent information service.

The Place2Be is currently working with 128 schools across the UK, supporting a child population of around 40,000, often in areas of great deprivation. They provide 1:1 and group counselling sessions and drop-in services and employ trained therapists.

Nurture groups or classes are discrete classes located in mainstream schools, based on attachment theory. The class provides a secure base with consistent adults where the child can explore from and return to. Increasingly, these classes are found in secondary schools as well as infant/primary schools.

There are also many strategies such as therapeutic story writing or circle time which can be used successfully by teachers in mainstream schools after some training, which use the existing educational curriculum as a therapeutic context.

---

* Website available at www.childpsychotherapy.org.uk.

QUESTIONS TO ASK ABOUT THERAPEUTIC INVOLVEMENT

1. Ask for the school's behaviour policy. It would be more helpful if this could be read before the visit, so that specific questions can be raised, particularly with respect to school discipline and the flexibility of the school to address the needs of individual children.

2. What is the whole-school strategy for promoting mental health, and for identifying difficulties that may arise? Does the school use therapists? It may be necessary to check formal qualifications and to ask whether therapy is being offered directly by a qualified therapist or a therapy assistant.

3. The Social and Emotional Aspects of Learning (SEAL) Programme in schools promotes the development of social and emotional skills. SEAL provides the small group work for children who need more support, but the programmes may not be sufficient for children who have severe behavioural or mental health problems who require specialist help. How has the school implemented this programme so far? What improvements have been seen — both inside and outside of the classroom? What additional support will be available over and beyond SEAL for those children who require more support?

4. What sanctions will be applied and who will apply them?

5. How will the school initiate a pastoral support programme (a school-based intervention to help individual children to manage their behaviour) and who will be involved in drawing this up?

6. What is the school's record of exclusions? How might the school avoid exclusion by taking pre-emptive action, particularly where a specific SEN is known, e.g. autistic children?

7. Are there any adjustments that the school can make to expectations and routines?

8. What specialist behavioural and cognitive approaches will be used? Does the school make referrals to outside agencies or is it better for parents to self-refer? Which is the quicker route?

9. How will the school attempt to rechannel behaviours, e.g. through extra-curricular activities?

10. Can a separate room be available for 'time-out' or quiet space?

11. How will links be made with the local Child and Adolescent Mental Health Services (CAMHS) for children who are withdrawn, anxious or depressed and multiple self-harming? What strategies will the school employ before this stage? For example, will the school draw up a Pastoral Support Plan (PSP)?

12. What is the school's past experience with the local CAMHS?

13. In what circumstances does the school disapply the National Curriculum?

14. What support will the child receive in personal and social development and, in particular, managing relationships with others in the classroom or during wider activities in and around the school?

15. Will the child have one identified adult (sometimes called a key worker) with whom they can discuss matters, causing them concern and, if so, will this be a teacher, learning mentor or an LSA? What is their experience and qualifications?

16. What practical learning activities or work experience outside the classroom can be undertaken, particularly at Key Stage 4? This may be very motivating for some children.

17. How will other support services be used?
    - educational psychology
    - behavioural advisory teachers
    - social care services
    - CAMHS
    - speech and language therapy
    - physiotherapy
    - occupational therapy.

18. Can the school access art therapy, music therapy, drama therapy, play therapy or psychotherapy? It may be possible to access some or all of these through local special schools as well as through other avenues.

19. What additional courses have teachers followed? It will be important to identify whether training has taken place, not only for teachers or assistants who are specifically involved with children, perhaps in a resource base or unit, but also for mainstream teachers if children are integrating back into class. Will other staff employed by the school, lunchtime supervisors, receptionists, etc., also receive training?

20. Are restraint procedures used in school? Who is trained to carry these out and does the school have experience in doing this?

21. Is the school experienced in carrying out Risk Assessments?

22. Are there any qualified counsellors in school? If so, what are their qualifications (it is important to ascertain that counsellors have experience in special needs, if relevant)?

23. Are there specific groups already taking place in the school, such as anger management or anxiety management? If so, how will the child access these? If not, can these be formed and is there the expertise to do so? How will the group be made up and will the other members

of the group have similar difficulties or will they be in the group to provide 'normalized' role models?

24. What is the range of interventions that the school is implementing during break and lunchtime? These may, for example, include circle of friends, play assistance or other schemes. Who will be supervising these activities?

25. What is the view on medication and will the school support children who are being medicated?

26. What is the role of parents within the school and how will the school liaise with parents and any family support workers?

27. Are there any peer/buddy schemes operating in school, where peers will support other peers?

28. Does the school use any of the published programmes on promoting alternative thinking strategies (PATHS), which have lessons on emotional awareness?

29. Does the school have any experience of mental health professionals, such as psychiatrists or psychologists, delivering short-term cognitive behavioural therapy? Has it been successful? How will liaison take place? Will the child miss lessons and how will they catch up work?

30. Does the school have experience with eating disorders?

31. What are the channels of communication with regard to children who self-harm or express suicidal behaviour?

32. Is circle time used (usually at primary school)? If so, what issues are addressed?

33. What is the school's policy on confidentiality? How will the policy be clarified with the child and parents to ensure they fully understand the implications of therapeutic intervention?

CHAPTER 20

Counselling and Mentoring

COUNSELLING

The British Association for Counselling and Psychotherapy (BACP) contains a division entitled 'Counselling for Children and Young Children' (CCYP). It advises schools on how to set up school-based counselling services and sets benchmarks for quality and standards. Types of problems for referral to counselling services, as indicated on the website, are:

Abuse	Personal/self	Relationships/other
Emotional	Anxiety/stress	Bereavement
Neglect	Attempted suicide	Boy/girlfriends
Physical	Criminal activity	Friends
Racial	Dangerous behaviour	Inappropriate sexual
Rape	Depression	behaviour
Sexual	Gender and sexuality	Isolation/loneliness
Violence	Identity	Peer relationships
Others (specify)	Obsessive-compulsive	Others (specify)
	Post-traumatic stress	
	Self-esteem	
	Self-harm	
	Transitions	
	Others (specify)	
Health	**Relationships/family**	**School**
Disability	Bereavement	Academic/not coping
Drugs/alcohol	Dysfunctional family	Attendance difficulties
Eating disorder	Parental needs/expectations	Behaviour
HIV/AIDS	Financial problems	Experience of school
Physical (e.g. illness)	Siblings	Stress
Pregnancy	Split family/separations	Phobic
STDs	Step-parents	Relationships with staff
Others (specify)	Others (specify)	Transitions
		Victim
		Others (specify)

Racial/cultural		
Discrimination		
Equal opportunities		
Identity		
Religious/cultural		

Reproduced by kind permission of the British Association for Counselling and Psychotherapy (BACP).

The difficulty with counselling is that, at present, there are no legal minimum qualifications necessary to practise as a counsellor in the UK. As one of its main aims, to develop and improve the standards of counselling in the UK, BACP has developed stringent ethical guidelines which should inform the practice of members. However, employers are increasingly requiring that their counsellors are BACP accredited. The United Kingdom Register of Counsellors (UKRC) is part of BACP and the register has a published list of independent counsellors/psychotherapists. There are few full-time counselling courses, and these tend to be for professionals, such as teachers, social workers and ministers, who may gain secondment from their employer if they will be using newly acquired skills in their post afterwards. There are many more part-time substantial certificate or diploma courses which often require the applicant to have a degree, other professional training or experience in a related field.

Courses range from shorter counselling skills courses for those with little or no experience of counselling, up to PhD level. Apart from the BACP Accreditation of Courses Scheme, there are a number of bodies which undertake courses, such as AQA, Edexcel, RSPH and others. Although there are standards laid down for them, the teaching may be quite variable. Some training institutions award internal certificates, which are only certificates of attendance. Schools and parents are well advised to check the value of any certificates offered. In general, where a course is offered and it is not BACP accredited, it is wise to ascertain from the course tutor which professional body and code of ethics they adhere to and to discuss the content of the course. It is also important to be satisfied as to the experience, training and qualifications of the counsellor. It would be unlikely that distance-learning courses done by correspondence can provide a useful introduction to counselling theory and such courses would not count towards the training requirements of the BACP Accreditation Scheme as there would be little, if any, formal contact between the tutor and student.

THE BACP DEFINITION OF COUNSELLING

Counselling takes place when a counsellor sees an individual in a private and confidential setting to explore a difficulty the individual is having, distress they may be experiencing or, perhaps, their dissatisfaction with life, or loss of a sense of direction and purpose. It is always at the request of the individual as no one can properly be 'sent' for counselling. By listening attentively and patiently, the counsellor can begin to perceive the difficulties from the individual's point of view and can help them to see things more clearly, possibly from a different perspective. Counselling is a way of enabling choice or change or of reducing confusion. It does not involve giving advice or directing an individual client to take a particular course of action. Counsellors do not judge or exploit the individual in any way. The counsellor may help the individual to examine in detail the behaviour or situations which are proving troublesome and to find an area where it would be possible to initiate some change as a start. The counsellor may help the individual to look at the options open to them and help them to decide the best for them. There will clearly be some overlap between the work done, for example, with a behavioural advisory teacher and a counsellor, and it is important to be clear of the different approaches. Counsellors working in schools usually concentrate more on the 'every day' problems and difficulties of life. The more severe psychological disorders may be referred to other therapists or health professionals.

The school counsellor is generally independent of the school staff and it may be that this facility is what the child needs rather than speaking to somebody they feel might feedback to other members on the staff group. The alternative view is to understand that the very success of the counselling service is the co-dependency of a relationship between school staff and counsellor, whereby counsellors in schools are part of the team system dependent on support from teachers and sharing information to benefit children. It may be necessary to clarify the role of the counsellor in relation to the child's particular needs and consider whether this type of relationship within a particular school will be conducive to success. In some cases, it may be preferable for the child to seek help off school premises.

MENTORING

Mentoring is another area which will be recommended by a school and can now appear on a Statement. The Mentoring and Befriending Foundation (MBF) provides guidance and support to organizations and practitioners involved in mentoring and befriending. It is committed to promoting voluntary regulation of mentoring and befriending projects through the approved provider standard, the national benchmark for safe and effective practice. Mentoring and befriending are similar activities with some differences of emphasis. In general, they both involve development of 1:1 relationships based on trust, confidentiality and mutual involvement. The relationship is often voluntary with a goal of providing practical assistance and support. The main difference between mentoring and befriending is usually the emphasis placed on working towards goals. Mentoring tends to focus more on goal-setting and operates within a clearly defined time-frame; whilst befriending tends to develop more informal and supportive social relationships, often over a longer time-frame. In schools, mentoring can be used quite loosely, either to define peer mentoring or providing adult mentors who can give time and support in any way that is deemed appropriate. Mentoring programmes meet the needs of various groups, including children with special educational needs. Mentoring can be an effective tool in helping to motivate, support and inspire children in many different ways. There are many types and models of mentoring, and mentoring can be suggested for many reasons. If the child is given the opportunity of having an adult mentor, either from within the school staff or outside of school, it is necessary to clarify the objectives and the accountability of the mentor within the school model.

School-based learning mentors may work with children facing barriers to learning; such as poor attendance/behaviour or social/emotional problems. Learning mentors are usually based within a specific school. Volunteer mentoring programmes generally rely on recruiting mentors from the business community and public sector or the wider community. These volunteer mentors may support children at key points of transition and develop their coping strategies for their future. The aim of this type of mentoring is to provide a role model and encourage learners to become more independent and take responsibility for themselves. Volunteer mentors are often attached to a specific school or recruited for a specific mentoring programme. Peer mentoring programmes may run concurrently, which involves older children mentoring younger ones, e.g. secondary-aged children mentoring primary-aged children going from primary to secondary school. E-mentoring may also occur to supplement face-to-face mentoring or where it is difficult for mentor and mentee to meet regularly. The Department for Children, Schools and Families have produced good practice guidelines for learning mentors, noting that the flexibility of the role means it can be adaptive to the needs of any variety of schools and of individual children.

The guideline sets out:

A learning mentor is a...	A learning mentor is NOT a...
• role model	• counsellor
• active listener	• classroom assistant
• observer	• babysitter
• encourager	• disciplinarian
• professional friend	• person to whom a pupil is sent when naughty.
• challenger of assumptions	
• guide	
• target negotiator	
• reliable, approachable, non-judgemental and realistic supporter – with pupils, parents and staff.	

It is necessary at the outset to address any potential clashes in primary schools between the roles of the learning mentor, classroom assistant and other support staff. There will need to be liaison between the SENCo, education welfare officer, pastoral team and, perhaps, head of year. If a learning mentor scheme is to work best, a whole-school awareness training programme is essential, with ongoing awareness sessions or meetings throughout the year for new staff. If the child is assigned a learning mentor, ask where sessions will take place and about the confidentiality and what whole-school awareness training has taken place. Guidance suggests that, in practice, 10–15 cases have proved manageable case loads balanced between short- and long-term intervention. It would be helpful to ask how many children the learning mentor is currently working with.

QUESTIONS TO ASK ABOUT COUNSELLING AND MENTORING

1. Has the school been involved with successful mentoring schemes in the past, what evidence do they have that these schemes are helpful? What are the objectives of the sessions?

2. How is the counselling or mentoring service additional to, or how does it complement, the usual pastoral system offered by the school? What level of additional personal support will the child be offered? Is the counselling or mentoring service a confidential service to children and, if so, how will the referral be made, e.g. will it be self-referral?

3. Does the school counsellor belong to a professional counselling body and hold counselling qualifications? Who will supervise the input and how will the counsellor communicate with the school?

4. Will the sessions be confidential and, if so, at what point would parents and/or the school be involved? How will they be kept informed of progress? Where will the sessions take place? If the child has to miss lesson times, how will they catch up? Are the other staff sympathetic to the timings of the sessions? Are any peer projects working in school, such as peer mentoring, peer mediation, peer listening and/or peer education? If so, how will the child be involved and how will these techniques be supervised and evaluated?

5. If the child does not want others to know about attendance to sessions, how can the school respect this? Can counselling or mentoring take place out of school? What impact will that have on lesson times? How will transport happen?

6. Who will keep records in the school of attendance at sessions and if a child does not attend, what further steps will the school take to ensure things do not fall through the net?

7. Has the school had an awareness training programme about learning mentor schemes, counselling or peer mentoring schemes taking place in school?

CHAPTER 21

Speech and Language Therapy*

WHAT IS A SPEECH AND LANGUAGE THERAPIST (SALT)?

There are around 10,000 practising SaLTs in the UK, mainly employed by the National Health Service. Some therapists work for education services or charities and others work independently and treat clients privately.

Speech and language therapists provide assessment and treatment for children and adults who have difficulties with speech (pronunciation), language (sentence structure, vocabulary, etc.) and communication (speech/language use) problems. They work in a variety of clinical/educational areas including the following:

- neurology (stroke, neurological disorders)
- voice, ear nose and throat (ENT)
- paediatrics
- neonatology
- eating, drinking and swallowing
- oncology (cancer) (working with those who have had laryngectomy, or removal of other speech organs)
- hearing impairment/deafness.

Speech and language therapists will work collaboratively with parents, carers and other professionals, including teachers, occupational therapists and the medical profession to achieve common goals associated with remediation.

---

* This chapter was authored by Myra Pontac, speech and language therapist.

QUALIFICATIONS OF A SPEECH AND LANGUAGE THERAPIST*

There are currently 18 universities and colleges in the UK offering recognized speech and language therapy courses.

The initials Cert MRCSLT show that a practitioner is a certified member of the Royal College of Speech and Language Therapists and that the individual has been awarded a licence to practise following the successful completion of an accredited degree course. Furthermore it confirms that the individual has agreed to adhere to the professional body's code of ethics and professional conduct. Registered therapists are committed to maintaining their competence and expertise through continuing education and active involvement in a range of professional activities. The Royal College of Speech and Language Therapists produce an annual register of practising members.

Since October 2000, speech and language therapists have not been able to practise legally without being registered with the Health Professions Council (HPC). Registration with the HPC requires that speech and language therapists undertake a stated minimum amount of continuing professional development each year. The HPC defines the following professional titles which are protected by law and these are:

- speech and language therapist
- speech therapist.

If a speech and language therapist chooses to work within the independent sector, and has a minimum of two years' post-graduate experience, they may register with The Association of Speech and Language Therapists in Independent Practice (ASLTIP). Members of ASLTIP must be registered with both the Health Professions Council and the Royal College of Speech and Language Therapists. ASLTIP keeps a register of therapists working independently in the UK and their areas of special interest. It also runs courses for speech and language therapists and has members who advise the Royal College of Speech and Language Therapists.

If a SaLT who speaks another language is required, the Royal College of Speech and Language Therapists should be contacted or ASLTIP or, of course, the Primary Care Trust, which is the employer of most of the local NHS Speech and Language Therapy Services.

Increasingly, speech and language therapy assistants (also called support practitioners) will be found working alongside speech and language therapists. The Royal College of Speech and Language Therapists state that SaLT assistants must have qualified speech and language therapists to direct them in:

---

* Reproduced by kind permission of the Royal College of Speech and Language Therapists (RCSLT).

- supporting clients to develop communication skills
- developing and preparing therapy materials.

Many SaLT assistants also support and facilitate group activities for individual clients. SaLT assistants are trained by speech and language therapists to undertake a variety of roles within schools and are mainly employed by the National Health Service. It should be noted that there are no formal educational or age requirements, although relevant skills, experience or qualifications from other areas are said to be beneficial. Training is often given on the job and assistants may have the chance to complete an NVQ or BTec qualification or a foundation degree course. The Royal College of Speech and Language Therapists has set up standards for working as a speech and language therapy support assistant (practitioner), but it is clear that the qualified SaLT holds the ethical and legal (duty of care) for the child and, consequently, for the standard of duties delegated to a support assistant (practitioner). All clinical decisions concerning the child are the responsibility of the qualified SaLT and the SaLT must be responsible for the work undertaken by a SaLT assistant. There is no specified amount or type of supervision and clinical advice required. This is based on the recorded knowledge and competence of the SaLT assistant, the needs of the child, the service setting and the tasks assigned.

The roles and responsibilities of a SaLT and a SaLT assistant must be clearly defined. For example, formal assessment using certain standardized tests, should be carried out by the qualified therapist. Some types of therapy will need to be carried out by the qualified therapist and others can be carried out by the assistant under the SaLT's guidance. Therapists use evidence-based research in order to make decisions as to who should carry out particular therapy tasks.

There are occasions when language work is carried out by professionals other than a speech and language therapist and it is important for parents and other professionals to check the status of that person and the qualifications they hold, e.g. a language teacher. Increasingly language work, particularly with children on the autistic spectrum, is carried out by professionals – usually teachers – within a 'communication and interaction team'. Usually, a speech and language therapist will play an advisory role within such a team.

Therapists who work with the NHS, Local Authorities or other organizations obtain a CRB check through them. Independent therapists will usually have CRB checks arranged through organizations with which they are involved or with whom they carry out work.

SaLTs will work with children of all cognitive abilities; mild, moderate, severe or profound, and with children who have difficulties with communication and interaction problems, as described in Chapter 2.

ASSESSMENT

The SaLT will consider the speech, language and communication difficulties the child has and the impact that these will have on their life. Assessment will usually include:

- gathering information from parents, families and teachers and anyone else involved in the child's life
- assessment of the understanding of spoken language and non-verbal communication (comprehension)
- assessment of expression through speaking and body language (expression)
- assessment of production and use of sounds (phonetics/phonology)
- assessment of the ability to use language in a social context (pragmatics)
- assessment of play skills
- assessment of eating, drinking and swallowing.

Depending on the child's cognitive level of ability and co-operation, these assessments may be formal, using standardized tests, or informal and will include observation. The decision of whether to offer further intervention will be based on the outcome of assessment and the impact of the difficulty on the child's life and the likelihood of effecting change with speech and language therapy at this time.

Following the assessments, the outcome is usually discussed with the parents and a written report is sent to the parents and the referral agent.

There are a range of interventions, some of which will involve working with and through parents, and others through classroom support assistants, speech and language therapy assistants, class teachers, nursery workers or, indeed, individual treatment by the SaLT. Possible ways of supporting the child may include one or more of the following:

- direct therapy with the child, individually or in a group
- provision of programmes of work
- supporting the child in different environments and by different people
- assessment and provision of communication aids and resources
- training and advice for parents/carers and other professionals involved with the child, including education and social work
- involvement with educational and transitional planning.

Interventions may be time-bound, either with series of treatments, punctuated by breaks, or work which is subject to evaluation and review. Children will be discharged from therapy either because the therapist recognizes that the child is not benefitting from therapy at this time, or the communication potential has been achieved. The decision to discharge from therapy should not be based on resources, but rather on the child's needs and the response to therapy. In some situations, it is the child or family who do not wish to continue with therapy.

SaLTs work closely with classroom support assistants and/or SaLT assistants who offer valuable input to the child. However, one of the difficulties of long-term input is that the support assistant's skills, due to lack of experience, may not be flexible enough to alter the programme as the child develops and so progress can be inhibited. There is also concern expressed that sometimes the knowledge gained by working with one child could be wrongly generalized to other children with different needs and if the school perceives the SaLT assistant as 'semi-qualified', this may stop them from seeking further advice from the SaLT themselves. It is always good practice for assistants to be frequently supported by a qualified speech and language therapist.

Increasingly, clinical supervision is a part of any speech and language therapist's professional life. Speech and language therapy assistants are also involved in this. Supervision is a process via which therapists and assistants can receive professional and supportive guidance in their day-to-day decision making.

PROVISION OF SPEECH AND LANGUAGE THERAPY IN THE ENVIRONMENT

Speech and language therapy may be delivered in different contexts.

Mainstream school

Sometimes therapists work within mainstream schools. Children in mainstream schools generally receive an indirect approach, with therapists providing a consultative or advisory service to teaching staff rather than working directly. However, if a child has a Statement of Special Educational Needs, direct therapy delivered within a mainstream context may be possible. Specialist teaching methods, such as the use of communication aids, are used less in mainstream schools, whereas comparable children in special schools use specialist strategies and communication aids much more. Some children make very good progress in mainstream schools, others make less progress. Therapists can usually provide a good indication of the appropriate placement for a child with speech and language difficulties (Conti-Ramsden *et al.* 2002: 'Different school placements following language unit attendance: which factors affect language outcome?'). Much depends on the child's individual needs; some children require the specialist context and training available in specialist schools, others benefit hugely from the models of language provided by other mainstream children. It is unusual for therapists to work on site within a mainstream school.

Units

Sometimes specialist provision is available in the form of a unit within a mainstream school. Usually this consists of a class, staffed by teachers trained in a particular area of SEN, e.g. language impairment, learning difficulties, hearing impairment, etc. Therapists will work with teaching staff within such units and support children integrating into mainstream activities.

Special schools

Within special schools, therapists are more likely to work on site. Therapists will work as part of the team of professionals providing education and support to children, e.g. teachers, occupational therapists, physiotherapists and psychologists. Some specialist schools have residential facilities, where SaLTs will also spend time working with care staff on language or feeding programmes.

The amount of therapy provided in any context will take account of various factors:

a. how communication strategies are being implemented by other professionals and what the therapist can add to this

b. how likely the child is to benefit from the therapy

c. the severity of the child's communication impairment

d. the amount of therapy specified in the child's Statement of Special Educational Needs.

WHAT DO SPEECH AND LANGUAGE THERAPISTS DO?

The first point of contact with a speech and language therapist is usually the assessment. Assessment has a number of functions:

a. It provides a baseline measure of a child's skills in speech, language and communication. This measure can then be compared with later measures in order to assess progress.

b. It provides a guide as to the type and frequency of therapy that should be carried out. The therapist, on the basis of information from the initial assessment will choose programmes to work with, depending on various factors, e.g. the child's likes/dislikes, temperament, attentional skills and so on.

c. After an initial assessment a report is written which provides a written record of the child's speech, language and communication skills at a particular time.

A typical speech and language therapy assessment report should provide information about the following:

- attention/listening/behaviour
- play skills (for younger children)
- comprehension or understanding
- non-verbal communication
- expressive language (grammar, word finding, vocabulary, etc.)
- speech (pronunciation)
- voice
- fluency (stammering).

Some assessments are very specialist and may be carried out in particular clinics, e.g. those for eating/drinking. In this case, reports will focus on that particular area.

Following assessment, a therapist will then formulate a therapy plan. This will usually consist of a *set of aims*. For example:

Child A – Aims of therapy:

a. to improve understanding of instructions containing two pieces of information, e.g. 'Give me the *yellow car*'

b. to improve use of two-word sentences, e.g. 'Mummy sock'

c. to improve attention skills.

Therapists try to make their aims realistic, achievable and measurable and they will state a time by which those aims should be achieved.

Thus, for the above example, the therapist might say that the child should be able to understand two-word level instructions 75 per cent of the time by the end of a three-month period of therapy. This could be measured by recording the number of times, within a SaLT session, that a child understands a two-word level instruction.

Knowing whether an aim is achievable or realistic will rely on experience. Therapists, for example, who have worked for many years with children with learning difficulties, will have a good idea about whether it is likely that a particular child will achieve the aim within the set period of time. There are certain factors that a speech and language therapist will look for to indicate progress. The level of comprehension is important, as is the presence or otherwise of significant learning difficulties. However, speech and language therapists will test out a child's response to therapy and this is also an important indicator.

As well as aims, the therapist will *plan resources*. The therapist may use published programmes and the advice may be planned for teaching staff. The therapist will think about who is going to implement the work. Increasingly, speech and language therapists recognize that individual sessions that are not backed up with advice to staff and carry-over work, are not effective. In the same way, advice without individual sessions may not be effective. Generally, children with communication difficulties require a lot of repeated practice in order to make progress. The speech and language therapist has to devise ways in which that repeated practice can occur. The therapist will think about everyday experiences that can be used to help. So, for example, a child who doesn't understand the concepts of 'wet' and 'dry' might be helped by engaging in a laundry sorting activity with their mother, putting all the dry clothes in one basket and all the wet clothes in another.

The therapist will liaise with teaching staff to find out which topics are being studied in the classroom and will devise activities that can be incorporated into the curriculum, e.g. a child who does not understand 'big' and 'little' in a class studying minibeasts will already be at a disadvantage. The speech and language therapist might suggest that the child use a story about a kitten that starts off small and grows big to develop the concept.

Some therapy activities, like this, sound very much like what a teacher might do and there will be overlap. However, the speech and language therapist will continually question and identify the barriers to communication that are apparent. The therapist will observe the child in the therapy activities, set and ask questions about how hearing/vision/motor skills/emotional status and so on are affecting the child's response.

Therapy, when provided by a qualified therapist, is a process of continually setting up hypotheses (or ideas) about why a child is communicating in the way they do and testing these, then modifying the activities (that may or may not be carried out by others) accordingly.

Some types of therapy are better done by qualified therapists simply because of the training that they have had, e.g. some work with speech sounds (phonology) requires the ability to write in phonetic script which would be better done by a qualified therapist because they will have been trained in this. However, other work with speech sounds can be delegated to others.

Sometimes, rather than designing and carrying out particular therapy tasks, a therapist will want to change the communicative environment. The therapist may have identified that the way that staff are communicating with a child with learning difficulties, for example, is not helping that child. The therapist will then advise on different ways of communicating. For example, a child with autism, showing aggressive behaviour and continually hitting the wall, might automatically be asked by staff to calm down and then is offered a drink. The therapist could produce an ABC chart (antecedent, behaviour, consequence) to explore the communicative behaviour. In this way, the therapist could observe that the behaviour (hitting the wall) was the child's way of communicating that they wanted a drink. The child had no verbal language and no signs but the hitting always worked. The therapist would then produce a picture symbol for the child to tap when they wanted a drink. Initially the child may hit the picture but over time and with the staff's support, the child would simply touch it. In this example, the therapist works with staff to change the communicative environment.

Sometimes, therapists will work with other professionals, such as occupational therapists to change the environment. For example, a child with cerebral palsy who is producing inadequate levels of voice might be helped by the provision of appropriate seating to avoid slumping and compression of the chest. The occupational therapist would advise on seating and the speech and language therapist would be considering breathing for speech.

Specific programmes are sometimes used, e.g. Hanen (Pepper and Weitzman 2004) or the Derbyshire Language Scheme, Talktools, the Nuffield Dyspraxia Programme, etc. Many specific programmes are available in different areas of clinical need. Hanen, for example, is used to teach parents and educators to facilitate interaction and communication in everyday situations and through play. The Derbyshire Language Scheme works at increasing the amounts of information children can process within instructions. So, using play materials, therapists work at improving understanding of one piece of information, e.g. 'Give me the BALL', through to two pieces of information 'Give me the LITTLE BALL', on to three 'Give me the LITTLE, YELLOW BALL', etc. Therapists will usually have to be trained to undertake these programmes and they are chosen according to the child's individual needs. Therapists using these tools will explain their principles and how to use them to carers, parents and other professionals, and will be able to provide written information about them. Often, parents can go on courses to be trained in these particular approaches. Parents should expect therapists to be aware of a wide range of specific programmes and be able to discuss the relative merits of using particular programmes with their children.

Social skills and social communication work will be carried out by the speech and language therapist for some children, particularly those on the autistic spectrum. Therapists will work either individually or in groups or in pairs on areas such as the following:

- Understanding and use of facial expressions.
- Understanding and use of tones of voice.
- Understanding and use of ambiguous language, e.g. idioms such as 'Pull your socks up'.
- Understanding and use of body language, personal space and gesture.

Therapists may use published programmes to work on these areas, for example The Social Use of Language Programme (SULP) by Wendy Rinaldi (Rinaldi 2001). They may also work through role play and drama. Frequently, therapists work alongside and with other professionals such as music therapists and drama teachers in facilitating social skills and social use of language.

Some therapists are involved in contributing to a child's waking day curriculum. In this case, the child will be educated via a curriculum that extends beyond the ordinary school day and into residential facilities after school. The therapist's role, in this case, will be:

- to liaise with care and support staff to ensure that strategies used within school are carried over to activities after school hours and in all daily living activities
- to share aims developed as part of the child's individual curriculum
- to train staff in the use of particular techniques for supporting communication
- to assess the child's communication skills in the residential situation.

The overall aim for the therapist working in a residential school, along with other professionals, will be to try to ensure that the approach to the child's communication development is as consistent and seamless as possible.

HOW DO YOU KNOW THERAPY HAS BEEN SUCCESSFUL?

There are various ways:

a. A therapist can measure progress using standardized tests. The therapist will compare results with those obtained at the initial assessment or compare observations. Standard scores and percentile ranks will show whether a child has changed over and above what one would expect just because the child has got older. Therapists will be able to advise, given the child's condition, whether progress is adequate. Again, the ability to do this will depend on experience.

b. The satisfaction of the child or their parents is important. Sometimes objective measurements are not possible but if the child feels better about their speech this can be a good indication of success. Child satisfaction is often extremely important in areas such as stammering. Often the stammer cannot just be 'cured' but the stammerer may be able to cope better with others hearing the stammer, which is a very positive change.

c. Improvements in the communicative environment. Sometimes a change in the communicative environment is the first sign of success of a therapy programme. There might not be an immediate effect on the child, but a longer term effect might be expected.

d. Research is important in measuring success of particular types and frequency of therapy. Various types of research can be carried out. The most powerful are usually randomized controlled trials. However, individual studies are also important. It is not easy to get a homogenous group of children with communication problems together. Children are very individual and there are considerable differences between them so there are all sorts of factors that can determine outcome and it can be very difficult to control these.

Clearly, the more speech and language therapy that a child needs, the more on site, qualified therapy will be required.

QUESTIONS TO ASK ABOUT SPEECH AND LANGUAGE THERAPY PROVISION IN A SCHOOL

When asking about therapy provision within a school there are a number of important questions:

1. How many children have speech and language difficulties in the school and what experience does the school have of working with a SaLT? Is the SaLT employed by the school or the NHS? If they are employed by the NHS, does the school have any control over the workload, amount of sessions or supervision? How will the child catch up on any lessons missed if they go for therapy sessions?

2. How often is the speech and language therapist in school? Is the focus on individual or group therapy? Does the SaLT spend time in the classroom? How much time?

3. How many qualified speech and language therapists are there?

4. To what extent does the speech and language therapist work as part of the team within a school (therapists, who are part of a team and have a good working relationship with the other professionals, will be more successful in achieving generalization and carry over of therapy) or do they just come in and out for sessions?

5. What support does the speech and language therapist have? Are there any SaLT assistants working with the SaLT? What training have they received? Will the SaLT or SaLT assistant be working with the child?

6. What training does the speech and language therapist provide to the school? Do mainstream teachers differentiate the pace and language content of the lesson, or is this left to the LSA to do, working directly with the child?

7. To what extent are the therapists involved in curriculum planning?

8. Are the therapists involved in the annual reviews and in writing targets for individual education plans? Is there a separate language programme?

9. In special schools it is also useful to ask what additional training does the SaLT have? For example, in a school for dyslexic children, one might expect the SaLT to have a post-graduate diploma in working with dyslexic children.

10. If a child uses a communication aid, have the staff been trained in its use? Will it always be available? Who will know what to do when it goes wrong?

11. What training have staff at the school received? When was this and has it been updated? Who gave the training and how long was the session? Did the content cover the necessary areas for a specific child's needs?

HOW DO SPEECH AND LANGUAGE THERAPISTS WORK WITH ALTERNATIVE COMMUNICATION SYSTEMS?

For children who have communication impairments it may be necessary and helpful to use alternative and augmentative systems of communication. For some children, these will represent their only way of communicating. For others, they will be used to support verbal communication. So a child with severe cerebral palsy who has very little ability to move their oral muscles may depend entirely on an electronic communication aid (alternative communication). Another child, who has some speech, that is very unclear, may be supported by using sign and gestures. In this case, the sign/gesture is being used as an augmentative system of communication, not a replacement. Parents are often worried about using alternative means of communication and feel that their children will have little motivation to talk. There is a considerable body of research showing that this is not the case at all. In fact, augmentative communication systems used with speech tend to enhance the development of verbal communication.

There are many types of alternative communication systems.

Sign

Various signing systems are available and particular systems are used in order to meet particular needs. Makaton® is a system that uses single words. It is frequently used for children with learning difficulties. Paget Gorman and British Sign Language both enable grammatical structures to be signed. British Sign Language is usually used for children with hearing impairment and Paget Gorman for those with language disorders. The latter is particularly suitable for teaching language structure.

Intensive interaction

This approach to teaching the pre-speech fundamentals of communication to children with severe learning difficulties and/or autism was developed during the 1980s at Harperbury Hospital School in Hertfordshire. Intensive interaction is a communication system based on body language and imitation which aims to increase sociability and communication intentions.

Communication aids

Either low-tech or high-tech communication aids can be used. High-tech aids are electronic aids, low-tech aids are those that do not usually involve the use of electronic equipment, e.g. an e-tran frame is a square of perspex onto which a speech and language therapist may place pictures. The child is then encouraged to eye point to pictures placed in the corners of the frame in order to request. VOCA (voice output communication aids) are usually used with children with severe motor difficulties such as cerebral palsy. There are many types available and the individual needs of the child (motor/sensory/communication) will be considered when choosing which VOCA to use, e.g. those with good comprehension/understanding will be able to use those with much more information stored on them than those with a lesser ability to understand; a voice output communication aid produces a spoken word/sentence when the child activates the device by pressing buttons.

Picture communication systems

PECS (Picture Exchange Communication System) (Bondy and Frost 2001) is a good example of a picture communication system. Children are taught to request by selecting a picture out of a choice of pictures and giving this in exchange for a desired object/activity. The system can then be extended to sentence level with the child combining pictures in sequence in order to request, e.g. I want chocolate/biscuit.

Speech and language therapists will use assessments and often work with other professionals such as occupational therapists and physiotherapists in order to consider which system of alternative/augmentative communication might be of most use to a child.

CHAPTER 22

Occupational Therapy*

WHAT IS AN OCCUPATIONAL THERAPIST (OT)?

Occupational therapists in the UK work in a variety of settings, including hospitals, schools, local communities, social care, businesses, prisons, charities and other environments. Occupational therapy is a health profession concerned with promoting independence, health and well-being through occupation. The College of Occupational Therapists (COT) website describes occupational therapy as helping 'people engage as independently as possible in the activities (occupations) which enhance their health and wellbeing'. Occupational therapists are trained to understand occupational needs and therapeutic interventions which enable them to work collaboratively with people of all ages and abilities who experience obstacles to participation. These obstacles may result from a limitation or change in function (thinking, doing, feeling) because of illness or disability (e.g. cognitive impairment, physical difficulties) and/or barriers in the social, institutional and/or physical environment.

OTs work with children with a wide range of disabilities and difficulties, including physical and multiple disabilities, mental health and social problems, learning difficulties including specific difficulties such as developmental dyspraxia or developmental co-ordination disorder (DCD) and behavioural problems.

QUALIFICATIONS OF A PAEDIATRIC OCCUPATIONAL THERAPIST

Paediatric occupational therapists are those who work specifically with children, enabling them to fulfil as many of their functional demands as independently as possible. Children between the ages of 0 to 16 years will

---

* This chapter was authored by Elisheva Birnbaum, occupational therapist.

fall under the care of a paediatric OT. Children's productivity is *play and learning*, both of which are crucial for development. When a child's ability is affected as a result of injury, illness, disability or disease, an occupational therapist can evaluate a child's skills for daily activities, school performance and self-care activities and compare them to what is developmentally appropriate for a particular age group. Treatment is focused on improving a child's skill level and meeting their special educational needs as part of their overall development.

All occupational therapists are required to be registered with the regulatory body, the Health Professions Council (HPC). The HPC is responsible for the conduct, performance and ethical behaviour of all its registrants. Most occupational therapists are members of the British Association of Occupational Therapists (BAOT) and can receive referrals through doctors, local hospitals, social services, educational departments, parents, carers or the young people themselves. Parents may also seek out an OT independently. Occupational therapists who work independently can be found through the College of Occupational Therapists' Specialist Section – Independent Practice and many OTs will work in both sectors at the same time. Paediatric occupational therapists should be checked by the Criminal Records Bureau when working with children and vulnerable young adults.

The title 'occupational therapist' is a protected title and registrants can be checked on the register on the HPC website. Currently 31 universities in the UK offer pre-registration OT training. Some OTs will have diplomas, but increasingly they will have degrees. Once qualified, occupational therapists are expected to demonstrate continuing professional development (CPD) to ensure practice is up to date, current and relevant to their work. This can be done through a variety of ways including relevant courses, appropriate reading material, case discussions and supervision. Additionally, there are a number of masters and doctorate programmes for those wishing to further their professional development.

Occupational therapy assistants (also known as occupational therapy support workers or technical instructors) do not require formal qualifications for the job although, in practice, many will have some relevant formal academic or vocational qualifications, e.g. NVQ, and/or experience. The occupational therapy assistant carries out delegated duties given by the OT. Occupational therapy assistants must have regular supervision from an OT. The frequency of the supervision is dependent upon the work delegated and competence and experience of the assistant. In general, occupational therapy assistants will be working at NVQ Level 3, depending on their salary scale, experience and skills. There are a number of programmes at colleges and universities accredited by the College of Occupational Therapists and further information should be gleaned from the website.

ASSESSMENT

The paediatric OT will need to carry out a detailed assessment which is usually done with a parent or carer present and involves both standardized and non-standardized tests, screening, observations and questionnaires. The child's views must be taken into account. Parents' or carers' issues are placed on high priority and given much significance in order to make the treatment meaningful and orientated towards targets. Each therapy team may use slightly different assessments or frameworks to inform clinical practice but the fundamental points will be similar.

Following an assessment, the OT will formulate and prioritise objectives according to the assessed needs. The OT will also decide whether treatment will be most effective in an individualized session, part of a group or a combination of both. The decision on the number of sessions the child will receive will be based on the needs of the child and family, but other external factors will also be taken into consideration, e.g. the child's level of fatigue. The OT may also refer the child to other services if indicated from the assessment, for example a neurological evaluation, eye examination or speech therapy.

It is generally good practice for the parent to participate in the session, unless this is contraindicated either by the therapist or parent, in order to maximize the carry-over at home. If therapy takes place in school it is usually advised that the child's assistant is present in order to continue the programme in school. The parent and learning support assistant will then be able to observe and possibly participate in the therapy session and receive guidance on how to promote skills in the home or school environment. The OT is likely to set up a programme, in conjunction with the parent and/or teachers, of exercises and functional activities to be continued at home or school to support the therapy session. This will increase the child's success and overall improvement of their performance. In a mainstream school, it is good practice for OTs to work with and advise teachers and LSAs on how to include activities within the classroom, the school day and National Curriculum. This way, children are not excluded or stigmatized for being treated differently and/or being 'taken out of the classroom'.

Depending on the child's problems, the emphasis may be on:

- fine motor skills (in particular, hand function leading to effective handwriting)
- hand/eye co-ordination, sequencing, initiating activity, sensory processing needs, sensory integration/modulation, proprioception
- co-ordination and motor planning (gross motor skills)
- organizational skills
- self-help skills, such as eating, dressing, toileting

- perception, such as spatial and body awareness, visual discrimination
- concentration and attention span
- multi-tasking and executive functioning
- learning social skills, e.g. through therapeutic play
- postural management to facilitate functional activities.

The OT can also advise on the need for specialist equipment to compensate for a skill or to increase support so that independence in a task can be achieved, e.g. the use of a 'sit 'n' move' cushion to improve concentration. Equipment is also used as a therapeutic tool to aid development and/or recovery; to improve basic bodily functions, such as respiration and digestion; to enable carers to carry out their caring tasks; and to facilitate access to the National Curriculum. Equipment will have to be constantly reviewed and evaluated as the child grows or their needs change. Other types of equipment that may be suggested include:

- specific seating within classrooms – which may involve special seats or chairs
- mobility aids, e.g. buggies, wheelchairs
- utensils for eating and drinking
- equipment for washing and using the toilet
- equipment for handwriting, which may be as simple as pen grips or as complex as computer-aided technology
- hoists, postural management equipment, standing and transferring equipment, play equipment, etc.

The OT can also provide advice on lifting and handling the child safely and will liaise with other professionals and the family. The OT will have input into problem-solving to remove barriers to enable the child to participate in daily activities within their normal environment. This may involve adapting the environment to maximize the child's ability to engage in activities and also adapting the activity to permit the child to participate fully and access the curriculum. Sometimes, just providing a different pair of scissors will allow that child to participate in the same activity that their peers can do. The OT, being trained in physical and mental health and the psycho-social needs of individuals, uses activity as a therapeutic tool and the sessions go well beyond provision of merely handwriting techniques.

As part of Children's Services, specialized paediatric occupational therapists will also advise parents and offer support within the family. They will also assess the child's long-term needs in relation to major adaptations in the home and can assist in the process of designing facilities required for that individual. This may include changes to:

- access (within the home and external areas, such as entry to and from the garden)
- lifts (including stair lifts)
- hoists (and tracking)
- bathroom (to aid showering, washing facilities)
- kitchen (to increase self-help for teaching and life skills)
- extra heating or change of heating
- specific adaptations for children (security gates or alarms/sensors and wheelchair accessibility).

WHAT DO OCCUPATIONAL THERAPISTS DO?

Having assessed and identified the needs of the child, the OT will meet with the child for a session. Based on the objectives decided, the therapist will divide up the sessions, taking into consideration the child's stage of development, their concentration span and motivation. As play is a major part of a child's development, this will feature as a significant part of therapy and it will be through this medium that objectives can be achieved, particularly for a pre-schooler and infant/primary-aged child. Floor play and symbolic play is particularly important with a pre-schooler and young child, but strategy games, such as chess, Mastermind and Sudoku, can be part of an older child's play.

The occupational therapist will individualize the session according to the occupational demands on a child. A pre-schooler with identified issues in fine motor skills or hand function that is likely to impede handwriting later on, may be guided through play tasks such as play-doh, plasticine, lacing and beading which involve hand/finger strengthening, in-hand manipulation, and toys which encourage a correct pencil grip or games that involve similar skills. A primary school child struggling with handwriting may receive therapy to improve upper body strength, postural stability, hand function exercises and a pencil grip to improve their handwriting so that they can participate in class with their own age group. A secondary age child, however, who has poor handwriting might be advised to transfer to a computer for class work instead, due to the increased pressure and demand involved with work in secondary education and the reduced ability to change as one gets older.

The OT is likely to formulate long-term goals and then break these down into a number of short-term goals in order to achieve the main goal. These short-term goals will then structure the therapy session as the OT will choose tasks and games in order to attain them. Usually, there will be a number of goals and the therapist, using their clinical reasoning, may break up the session to work on the separate goals or may be able to combine the goals together.

Example of treatment plans

THE LONG-TERM GOAL FOR A PRE-SCHOOLER COULD BE:

- Child will be able to select a game from the toy cupboard and play on the floor with it with two peers for 20 minutes without the support of an adult.

SHORT-TERM GOALS MAY THEN INVOLVE:

- Child can select one toy from a choice of two familiar toys.
- Child can concentrate on one activity for 15 minutes without losing interest or requiring intervention from somewhere else.
- Child will play appropriately with one playmate with a specified toy and adult assistance.
- Child will be able to tolerate the floor environment for 15 minutes following 10 minutes of sensory integration input (see later for information on sensory integration).

THE LONG-TERM GOAL OF A PRIMARY SCHOOL CHILD COULD BE:

- Child will be able to copy a paragraph (50 words) from the whiteboard in an appropriate time-frame whilst maintaining a correct seating position, pencil grip and organization of letters and paper.

SHORT-TERM GOALS MAY THEN INVOLVE:

- Child will choose a pencil grip that allows a dynamic and effective tripod position to be maintained.
- Child will carry out weight-bearing exercises daily (wheelbarrow, press-ups) to strengthen their upper body to improve postural control.
- In 10 minutes, child will be able to complete a 24-piece puzzle using the picture.
- Child will use Cognitive Orientation to Daily Occupational Performance (COOP) strategies to encourage organization of the letters on the page. COOP is a therapeutic treatment approach for children with difficulties performing motor-based skills. It will be individualized to the child and is designed to guide children to

use metacognitive skills to achieve goals, e.g. writing and skipping, through discovery and development of effective cognitive strategies.

THE LONG-TERM GOAL OF A SECONDARY SCHOOL CHILD COULD BE:

- Child will be able to remember a list of five school stationery items and buy them from a familiar shop, using different amounts of money and overcoming any unexpected scenarios, independently.

SHORT-TERM GOALS MAY THEN INVOLVE:

- Child will learn to play a number of strategy games (chess, Othello, set) with another peer.
- Child will learn sensory techniques to do before carrying out a task to aid concentration and organization.
- Child will learn techniques to help in remembering a list of items.
- Child will learn and practice using different amounts of money to buy an item in a 'safe' environment and be able to check the change given.
- Child will use COOP strategies to carry out the task effectively.
- Child will remember two items and complete the above goal.

HOW DO YOU KNOW THERAPY HAS BEEN SUCCESSFUL?

The occupational therapist will be using clinical reasoning to inform their practice in every session. Therefore, success of treatment is continuously evaluated based on the child's progress. After each session, the OT will write case notes, reflecting on the treatment session and adapt these notes accordingly to ensure continuing accomplishment of the short-term goals. The OT will use standardized assessments according to need to accurately measure whether the child's baseline has improved in specific areas such as visual motor control or visual perception. Predicted outcomes can then be compared and results can be measured against expected scores for that age.

Discussion with parents and the school about the child's occupational performance will also provide information as to whether the goals are being achieved in a functional sense. For example, is the child better able to copy from the whiteboard? Or, have the parents been able to send their child independently to the shops with successful outcomes?

If the parent receives homework to do at home with the child, the parent can self-evaluate progress as well by judging the time taken, the amount of dependence needed and carry over into other functional areas of the child's life. A parent and/or LSA can also observe treatment sessions and see the level of progress within the treatment session. For example, how much sensory input a child needs in order to concentrate on a task for 30 minutes? Or how much intervention is the therapist giving in order for the child to accomplish a set task?

The use of a prioritized list of outcome measures, relevant to the child's needs are formulated with the parent and/or child and is another way to measure success of goal achievement and incorporates an aspect of whether the goal is less or more important to the child, school or parent. The OT can continually adapt interventions to ensure the occupational therapy continues to meet the improving developing needs of the child.

SENSORY INTEGRATION

Sensory integration is one of the frames of reference that can inform the intervention process. Others treatments offered by OTs, including Bobath and conductive education are discussed in 'Physiotherapy', Chapter 23. Most OTs in the UK use sensory integration within their therapy. It is used in treating sensory processing disorders. All occupational therapists will learn the principles of sensory integration as part of their professional training; some will then pursue advanced training, although formal sensory integration training within the UK is still rare. Other members of the multi-disciplinary team, if specifically trained in sensory integration therapy, may also offer this treatment, e.g. physiotherapists.

A regulatory disorder is when the body cannot regulate itself in response to change from the environment. When babies are born, their sensory response system needs to cope with a new environment. The nervous system receives messages and responds to them causing the baby to cry, settle, alert, and be frightened or angry. As a baby grows older, they learn how to adapt to the environment so that they feel comfortable and in control. This is a major developmental task as the brain expands and modulates its response in an integrated fashion so that they can self-soothe, be alert to stimuli and engage in interaction and learning. As the child matures, the need for regulation and modulation within their multi-sensory environment increases. For example, whilst a newborn baby has to adapt between the cot, the floor and pushchair and a handful of carers, an older child will be making the transition from a home environment to a car, a noisy school playground and then to a busy classroom in a short space of time of maybe just one hour.

As the brain receives sensory responses that bombard our body, it sorts, regulates, organizes and interprets the experience in order to create an appropriate sensory response. For example, if a jumper feels uncomfortable the brain's response might be to take it off, as it is twisted, back to front, or inside out. However, sometimes if there are difficulties with sensory regulation so that sensory signals do not get organized into a fitting response, it can cause a dysfunction. The child may then exhibit hypersensitivities, hyposensitivities and/or sensory-seeking behaviour.

Therefore, sensory integration therapy will attempt to regulate the body to avoid or reduce the inappropriate response and to encourage suitable adaptive response. It should also encourage general orientation, focus and exploration which will transfer into improved functional performance. It is important to remember that it is the pattern of frequency and intensity of the issue that will decide how significant the problem is and hence what and how much therapy the child should receive.

In sensory integration therapy, the therapist will encourage a child through a number of different sensory experiences. The frequency, intensity, duration, time of recovery and temporal summation are all qualities of stimulus that the therapist observes in order to help modulate and regulate their response.

This therapy may take place in a specialized room called a 'snoezelen' room or sensory room, where very specific equipment is used to stimulate all the senses especially vision, hearing and touch. However, this form of therapy is normally used for children with severe or profound disabilities with the purpose of educating and engaging the child through this stimulation.

Generally, sensory integration therapy can be given in a specifically designed OT room where there is lots of equipment including swings, balls and barrels to provide a varied range of sensory experiences. The equipment will be designed or used to give much proprioceptive (heavy work), vestibular (movement) and kinaesthetic (tactile) input.

The therapist can then guide parents and educators to carry this over outside of the sensory room. ASECRET (which stands for seven elements – Attention, Sensation, Emotion, Culture, Relationship, Environment, Task, comes from L.J. Miller's book (*Sensational Kids* 2006) and is her own acronym), is a technique where those involved with the child learn how to adapt an element in the internal or external environment in order to help a child regulate. Although not all therapists may use the above acronym, they will use their clinical reasoning to be creative and flexible so that functional success is achieved. This is done through observation, participation of the sensory integration therapy session and with the support of the therapist.

A sensory diet (a term coined by OT Patricia Wilbarger) is an individualized activity schedule that provides the sensory input to a child's nervous system so that the child stays focused and organized throughout the day (Wilbarger and Wilbarger 1991). Some children will need a calming input, while others who are sluggish may need arousal exercises which may also be given to the parent and the school to be used away from the therapy session. The diet will include regular intervals during the day (approximately five) where the therapist will recommend sensory input. The suggestions are expected to be adapted either in the home environment and/or in the school, and, thus, do not require expensive purchases. At home, it may include the use of an electric toothbrush, regulated jumping on a mini-trampoline or gym-ball, and using a weighted blanket at night.

Ideas to increase sensory input through food are also effective, such as drinking yoghurt with a straw, crunchy foods (carrots, apples) or chewy foods (dried fruit, chewing gum). At school, the teacher can be guided to provide sensory input at specific times of the day. This may include the child setting up the classroom at the beginning and end of the day (heavy work/ proprioceptive input) or running an errand up two flights of stairs (vestibular input). The use of a 'move 'n' sit' cushion, to provide sensory movement in class, and fidget toys, such as a soft ball underneath the table, would further encourage concentration through class. The therapist may use rhythmic swinging in order to organize and calm one child or alternating jumps to alert another.

Each child is unique and the therapist will provide individualized treatment approaches to provide for their needs, watching for the critical time when they can no longer adapt to the changing environment (e.g. faster swinging). The therapist will aim to achieve a 'zone' of optimal organization where their behaviour does not become more disorganized or below the threshold of just right stimulation. The child should then be able to carry out an expected task with greater independence and efficiency, for example being able to copy a paragraph from the whiteboard.

The purpose of the sensory integration therapy is to allow a child to fulfil their functional activities of daily living without the difficulties caused by a sensory processing disorder. Specific goals that might be expected after sensory integration therapy may be an increased ability to orientate and pay attention to a task, more generalized controlled and calm behaviour and/ or improved postural control due to better body awareness. It will always be necessary to monitor that success in OT sessions is being generalized and transferred to different contexts.

Within sensory integration therapy the therapist may recommend making adaptations to the environment. An adaptive suggestion may be to reduce the sensory issues identified through a detailed questionnaire or interview. This might be requesting a classroom change to avoid fluorescent lighting. However, usually this is not sufficient and regular sensory integration therapy is needed to provide the correct amount of sensory input in order to allow the child to participate effectively in class. For instance, if a child is so bothered by the type of jumper they are wearing that it is perceived to feel like sandpaper, it is exceedingly difficult to concentrate in a class. Therefore, therapy intervention is given to regulate the child's sensitivities to allow functional participation.

Initially, the therapist may have to spend increasing amounts of time with sensory integration therapy to achieve the right balance of stimulation to allow for effective and functional behaviour, so that a child can cope in a class setting. Over time, this will be reduced as the therapist and child learn what is needed to be administered in order to attain the optimal zone (Anzalone 2001). Also, the child and family, with the support of the therapist, will learn how to create situations to stimulate or satiate sensory behaviour or adapt a situation so that sensory integration therapy does not need to be ongoing. Periodic check-ups with the therapist may be advisable to monitor progress and evaluation of the intervention.

An example of this could be a sensory-seeking child who cannot sit still for more than five minutes without sensory integration therapy, will learn how to provide the input needed to regulate themselves. It might be going for a run for 20 minutes followed by a deep pressure massage before school starts to allow appropriate performance in morning school. The teacher may also support the child by choosing them to do a couple of errands in the school to give an opportunity of moving around. A child who is under-responsive to their environment could learn how to use jumping on a trampoline as they dress in the morning and a cold shower with a sponge in order to alert them for morning school. They might also like to use a gym ball in place of a chair and sip ice-cold water.

QUESTIONS TO ASK ABOUT OCCUPATIONAL THERAPY PROVISION IN A SCHOOL

1. How many children already receive occupational therapy in the school and what expertise does the school have in this area? How will the child catch up on any lessons missed if they go for therapy sessions?

2. How often is the OT in school? If there is an OT department, what is it like? How many registered OTs are there? How many OT assistants?

3. Is there space in school for occupational therapy to take place and will the recommendations given by the OT assessment fit in with the resources of the school, e.g. availability of a snoezelen or sensory room in a special school, a space to work, such as a gym, in a mainstream school?

4. Who will organize occupational therapy? If occupational therapy is specified on a Statement of Special Educational Needs under Part 2 as an educational need and in Part 3 as special educational provision, the Local Authority is obligated by law to arrange provision. If occupational therapy is not specified as an educational need it will count as a medical need and is then the responsibility of the NHS to organize.

5. Who will provide occupational therapy? Will it be an OT or OT assistant, under supervision? Local Authorities have a duty to provide occupational therapy for those with Statements, but, occasionally the Local Authority might arrange for an independent occupational therapist to be provided to meet the provision in the Statement. Many special schools employ OTs, while others have a local contract for services with the NHS. It is important to clarify who will provide the OT services.

6. How will the OT link with other therapists and the school staff? How are occupational therapy objectives included in individual education plans and through the curriculum?

7. How will the OT keep parents/teachers informed of progress? How often can parents expect contact from the OT or a report of progress? Is there an option to increase sessions? This will need to be discussed with the OT, but may include writing in a home/school book, email or telephone. The OT should complete written reports for the annual review and contribute to the IEP.

8. How good are the teachers/parents/LSAs at carrying out recommendations or exercises given by the OT? How are the child's occupational therapy needs integrated into the classroom? Is the child transferring skills learnt in the occupational therapy sessions across different environments?

9. Does the child's OT have the relevant experience? Check that the OT is registered with the HPC. The HPC gives no indication of relevant experience, so this information will need to be sought in another way.

10. Has the OT discussed the curriculum with the teacher to see how accessibility can be improved through strategies or equipment? This will be the case in mainstream or special schools.

11. Does the child's OT have any specific training in assessing and treating children with sensory processing disorder? Do they have the relevant skills, even if they do not have formal training? Who will supervise the work?

12. How much experience does the OT have in working with children with developmental problems and/or with sensory processing disorder?

13. Is the OT trained or certified in the use of any standardized diagnostic tools that are used to assess children who might have sensory processing disorder?

14. What training have staff at the school received? When was this and has it been updated? Who gave the training and how long was the

session? Did the content cover the necessary areas for a specific child's needs?

15. Prior to a child joining a school, has the necessary equipment/ resources been discussed to ensure the child will be able to access the curriculum?

There are many techniques that can fit well into the school day with advice from the OT. Sometimes, advice is all that is necessary on a periodic basis, while for other children, more intensive programmes and individual OT will be required.

SPECIALIZED PROGRAMMES THAT MAY BE HELPFUL TO THE CHILD

Occupational therapists may offer the child a specific programme to follow to achieve functional goals. The following approaches are ones that frequently appear in OT reports. They are just examples and there are many others.

- *The Teodorescu Perceptuo-Motor programme, 'Write from the Start'* is a specific approach which is designed to enable the child to achieve fluent and legible handwriting easily. It encourages the child to acquire perceptual skills so that fluid orientation and organization of the letters are achieved. It also develops the muscles of the hand through regular practice.

  The programme contains 400 graded exercises and activities to help complete the goals. This involves hand/eye co-ordination, figure ground discrimination, form constancy, orientation and laterality and spatial organization.

  Generally the programmes are suitable for mainstream children between the ages of 4 to 6 years, children with developmental co-ordination disorder (DCD) and older children with mild to moderate learning difficulties.

  The programme is cumulative and split into eight stages each developing a perceptual and motor skill.

- *The Jump Ahead programme* is a graded intervention programme for children with motor co-ordination difficulties focusing on sensory motor integration and perceptual motor skills. It was devised by West Sussex County Council to support schools.

- *The ALERT programme, 'How Does Your Engine Run?'*, supports children, teachers, parents and therapists to choose appropriate strategies to change or maintain states of alertness and identify how to help the nervous system change from different states of alertness to suit the task or time of day.

- *The Wilbarger Deep Pressure and Proprioceptive Technique (DPPT) and Oral Tactile Technique (OTT),* formerly referred to as the Wilbarger Brushing Protocol (WBP). This technique has its origins in sensory integration theory and has evolved through clinical use. It involves deep-touch pressure, to the skin on the arms, back and legs, through the use of a special surgical brush. Many parents of children with autism report that their children have responded positively to this technique and noted a reduction in sensory defensiveness, decreased anxiety and increased comfort in their environment. The programme needs to be taught and supervised by an OT who has been trained in the technique, as it could be uncomfortable for the child, leading to undesired results if carried out without proper instruction.

- *The Listening Program*™ uses psychoacoustically modified music to 'exercise' the different functions of the auditory processing system. It is used by OTs for sensory integration as the lower frequencies are thought to stimulate functions such as balance, co-ordination, motor skills and give an overall 'organizing' experience.

CHAPTER 23

Physiotherapy*

All practising physiotherapists must be registered with the regulatory body for health professions: the Health Professions Council (HPC). In order to be HPC registered physiotherapists must have a recognized physiotherapy qualification. Physiotherapists working within the private sector should also be HPC registered.

WHAT IS A PHYSIOTHERAPIST (PT)?

There are 48,000 chartered physiotherapists, physiotherapy students and assistants in the UK. Physiotherapy helps to develop and/or restore movement and function to as near to normal as possible when someone is affected by injury, illness, or by developmental or other disability. They have the title Chartered Physiotherapist and are members of the Chartered Society of Physiotherapy (CSP). Membership is gained through successful completion of a recognized undergraduate training course in physiotherapy. The title Chartered Physiotherapist is protected and all practising members have professional liability insurance through the Society and also adhere to a Professional Code of Conduct. This maintains high professional standards of practice, which protects the public.

All professionals working with children and vulnerable young adults must be checked by the Criminal Records Bureau (CRB) to make sure they do not have a criminal record that would put the children they work with at risk. It is the responsibility of the organization they work for to do this or, in the case of independent therapists, checks can be arranged through recognized agencies and organizations they are involved with or for whom they carry out work.

---

* This chapter was authored by Sally Wright, physiotherapist.

QUALIFICATIONS OF A PHYSIOTHERAPIST

A physiotherapist has either one of the following sets of initials after their name:

- MCSP (Member of the Chartered Society of Physiotherapy)
- FCSP (Fellow of the Chartered Society of Physiotherapy)
- and/or is a registered physiotherapist/physical therapist.

Physiotherapists gain clinical experience by working directly with clients in various settings, by working alongside more experienced physiotherapy colleagues, by working with other health professionals in multi-disciplinary settings, by attending clinics and gaining expertise through work experience. Physiotherapists support their clinical experience by attending courses, subscribing to journals and special interest groups and by case discussions – this is called continual professional development (CPD). Some physiotherapists go on to take a masters qualification in aspects of healthcare. A physiotherapist can be asked about their particular experience and what courses they have attended to assess the relevance to the child in question.

WHAT DO PAEDIATRIC PHYSIOTHERAPISTS DO?

Paediatric physiotherapists work with babies, children and adolescents in a variety of settings including hospitals, child development centres, schools and nurseries, and family homes. They frequently work together with other members of the multi-professional team but can also be the only therapist a child sees. In hospitals, paediatric physiotherapists work mostly with babies and children who have medical and surgical problems, including cystic fibrosis, cardiac surgery, orthopaedic surgery, neonatal care, cancer and intensive care. In child development centres, schools and nurseries (working within the community) paediatric physiotherapists work mostly with infants and children whose physical development is atypical in some way. These children fall broadly into three categories; those whose way of moving is grossly 'normal' but who achieve their early developmental milestones such as sitting, standing and walking either later than average, or not at all; those who achieve their early motor milestones within average time-frames but later present with mild to moderate difficulties carrying out motor skills smoothly and efficiently; and those who do not move normally and may not progress through typical developmental sequence. Children in the first group might have low muscle tone, loose ligaments, Down's or other syndromes. Those in the second group might have dyspraxia, developmental co-ordination disorder. Children in the latter group might have cerebral palsy.

All these groups of children are at risk of having special educational needs though not all go on to do so.

WHY ARE CHILDREN WITH ATYPICAL DEVELOPMENT AT RISK OF HAVING SPECIAL EDUCATIONAL NEEDS?

Early motor development is a sensory learning experience that provides the foundations for postural, gross motor, spatial, fine motor, perceptual and cognitive learning skills. The baby's very first learning experience is to problem solve how to co-ordinate breathing, sucking and swallowing without milk going into the lungs. This provides the foundation for postural control as it activates the neck and tummy muscles and is an early organizational skill. Babies have to learn to adapt to changes in the pull of gravity as they move, e.g. with rolling. This activates specialized sensory cells in the inner ear (called vestibular cells) which register the direction of the pull of gravity and the brain uses this information to adapt balance responses. Most of the time babies become more and more successful at mastering these challenges and thus enjoy them. Success drives them on to become experts at adapting their posture. Being able to keep their balance (postural security) no matter what they are doing is a fundamental pre-requisite for learning as it inspires physical and emotional confidence and frees the hands for fine motor skills. Children who do not develop postural security may have exaggerated fear response, which blocks their receptiveness to learning. Once postural responses are adaptive the infant can move within and explore their physical environment with confidence and this is the beginning of learning about spatial concepts such as distance, depth, height and spatial boundaries. One way of doing this is by crawling. Crawling strengthens the shoulder muscles and co-ordinates arms and legs together in opposite actions. This lays the foundations for more complex gross and fine motor skills and activates communication between the two sides of the brain, which is needed for learning.

All this is achieved through a process of trial and error, which results in neurological networks being laid down in the brain. Successful pathways will be reinforced and less successful pathways will be discarded.

Paediatric physiotherapists use their knowledge of sensory motor development to facilitate learning holistically.

ASSESSMENT

Before treatment can start, underlying reasons for concerns need to be evaluated by way of an assessment and this is usually accompanied by a written report.

Assessment involves:

- clearly defining concerns
- gathering relevant background information such as early developmental and medical information

- gathering specific information through parent, teacher and child questionnaires
- gathering information from other therapists and professionals involved with the child
- direct evaluation of:
  - musculo-skeletal system
  - posture
  - balance
  - gross motor skills
- interpretation of findings
- drawing up a treatment plan
- modification of treatment according to response.

Assessment is ongoing and an integral part of treatment. Assessment identifies underlying reasons for concerns, e.g. for a child there are many different reasons why they could be having difficulties catching a ball.

One reason may be because they cannot adapt or stabilize their background posture enough to maintain a steady stance as the ball comes towards them. A second reason may be that they have not yet integrated early reflexes such as the blink reflex which means they will push the ball away defensively rather than catch. A third reason may be that they cannot organize their background posture to get their hands in just the right place at just the right time to catch the ball. A fourth reason may be that they cannot close their hands around the ball at just the right time with just the right amount of force. A fifth reason may be that the child has visual pursuit issues.

TREATMENT PLAN

Following assessment an individual treatment plan is drawn up. This plots the route from cause to remediation of concern. Underlying issues identified at assessment are tackled with reference to typical development and where possible ordered in typical developmental sequence. In other words treatment starts at the lowest level of development where gaps/anomalies have been identified and builds on this.

The following examples will help to explain the variety of ways physiotherapy can help children with special needs.

EXAMPLE 1: 4-YEAR-OLD CHILD WITH DELAYED GROSS MOTOR AND FINE MOTOR DEVELOPMENT

Objective: Develop adaptive balance responses

Target: For child to be able to sit on gym ball with feet on floor and catch a kindly thrown ball two out of three times

How to achieve	What this helps
Sit on trolley plus pull self along on overhead rope	Helps develop sitting balance and upper body strength. Also develops spatial awareness
Lie on trolley plus pull self along hand over hand on rope	Helps strengthen arm and back muscles
Climbing large inflated cylinder	Helps develop strength generally
Lying on trolley plus pull self along overhead rope	Helps develop strength of tummy muscles
Hold body in tuck position	Helps strengthen anti-gravity flexion
Take feet over head to touch ball	Helps strengthen tummy muscles
Sit on ball and lift stick above head with two hands	Helps develop sitting balance
Sitting on ball; place ball in child's hands and child throws to therapist	Prepares for target by breaking it down

EXAMPLE 2: 9-YEAR-OLD CHILD WITH POOR CO-ORDINATION

Objective: Improve muscular stability around hips

Target: For child to be able to stand on either leg with knees slightly bent and eyes closed for 10 seconds

How to achieve	What this helps
Raising bottom from lying on back with knees bent	Strengthens hip muscles
Leg raises from side lying	Strengthens hip muscles
Rolling with arms above head plus stop and balance on side	Strengthens hip muscles and improves the way they work together dynamically to stabilise hips
Balancing in half kneeling with one foot forwards	Develops dynamic stability of hips
Kicking with alternate feet from standing on wobble board	Develops dynamic stability of hips and adaptive postural responses generally
Standing on right leg with knee bent	Develops dynamic muscular stability around hips

Objective: Combine above with rotation

Target: For child to be able to move in and out of straight legged sitting via side sitting with arms folded

How to achieve	What this helps
Move from hands and knees to side sitting	Lengthens trunk muscles

Objective: Develop bilateral co-ordination

Target: For child to be able to do 20 scissor jumps in a row

How to achieve	What this helps
Cross crawling	Develops co-ordination
Touch opposite knee	Develops crossing the midline
Scissor jumps	Develops bilateral co-ordination

EXAMPLE 3: 16-YEAR-OLD BOY WITH POOR HANDWRITING

Objective: Improve sitting posture when writing

Target: For child to sit correctly during English and for homework

How to achieve	What this helps
Lengthen hamstrings and mobilize pelvis	Allows pelvis to be tipped slightly forwards
Mobilize upper spine	Enables spine to be positioned in upright position
Strengthen back muscles	Enables child to sit with upright spine
Educate about good posture	Increases awareness
Adapt chair and desk as possible	Supports good posture

The above treatment plans give examples of some of the treatment tools that paediatric physiotherapists have in their toolbox. Their core tools are:

- musculo-skeletal techniques
- posture and balance therapies
- neuro-developmental therapy
- sensory integration.

These therapies can be mixed and matched as needed.

Many children with special educational needs have difficulties carrying out gross and fine motor skills due to associated postural, balance, developmental and sensory processing issues, which can be improved through physiotherapy, though of course this may not be the only therapy needed. If this need and provision of physiotherapy is detailed in Part 3 of a Statement of Special Educational Needs then physiotherapy is the responsibility of the Local

Authority. If treatment is not specified or the child does not have a Statement of Special Educational Needs, the NHS can give advice. A child can be referred to the local paediatric physiotherapy service via their GP or consultant. A parent can also refer their child to an independent physiotherapist. This may be covered by private medical insurance.

If the child is in a special school, staff will already have knowledge of how to help children with special needs. The physiotherapist will be part of a team that works towards helping the child achieve their educational targets. In a mainstream school, staff may or may not have experience of the particular special needs the child has and more training may be needed. The physiotherapist will assess training needs.

Physiotherapy intervention can take many forms including the following:

- assessment
- review of progress
- report writing
- teaching postural management including how to use special chairs/ standing frames
- teaching handling techniques needed within the classroom
- teaching programmes to staff
- advice
- direct hands-on treatment
- liaison with other professionals
- liaison with parents
- for children with physiotherapy specified on their Statement, the physiotherapist must contribute towards the individual education plan and annual review.

HOW DO YOU KNOW THERAPY HAS BEEN SUCCESSFUL?

Physiotherapists use outcome measures to ascertain progress. These may be the successful achievement of targets, improvement in standardized test result and/or other noted improvements in function.

Progress is evaluated through response to treatment and treatment adjusted accordingly.

Progress is formally reviewed at relevant stages of treatment and this is normally accompanied by a written report, a copy of which is given to parents.

QUESTIONS TO ASK ABOUT PHYSIOTHERAPY PROVISION IN A SCHOOL

1. How many children have physiotherapy in the school and what experience does the school have of working with a physiotherapist? How will the child catch up on any lessons missed if they go for therapy sessions?

2. Is there space in school for physiotherapy to take place?

3. How will the physiotherapist link with other therapists and the school staff?

4. Who will organize physiotherapy? If physiotherapy is specified on a Statement of Special Educational Needs under Part 3 (special educational provision), the Local Authority is obligated, by law, to arrange provision. If physiotherapy is not specified as an educational need, it will count as a medical need and is then the responsibility of the NHS to organize.

5. Who will provide physiotherapy? Will it be a physiotherapist or a physiotherapist assistant? This is usually through the NHS, but the Local Authority may arrange for an independent physiotherapist to provide physiotherapy as detailed in the Statement of Special Educational Needs.

6. How will the physiotherapist keep parents/teachers informed of progress? This will need to be discussed with the therapist, but ways may include writing in home/school book, email, telephone. Copies of all written reports about the child should be sent home. Written reports will be completed for the annual review and the physiotherapist may contribute towards the individual education plan.

7. How are the child's physical needs integrated into the classroom? This may be via the learning support assistant (LSA). Ask who has trained the LSA for this work.

8. Does the child's physiotherapist have the relevant experience? Ask the therapist themselves or the head of physiotherapy. The NHS is a teaching institution and the amount of experience the child's therapist has will vary. If the therapist is not as experienced as they need to be, ask how they will be supervised. Within the private sector, it is possible to seek out a physiotherapist with the particular expertise a child needs. Ask what courses the physiotherapist has attended and consider the relevance to the child in question.

9. How will a parent or LSA know what exercises/activities to do with the child? Ask the physiotherapist to advise on this. Ask to observe a session in school or at home.

10. If a parent/teacher is not happy about physiotherapy provision or the quantity, ask to speak to the physiotherapist, SENCo, head of physiotherapy services and/or the Local Authority.

11. Ask if staff at school have received any training about the importance of physiotherapy intervention and the particular child's needs.

SPECIALIZED PROGRAMMES THAT MAY BE HELPFUL TO THE CHILD

There are several specialized treatment approaches that have been developed over the years – many have a developmental basis. Most physiotherapists in this country use developmental therapy as their core and many paediatric physiotherapists have attended Bobath and sensory integration courses. Physiotherapists can only use approaches they have experience of in their work. Other programmes are carried out by other professionals in centres outside the NHS and usually have to be funded privately.

Developmental therapy

This is where the physiotherapist will help a child progress through the various stages of typical development by providing them with opportunities to do this. For example being placed on their tummies while awake will provide opportunities for the child to learn to support themselves on their elbows thereby helping to strengthen muscles that act around the shoulder girdle. This will help the child to push up through straight arms which will further strengthen these muscles and also stretch out the small hand muscles which activates them for fine motor skills. Facilitation of crawling will help the child dissociate movement of one limb from another and learn to move within space thereby gaining spatial awareness. Integration of early reflexes helps facilitate balance and equilibrium and so on. This approach is likely to be used in cases where the child is moving in normal ways but is late to achieve milestones.

Bobath therapy

This approach is mostly used in the treatment of cerebral palsy where children are not moving in typical ways. Many paediatric physiotherapists in this country have attended Bobath courses and would integrate some or all of the principles into their work. Ask the therapist if they have Bobath training.

The Bobath approach was developed by Berta Bobath (a remedial gymnast) and Karel Bobath (a neuropsychiatrist) and continues to evolve today as a treatment approach in various Bobath Centres around the world.

In the UK, there are Bobath Centres in London, Cardiff and Edinburgh. The Bobaths recognized that controlled movement can only occur against an adaptive postural background. An adaptive postural background emerges as early postural reflexes become integrated. In cerebral palsy, to varying degrees depending on severity, these postural reflexes can persist and prevent more sophisticated postural response systems from emerging, thus controlled movement is compromised. Bobath therapy positions and handles children in ways which inhibit and/or stabilize abnormal postural tone, and thus facilitates more typical postural responses. Parents are shown ways to integrate gains made in treatment into the home and learning support assistants can be shown how to incorporate principles of treatment into the school setting.

Conductive education

Conductive education was developed in the late 1940s by Professor Andreas Peto at what is now the Peto Institute in Budapest, Hungary. Conductive education helps children with physical difficulties who are able to follow verbal instructions. It is unique in that it addresses all aspects of the child's development (motor, language, self-care, cognitive and social) within a classroom setting. Children work in small groups on carefully designed programmes, which use special wooden furniture such as slatted plinths and box seats. Programmes are highly structured and progressive and challenge the child to respond to physical challenges. Physical challenges are broken down into small components, which are later integrated into functional skills. Conductors undergo four years training where they learn about the physical, language, cognitive and functional implications of physical disability and how to address these with structured programmes in group settings. Conductors are effectively teacher, physiotherapist, occupational therapist and speech therapist rolled into one. Conductive education was introduced to this country by a physiotherapist, Ester Cotton in the late 1960s. Now there is a national centre in Birmingham and several smaller centres which offer the conductive education approach.

Parents are advised to discuss the suitability of any approach outside that offered by the NHS with their physiotherapist and doctor.

PART 5

OTHER IMPORTANT
ISSUES to CONSIDER

CHAPTER 24

Integration and Inclusion

The terms integration and inclusion are sometimes used synonymously. Integration was the term used in the 1980s following the Warnock Report (1978), but this resulted in children with special educational needs attending a mainstream setting, often without the level of support they required. In effect, this was almost like paying 'lip-service' and permitting children with special educational needs to attend mainstream schools as long as they were able to fit into the existing systems and routines and did not disrupt the education of the other children. There is now an acknowledgement that the term 'inclusion' means much more than integration and is about a child's right to belong to their mainstream school and community. This will involve restructuring the environment with the school changing its policies, practices, attitudes and responses to ensure that the child is a full participant and contributes to the community as a whole. For inclusion to be successful, the child and their parent must play a full part in the process. It requires commitment from the whole staff and an understanding that it is a continuous and evolving process of change. Whilst inclusion is relevant to all children in a school, it is used particularly to focus on children with special educational needs as a way of removing or minimizing the barriers to learning as a result of their special educational needs. Ofsted now inspects 'educational inclusion' defining an educationally inclusive school as one in which the teaching and learning, achievements, attitudes and well-being of every young person matters. To ensure appropriate inclusive practice, Ofsted identifies the importance of an inclusive experience for the following groups: girls and boys; men and women; black and minority groups, ethnic and faith groups; travellers; asylum seekers and refugees; learners with special educational needs; gifted/talented learners; children looked after by the Local Authority; sick children; young carers; children from families under stress and learners at risk of disaffection and exclusion.

In this chapter, the focus will be on inclusion for children with special educational needs. This will, of necessity, encompass both educational inclusion and also social inclusion.

Inclusion could be seen as a continuum with one extreme being full inclusion, whereby all children, regardless of the extent of their learning difficulties or specialist support, are educated in mainstream schools to many other different interpretations which may involve inclusion for some lessons, at some times, and even some children moving between schools or bases. The 1996 Education Act made its inclusion procedures, which, until that point, had only the status of advisory guidelines, a legal obligation upon all Local Authorities. Although, in practice, schools had been working towards inclusion since the early 1980s, following the Education Act, it was no longer seen solely as something the SENCo/Local Authority officers were working on. Inclusion now became the concern of every staff member in every school in all sectors. In some Local Authorities, this has resulted in a large-scale transfer of children with special educational needs into mainstream schools, inevitably resulting in closure of many special schools. Parents of children with special educational needs have their advocates in both camps, and there are advantages and disadvantages to the placement of children in mainstream or special schools. However, opposition to inclusion may just be a reflection that not all parents and children will respond in the same way and diversity is a fact of life and different circumstances will present different challenges to individuals. Ultimately, inclusion must be about being included where a child learns best, be it a special school, a mainstream school or an inclusive system that involves both.

The *Index for Inclusion* (published by the Centre for Studies on Inclusive Education), sent to all schools in 2000, emphasizes that developing inclusion involves reducing exclusionary pressures. Barriers to learning and participation provide an alternative to the concept of special educational needs. The authors state that the idea that educational difficulties can be resolved by identifying some children as having special educational needs has considerable limitations. They prefer the notion of barriers to learning and participation, which can be used to direct attention at what needs to be done to improve the education for any child. Increasingly, the title of special educational needs co-ordinator (SENCo) is being changed to alternative titles such as inclusion co-ordinator or learning development co-ordinator. These terms stress the idea of inclusion. When considering the question of inclusion, it is, therefore, not only about what the school can do for a specific child to include them into the school, but also about a much more over-arching concept of whether the school, itself, is an inclusive school and whether the culture has sufficiently changed to accommodate all children. Booth and Ainscow, authors of *Index for Inclusion* note that inclusion involves change:

It is an unending *process* of increasing learning and participation for all students. It is an ideal to which schools can aspire but which is never fully reached. But inclusion happens as soon as the process of increasing participation is started. An inclusive school is one that is on the move. (Booth and Ainscow 2002, p.3)

Schools can now apply to Ofsted to gain an inclusion Quality Mark. The school is reassessed every three years and it reflects an overall recognition of the work going on in schools on inclusion.

As part of an inclusive school, all children have a common entitlement to a broad and balanced curriculum and all teachers have a responsibility to offer a curriculum that meets the needs of all children. As a consequence, the curriculum must be differentiated to respond to different children's learning needs and provide suitable learning challenges. Differentiation may take different forms:

- presentation – using a variety of media to present ideas
- content – selecting appropriately from the programme of study
- resource – using resources that support children's needs
- grouping – grouping children of similar ability for targeted support or pairing with a more able child
- task – matching tasks to children's abilities
- support – offering additional adult or peer assistance
- time – giving more or less time to complete a given task
- outcome – reducing the number of tasks and the amount or quality of work required.

These details can be discussed to find out exactly what type of differentiation is taking place within the school. It will be necessary to consider with teaching staff whether the strategies are appropriate and whether they are getting the results they would like.

A survey in 2008 (Ofsted, *How Well New Teachers are Prepared to Teach Pupils with Learning Difficulties and/or Disabilities*) identified considerable variations in practice and quality across initial teacher training courses and raised concerns that there was a high reliance on schools to provide training in this area which led to 'considerable differences in the quality of provision'. It therefore cannot be assumed that all teachers in mainstream schools, particularly new teachers, are well-prepared to teach children with special educational needs. It will be necessary to ask about the range of in-service training courses which will be provided for teachers in a school and any specific training which will be put in place to meet a particular child's needs.

When Ofsted carried out a survey in 2005, based on the five outcomes of Every Child Matters, to look at good practice for children with special needs in early years childcare and education in the private and voluntary sectors, they recognized the provider who was positive, welcoming and displayed a 'can-do' approach as being fundamental to achieving successful outcomes for children in overcoming barriers to inclusion. They recognized that children who have complex health needs, and children with challenging behaviour, presented the most difficulties for providers to create an inclusive environment, but to overcome these challenges, providers needed access to specialist/well-informed training and co-ordinated multi-agency support from Local Authorities, health professionals and voluntary organizations. Unfortunately, they found inconsistency across the country and, as a result, they stated 'services for children with special needs depend on where they live, not on what they need'. However, they also noted that 'modest, imaginative, but low cost changes to equipment and buildings, can have a disproportionately positive effect on removing barriers' and one would hope that some of these initiatives have now been put into place. Clearly, different ideas will be needed at different stages of schooling.

QUESTIONS TO ASK ABOUT INCLUSION

1. Why is inclusion being recommended now and for what purpose? It may be that both sides are very positive about inclusion, but there is a need to be clear that the objective is commonly understood. Is there an agreement about the advantages and disadvantages, and do they apply equally to social and educational inclusion?

2. Try to get a sense of whether the school has a 'can-do' rather than a 'can't do' approach. Observe how positive and welcoming the staff are. It is important to ensure that it is not only the head teacher and SENCo who feel positive, but, equally as important, the teacher where the child will be spending most of their time. If there is a sense that the teacher is concerned about the child being included, e.g. in a mainstream class, try and identify what the concerns are about, as they might be just lack of confidence or they might be more far-reaching.

3. Has the school already thought, or put into place, any training to create awareness, change staff attitudes and develop their skills and confidence in including children with special needs? What training has the school already organized for the future and are they open to any other suggestions, particularly if a parent or professional feels some specific training is needed for the child?

4. Some Local Authorities and organizations have been working to overcome healthcare barriers for children with special needs who require invasive procedures. This might involve employing 'dual

workers', trained to meet both the healthcare and education needs of the child. Does this kind of thing exist and could this help overcome some of the doubts expressed in schools?

5. All children learn and develop by exploring what they can do, experimenting and taking risks. How does the school ensure that independence is rewarded, whilst at the same time, recognizing and minimizing the risks? If the child has behavioural difficulties and personal restraint may be needed, ask who is trained and whether they are confident in dealing with this behaviour. Sometimes, children are not included because of difficulty in managing behaviour and the risk this poses to their safety. However, training can be given and should be accessed.

6. Does the school have resources so that books, posters and equipment reflect diversity and give positive images of disabled children?

7. If the child cannot speak, does the school understand the preferred means of communication? Does the school use augmented communication techniques, such as Makaton® or sign language, and if not, how will they be trained to do so? Has the school visited other settings where inclusion is working well to receive direction or support on how to include children with special educational needs?

8. What is the relationship with outside professionals and the Local Authority, if appropriate? Has the school considered making adjustments to increase accessibility? This may include:

   • small group work so children with special educational needs are able to participate

   • sectioning off areas to make the environment quieter and provide more opportunities for 1:1

   • making different arrangements for a child with ASD, e.g. to leave early or late at the beginning and end of sessions

   • using visual timetables

   • altering the heights of tables and chairs

   • fitting soft furnishings to reduce background noise for children with hearing impairments and changing lighting for children with visual impairment and other strategies which can be reasonably easily put in place.

9. Ask if the school will undertake a home visit. It might be helpful to discuss concerns with a parent in a more informal environment and, also, give the school a different perspective on the child.

10. Ask what level of communication the school will be having with parents and other professionals. How will the school communicate if a parent has a disability themselves?

11. If the school is not well equipped, ask if there are any equipment loan services for children with special needs, as some Local Authorities provide specialist equipment (such as mobile sensory toys) or these might be available from voluntary organizations (such as toy libraries).

12. Discuss how the school uses their individual education plans (IEPs) and whether targets which also relate to difficulties at home, such as toileting or eating, can be put on the plan and discussed with parents.

13. Ask how other children will communicate with the child if they are the only one using sign or other forms of augmented communication. Can their peers be taught, for example, some Makaton® signs?

The *Index for Inclusion* sets out a number of questions looking at:

- creating inclusive cultures
- producing inclusive policies
- evolving inclusive practices.

It is not expected that parents or professionals will be asking all the questions in the Index and nor will they be relevant for every child. However, some of the questions posed may be very pertinent to a specific situation and reference should be made to the Centre for Studies on Inclusive Education (CSIE).

Although inclusion is primarily seen as an opportunity for children with special educational needs to be included within mainstream school, in fact inclusive practices should be questioned in whatever type of school the child attends. A child can, effectively, be excluded even within a specialist placement if they are constantly withdrawn or given special support. Similarly, there may be many opportunities for encouraging inclusion for a child in a special school by creative thinking, either within the school itself, e.g. attending other classes for some of the school day with, perhaps, more mobile children, or looking at the question of dual placements.

CHAPTER 25

Religious Beliefs, Co-Education, School Size, Small Classes and Transition

RELIGIOUS BELIEFS

A Statement of Special Educational Needs is set out in six parts. Part 1 asks for factual details, including religion. If religion is important to the family it is helpful to complete this section.

It should be noted that although a child's religion and identity cannot constitute a special educational need, the Local Authority must have regard to a child's religion and identity if these are relevant to that child's special educational needs or the manner in which these aspects may be met.

If, for example, religious adherence will impact on certain lessons and activities and the child needs to be withdrawn, then this may have to be considered by the school in terms of the effect on access to the curriculum. Similarly, there may be concerns about dietary issues which may not be confined merely to the lunch hour, but also affect the child's inclusion in lessons involving food items. This may be particularly relevant in a special school setting where the child's level of understanding may not prevent them from taking food or participating in lessons which the parents may not permit.

Frequently, a child's religious, cultural and social needs are inextricably intertwined with their special educational needs and the question of what constitutes 'having regard to' the child's religious background and the ability of the school to take this into account may well need to be challenged should the parents consider this an essential part of the child's education.

There is case law on religion and special educational needs, notably A v SENDIST and London Borough of Barnet (November 2003), where the Court stated that both a Local Authority and a Tribunal need to take proper account of the impact of a child's religion in assessing his/her special educational needs and the provision to be made for them.

Freedom of thought, religion and belief enshrined in Article 9 of the Human Rights Act, which states, under Article 14, 'A person should not be treated unfairly because of their race, religion, sex, age, political views, disability or anything else' must also be adhered to.

It may also be necessary to consider the concept of inclusion within this context. Some children, because of their culture, religion and social background, may experience barriers to learning as a result of their disability, heritage, gender, special educational need, ethnicity, social group, sexual orientation, race or culture. This may lead to disaffection, low self-esteem, marginalization and informal or formal exclusion. When a school is looking at how they will meet the needs of all their children from diverse backgrounds, religion is one of the areas which they will need to consider as part of being a fully inclusive environment. There are, of course, a number of faith schools both in the maintained and independent sectors which have a religious character which help meet the needs of children in their own faith communities and enable them to integrate into society. Schools in the maintained sector have a duty to promote community cohesion, and faith schools should be able to demonstrate their working together with the wider community and in partnership with other schools and groups.

CO-EDUCATION

There may be strong feelings about whether a child attends a single-sex or co-educational school. Sometimes, single-sex education is preferred on the basis of religious or cultural values. In the more traditional situation of independent schools, many schools remain single-sex, although there is now a move towards becoming co-educational in many of these schools. The research on whether single sex-education makes any difference to children's achievements is very mixed, and it would be necessary to look at other aspects, including the impact on socialization.

This issue could be relevant in a case of a child with special educational needs and some parents have argued that a child particularly with precocious sexuality may be vulnerable in a co-educational school.

SCHOOL SIZE

Ofsted and the National Association for Small Schools (NASS) have defined small schools as schools with less than 100 pupils. Those with less than 50 are described as 'very small', but these numbers should not be taken rigidly as other organizations include some schools as small with up to 200 pupils. In a small school there is sometimes a struggle between effectiveness and viability. However, Local Authorities often use small schools for children with special educational needs.

It is argued that some children with special educational needs have much greater difficulties in large schools,* particularly at secondary level, for many reasons, including:

- logistical difficulties in moving around a spread out site
- organizational problems
- sensory difficulties
- socialization.

Each individual case needs to be considered, particularly in view of the fact that large schools may well be advantageous for some children as they can provide more resources or options, particularly at Key Stage 4.

Inevitably, most special schools will be smaller, although they can vary considerably in numbers of children and physical size.

SMALL CLASSES

In this context, small classes are defined as being between 15 and 20 children in a class and in relation to children with special educational needs, research shows:

- there is more individual interaction between teachers and children
- there is more teacher support for learning per child
- there is more attentiveness to the teacher and therefore less disruptive behaviour from children
- teachers spend more time teaching rather than managing children (both behaviour-wise and in terms of assessment duties)
- teachers are better able to identify children's problems and specific needs
- the level of distraction is less.

In relation to children with special educational needs, small classes is often cited as one of the main reasons, alongside specialism, for special school placements or unit provisions. Consideration of a child's individual needs will lead to a conclusion of whether small classes would be beneficial, particularly in terms of issues, such as friendship groups, concentration patterns and access to the curriculum.

---

* One in seven children in England are now in a secondary school with over 1500 children, and the number of children in schools of over 2000 has doubled since 1997 (*Special Children*, June/July 2007/8, p.17).

TRANSITION

Transitions will occur at normal junctures for all children between pre-school and nursery/reception; between primary and secondary; and possibly, at post-16, but for children with special educational needs, there may be movements between schools at other times, and the difficulties of moving may be exaggerated because of their individual problems.

Moving can be one of the most stressful life experiences and, given that school plays such a large part in a young child's life, transitions should be handled carefully. If a child has a Statement of Special Educational Needs, it cannot be assumed that the Statement will automatically be financed by a new Authority, and parents must be made aware of that before a family move takes place.

When a child with special educational needs moves schools, in addition to the practical considerations, there will be very specific things that a parent/teacher will need to be aware of, e.g. for an autistic child, it may be necessary to provide photographs not only of buildings but also of teachers, and, perhaps, to undertake a few visits before the child actually starts. For a child who has difficulty in making friends and establishing friendship groups, it may be helpful for the child to meet up with peers before they begin. Many schools will operate a buddy pairing system so the child is not left on their own during the first couple of days to find their own way around.

For some children, just being singled out as 'different' will make them nervous and discussions will need to take place with the receiving school, how the 'new' child can receive extra input without making them the focus of attention.

Secondary school poses different challenges to primary school. It is helpful if a meeting between parents and the form tutor takes place before the child begins. An informal meeting should also be set up between the form tutor and the child. This will enable the tutor to ensure that they are aware of any special educational needs and give them time to plan and organize any strategies to address the child's needs and, perhaps, their worries or concerns which they express during the informal meeting. Thought needs to go into seating plans in classes, particularly for children with sensory difficulties, but also with respect to thinking about who is already in the class (if known) to ensure that children do not react negatively towards each other.

The child's current school can pre-prepare them beforehand, by identifying their feelings about change and transition and working with the child to think about their main concerns and hopes when moving schools. There are opportunities within the curriculum to undertake this work without singling an individual out, such as in lessons on citizenship or personal, social and health education (PSHE).

Transitions also occur throughout the school day, between home and school, one lesson to another, as well as from one school to another or from a school to a post-16 provider. It is important to be aware that any of these transitions could be problematic for a child with special educational needs if they find change difficult.

The Connexions Service, the advice and guidance service for all 13–19 year olds, has particular responsibilities for young people with special educational needs. The Connexions Personal Advisor must attend the Year 9 review of a young person's Statement and they are responsible for then overseeing the implementation of the Transition Plan which is drawn up as a result of that review. For a young person with a Statement, in the final year of compulsory school, the Connexions Advisor is under a duty to arrange assessments of their needs and the provision required to meet those needs in the post-16 sector. It will be necessary to ensure the Connexions Advisor is present at the transition review, even if the child is in a non-maintained school.

Parents and professionals need to consult the Local Authority as to their procedures and investigate whether there are local providers who can work together, particularly if a young person has been away at a residential school and is returning to local-based provision.

It is helpful to think about any potential problems that could arise over transitions as forward planning can make a transition go smoothly even for a child with special educational needs.

CHAPTER 26

Equality and Discrimination

There are several areas in which discrimination may occur within a school:

- disability
- religion and belief
- gender
- race
- sexual orientation
- age.

The Code of Practice on Special Educational Needs makes it clear that when assessment takes place it is necessary to consider the child 'within the context of their home, culture and community'. It also notes that lack of competence in English must not be equated with learning difficulties, as understood in the Code. At the same time, when children have English as an additional language, and they make slow progress, it cannot be assumed that their language status is the only reason, as they may also have learning difficulties. Clearly, when looking at inclusion, the school needs to ensure that particular groups are not disadvantaged, and specifically, the school needs to prevent and address racism, sexism and other forms of discrimination. When working with children from a variety of cultural backgrounds, the school must ensure that work provided gives a positive image of different cultures and also draws on the children's experience. This is particularly important for children with special educational needs who may have additional difficulties in making sense of their world and so require sensitive, culturally aware teachers and resources.

The National Autistic Society published a report in 2007 – *Missing Out? Autism, Education and Ethnicity: The Reality for Families Today* (Corbett and Perepa 2007),* which specifically looked at children with autism from black and minority ethnic communities. The term black and minority ethnic (BME)

---

* Reproduced with permission of the National Autistic Society.

communities used in the report represented anyone who did not come from a white British background. This included visible minority ethnic communities, including those from mixed backgrounds and those who were not visibly different but who experienced disadvantage by virtue of minority status, such as travellers, asylum seekers, refugees or new immigrants. Although this study was limited to a sample of children with autism, they stated 'the neglect of BME families by researchers, professionals and service providers is unacceptable and must be addressed with urgency'. They highlighted the way in which autism was perceived differently by different communities and sometimes by different members from the same community and the impact that had on gaining services. They also looked at the way in which some developmental milestones used to diagnose ASD were culture specific, which may result in under-diagnosis, e.g. not making direct eye-contact (one of the diagnostic criteria for ASD) is viewed by some communities as a sign of respect. Some languages do not have a word for autism and many interpreters substituted terms that meant 'mental health' or 'learning disability' which caused confusion for families. Communities for whom English is an additional language and other communities, including travellers, also had reduced opportunities for learning about autism. The report made a number of recommendations, including the need for professionals working with children to develop cultural awareness to address the needs of diverse communities and for speech and language therapists working with children from bi- or multi-lingual families to be aware of strategies to teach communication skills to these children.

There is also a need to encourage refugees, immigrants and other new arrivals the opportunity to settle into school and to help existing school populations to empathize with their experiences and understand their personal histories. This may include school-based projects, e.g. one school introduced voices for computer programmes in Gujarati, Punjabi and Urdu, so that Asian children could move between their native language on the computer and English as they became bi-lingual.

In 2007, the Department for Children, Schools and Families estimated that 12 per cent of the school population in primary and secondary maintained schools were learning English as an additional language. Over 50 per cent of children in Inner London were learning English as an additional language. The *New Arrivals Excellence Programme; Primary and Secondary National Strategies*, published in 2007, defined 'new arrivals' as:

- International migrants – including refugees, asylum seekers and economic migrants from overseas.
- Internal migrants – including children and young people joining schools as a result of moving home within the UK, e.g. traveller children.

- Institutional movers – children and young people who change schools without moving home, including exclusions and voluntary transfers.
- Individual movers – children who move without their family, e.g. looked-after children.

They then highlighted principles for support:

- Every child in school has an entitlement to fulfil their potential through access to the National Curriculum.
- This is best achieved within a whole-school context where children are educated with their peers.
- Children and young people learn best when they feel secure and valued.
- Schools need to ensure that there is a process to support the integration of new arrivals.
- Schools have a responsibility to promote race equality, so should be clear about the requirements of the Race Relations (Amendment) Act 2000.
- Schools need to focus on the positive contributions made by new arrivals and mobile children.
- Provision for children and young people should be based on a meaningful assessment of their prior knowledge, experience and their language proficiency.
- Support needs to be made available for parents of new arrivals to familiarize themselves with the new education system of which their child is now part.

QUESTIONS TO ASK IF A CHILD IS FROM A DIFFERENT BACKGROUND AND/OR CULTURE

1. Will the parent have access to an interpreter when meeting with the school or attending annual reviews? Will appointment letters be sent out in the family's language?
2. How will the curriculum reflect different cultural backgrounds and/or challenge stereotypes?
3. Will teachers use culturally sensitive language and be alert to the cultural differences in non-communication?
4. How will the school assure parents that they do not condone racism and bullying?

5. Do learning resources show sensitivity to different groups and cultures and how will teachers or assistants ensure that children are not offended by certain images or stereotypes?

6. Will children joining the school be given support systems, such as buddies, mentors or support staff? Will these children be able to communicate in the same language?

7. How will children acquire English?

8. How will the school encourage use of the first language as a tool for learning?

9. When tracking progress, is the school aware of the changing needs of children as they become more fluent in English? What special arrangements can be made for new arrivals, e.g. access to GCSE and A Level exams in their first language?

10. Will the school be providing training for staff and, if so, will trainers be knowledgeable about the particular groups that are being considered?

11. Is there a sharing of resources between schools, e.g. employing bi-lingual teaching assistants between schools and a sharing of good practice?

12. How do teachers ensure that, as far as possible, they are free from cultural bias and positively reflect cultural, religious and linguistic diversity?

13. What suggestions can parents make to the school to ease their child's transition and will the school listen?

14. Can the child be paired up for work with stronger peer language models?

15. Does the teacher know of differences between the home language and English, e.g. intonation and stress, the direction of handwriting and can the teacher get a dictionary?

16. Is the teacher aware of the amount of time the child may have spent in formal schooling in the country of origin? (This may address difficulties observed with concentration or learning styles which may be due to factors that have not been realized.)

17. If a child is silent in class, it should not be construed that they are having difficulty learning. An initial silent period is a normal part of second language development, during which the child is 'tuning in' to the new language. They may not feel confident enough to actively vocalize in classroom activities and use English. (Teachers should, themselves, think back to what learning a language in school was like.)

Many of the feelings that new arrivals face are common to the difficulties faced by children with special educational needs, e.g. managing transitions, feelings of insecurity, lack of friends, previous lack of opportunities, feeling misunderstood or unvalued. In addition, these children may have English as a second language and feelings of alienation if they cannot see their culture, language and experiences reflected around the school or in the classroom. Schools need to value the richness and the positive contributions that these children can make.

It is sometimes difficult for school staff to identify what the differences are between special educational needs and English as a second language, when newly arrived bi-lingual children appear in school, but this is crucial, so that they are not inappropriately taught. In most situations, withdrawal arrangements for bi-lingual children will be time limited and carefully monitored to ensure their full access to the curriculum and their rate of progress will help schools to decide if the child also has special educational needs.

Susan Shaw (1995) has developed a set of filter questions that teachers can use to guide their thinking to differentiate whether the child has English as a second language (EAL) or special educational needs (*Bilingual Pupils and Special Educational Needs – A Teacher's Guide to Appropriate Support and Referral*), and these are accessible from the Portsmouth Ethnic Minority Achievement Service website.

PART 6

DIFFERENT SCHOOL MODELS

Chapter 27

Mainstream Schools

Section 316 (4) of the Education Act 1996 defines a mainstream school as:

> Any school that is not a special school or an independent school. Exceptionally, City Technology Colleges, City Colleges for the Technology of the Arts and City Academies all count as mainstream schools as do Pupil Referral Units.

In England and Wales, compulsory school is for children from ages 5 to 16 years, with a transfer to secondary school at age 11 years. A mainstream school is, by definition, a school other than a special school. There are many types of mainstream schools, as described in Chapter 10.

When looking at provision in a mainstream school, one should consider the staffing, resources and the curriculum. Every teacher in a mainstream school should expect to teach children with special educational needs and both the teacher and the school should feel they have the necessary skills to do this effectively.

Some of these skills should be developed during initial teacher training and subsequent training during the induction year. More trainee teachers are taking school-based routes to qualified teacher status (QTS), so schools and the training providers (usually Local Authorities) have particular responsibility for trainees on the job and also for newly qualified teachers (NQT).

Since March 2008, the Inclusion Development Programme (IDP) has been available for all school staff (not only teachers), with separate versions for early years and initial teacher training. This is a four-year programme on interactive DVD looking at strategies and resources to support learning in all areas. The programme does not have to be followed in a linear way, but it will provide tangible evidence for parents or professionals that the topic of special educational needs has been covered.

The Inclusion Development programme:

Year 1 (2008):	Speech, language and communication needs and dyslexia.
Year 2 (2009):	Autistic spectrum disorders.
Year 3 (2010):	Behavioural, emotional and social difficulties.
Year 4 (2011):	Moderate learning difficulties.

In mainstream schools the aim is for all schools to have a qualified teacher as a SENCo by 2011 and mandatory training is now being developed for all new SENCos and inclusion managers. There should no longer be teaching assistants fulfilling the role of SENCo, although some teaching assistants may opt to train as teachers and perhaps then continue in their existing role as SENCo.

The highest level of training for mainstream teachers is for those who want to develop a more specialist role. There will be mandatory training for teachers of classes with a sensory impairment from September 2009. Also from September 2009, a new qualification is being introduced to make teaching a masters level profession. The Masters in Teaching in Learning (MTL) will be a practice-based qualification and some areas may be extended by those wanting to specialize in areas focusing on learning difficulties and/ or disabilities. In the not too distant future, it will, therefore, be possible to ask about accredited qualifications of mainstream teaching staff as well as in-service training and whole-school training.

THE NATIONAL CURRICULUM

The National Curriculum was first introduced in England in 1998. It applies to children of compulsory school age (5–16 years) in maintained schools and is organized on the basis of four Key Stages and the subjects which must be covered in each of these stages. The core subjects are English, mathematics and science. The Foundation subjects are design and technology, information and communication technology, history, geography, modern foreign languages, art and design, music, physical education and citizenship.

The National Curriculum consists of four Key Stages plus the Early Years Foundation Stage, which covers education for children before they reach 5 years of age (compulsory school age).

At Key Stage 4, there are entitlement elements, including work-related courses like Young Apprenticeships, and subjects from which the children may choose. In addition, there are non-statutory programmes of study. There is less prescription in the content of programmes for each curriculum subject, and an emphasis on teaching the essential concepts and skills underpinning

TABLE 7.1 STAGES OF THE NATIONAL CURRICULUM

Age		Year(s) group	Stage
3–5	Nursery and Reception	Nursery and Reception	Foundation
5–7	Infants	1 and 2	Key Stage 1
7–11	Juniors	3, 4, 5 and 6	Key Stage 2
11–14	Secondary	7, 8 and 9	Key Stage 3
14–16	Secondary	10 and 11	Key Stage 4

curriculum subjects rather than coverage of detailed lists of content. There are opportunities, both within and outside of the classroom, and emphasis on the development of personal learning and thinking skills. Practical life skills, such as money management, are also highlighted.

Within the statutory framework and the assessments at the end of each Key Stage, it is important to consider where children with special educational needs fit in. These children are represented across the whole range of attainment levels, but many are not entered for examinations as they perform below the necessary standards and many achieve only lower level qualifications. A key feature of the updated secondary curriculum is the flexibility it gives to schools to meet the needs of children who may not be learning in a regular way. When looking at schools, and the range of opportunities that are available within the curriculum to match the child's special educational needs, it is important to consider the way in which the curriculum can be flexible and how teachers are able to integrate the child's level and style of learning, whilst still having access to a broad curriculum. It should be noted that non-maintained schools do not have to offer the National Curriculum. For some independent schools, it offers a basic minimum standard, others offer alternatives, such as the International Baccalaureate, although most children are prepared for the same final exams, such as GCSE and A levels. Some independent special schools offer an alternative curriculum and it may be necessary to ensure the school can be named in a child's Statement if it does not offer access to the National Curriculum.

The National Curriculum only applies to state schools. If a child is educated at home, they do not have to follow the National Curriculum, although Local Authorities assert that parents have to provide a 'broad and balanced' education, as in the National Curriculum. The Statutory Inclusion Statement of the National Curriculum sets out three principles for developing an inclusive curriculum:

- to set suitable learning challenges
- to respond to children's diverse learning needs
- to overcome potential barriers to learning and assessment for individuals and groups of children.

These statements emphasize that all children should experience success in learning and be provided with programmes of study to suit their abilities. They establish the need for differentiation for children whose attainments fall significantly below the expected levels of a particular Key Stage, and expect teachers to plan for the full range of children's needs in their classrooms. For children with special educational needs, teachers should take specific action to provide access to learning by:

- providing for children who need help with communication, language and literacy
- planning, where necessary, to develop the child's understanding through the use of all available senses and experiences
- planning for children's participation in learning and in physical and practical activities
- helping children to manage their behaviour, to take part in learning effectively and safely and at Key Stage 4 to prepare for work
- helping children to manage their emotions, particularly trauma or stress and to take part in learning.

Not all children with disabilities will necessarily have special educational needs, but these children would learn alongside their peers and, again, teachers should take action to ensure these children are included and enabled to follow the National Curriculum.

Depending on the age of the child, it will, therefore, be necessary to look at all aspects of the curriculum within the classroom, in addition to considering access to the wider curriculum in relation to the child's special educational needs. (If the child requires additional specialist teaching and/or therapy, consult the questions in the specific chapters.)

QUESTIONS TO ASK WITH REGARD TO MAINSTREAM SCHOOLING

1. What is the staff/child ratio in the class or group that the child will be placed in, also the male/female make up of the school and the class?
2. If there are concerns about staff/child ratios, ascertain how many of the adults are qualified teachers, nursery nurses (if relevant) and how many are unqualified LSAs. These ratios can be checked against the current statutory framework (Ofsted).
3. Is the National Curriculum offered, and if not, what has been substituted? For example, some independent schools offer the International Baccalaureate, but they do take children with special needs.

4. How flexible, or rigid, is the school's approach and will the child be disapplied from any aspect of the curriculum? If so, how and why?

5. Are children streamed according to ability? Are children in mixed ability classes for some subjects and put into separate sets for some subjects, like maths? How will this suit a child with special educational needs (e.g. will a bright child with dyslexia always be placed in low sets because of their attainment levels and become demoralized)?

6. What are the Key Stage 4 options, both in terms of specific courses, but also with regard to work experience, etc.? Does the school offer vocational courses as well as GCSE and AS/A2 levels?

7. If a child has to be withdrawn from lessons for extra help or therapy, how will the teacher minimize the possible difficulties which result from missing work in the classroom and how will the child catch up?

8. How will the child's strengths be encouraged and will there be any extra-curricular opportunities to develop the child's interests and strengths? What are they? How will the child access these, particularly if there are transport issues? Could any of these take place during school time?

9. Does the school offer lunchtime or after-school homework clubs, particularly if this is a difficult task to do at home? Is there a homework timetable and do teachers or LSAs support homework time in school? Is there a homework diary? Who will check that homework is written down?

10. How do teachers incorporate information from Statements, annual reviews or individual education plans, in their day-to-day planning, and can they involve a group of children in aspects of teaching the specific targets, or will the child, effectively, be taught alone on an individual programme (this will have implications for social inclusion)?

11. How will the school ensure that appropriate language is used in lessons, so children with learning difficulties can access work directly from the teacher? This may involve the teacher changing the content, pace and delivery of language in the classroom.

12. Will reading materials be suitable and accessible, and, if not, who will ensure that this occurs?

13. What access to ICT will there be to enable children who need help to communicate what they know and want to say in writing? Will training be available?

14. Ask about seating positions, provision of aids or access to equipment if this is necessary for children with sensory or physical difficulties. Is there enough space in the classroom?

15. How does the school provide a positive image of different cultures and draw on the child's experiences, particularly for those children with special educational needs?

16. How do teachers relate to support staff and what kind of support, training and resources are support staff given? How frequently do support staff meet with each other, the class teacher, SENCo and outside professionals? Do they have time in their timetable for this?

17. When resources need to be modified, or broken down into smaller steps, who is responsible for doing this and what time is available? Are there facilities in the school?

18. What teaching strategies are used, e.g. visual, auditory, multi-sensory, formal, informal and practical?

19. Where relevant, do IEPs contain targets for life skills and self-care skills?

20. Look at an example of an individual education plan. Are IEP targets relevant to the school day as a whole and can they be generalized to be of use in different settings?

21. How are IEP targets monitored and with whom are they discussed, both before setting them and then reviewing them? How are parents involved? How is the child involved?

22. If the child needs to sign, how many other children are using signing and are enough of them able to use signing to include the child? If not, what arrangements are being made to ensure that the school is a 'Signing Community'?

23. If there is a particular philosophy used at the school, e.g. Steiner School or conductive education, ask whether it is used throughout the school and in what way. (Many of these approaches are used, but in a much diluted form.)

24. Ask about general results and also specifically for children with special educational needs. What is the evidence that the methods and strategies have been successful?

25. How is the school evaluating their work, aside from attainment data?

26. How does the school evaluate their success with inclusion, social and emotional aspects and behavioural issues?

CHAPTER 28

Special Units in Mainstream Schools

Special units (sometimes called resource bases or resource classes) can be found in mainstream and special schools. In some special schools there may be discrete provisions; such as a specialist class or unit for autistic children or a specialist PMLD class running alongside other more generic classes. Special units within mainstream schools are part of the continuum of provision within a Local Authority and for many children, provide access to a mainstream school for part or most of the school day.

Many of the advantages of special units or classes are similar to those described for special schools. They are usually small with high adult/child ratios and staffed by teachers with appropriate qualifications and expertise. Units can be highly structured with teaching geared to individual needs. The concentration of resources, specialist teaching, 1:1 attention and a less threatening environment and opportunity to be with peers who have similar needs are usually considered as the benefits of a special unit provision. Special units located in mainstream schools, however, offer far greater opportunities than special schools for children to participate in mainstream activities. In most schools, special units tend to cater for specific categories of special educational needs rather than offering a generic provision. Thus, it is not unusual to find, for example, special units for autism, dyslexia or physical difficulties within mainstream schools.

QUESTIONS TO ASK ABOUT SPECIAL UNITS IN MAINSTREAM SCHOOLS

1. The obvious question to ask is what are the admissions criteria for the unit and the range of needs and abilities within it, e.g. if the child has high functioning autism or Asperger's syndrome, check that the Unit

is not for all types of children with autism, who may have a range of cognitive abilities, as the child with Asperger's syndrome may be cognitively well above others. Does a child need a Statement which names the provision?

2. How many children are in the unit and how is it staffed? What is the adult to child ratio? What year groups are the children in? Are they boys or girls? How is the unit funded?

3. What are the qualifications of the teachers and learning support assistants? Do they have specialist qualifications or are they just drawn from the resources of the school? What recent in-service training have they had? What is planned?

4. What is the communication like between staff in the special unit and the SENCo of the school and how does communication take place?

5. What is the general attitude towards the special unit in the school? Is it accepted as part of the school? Look at where it is situated and ask whether any work has been done with the children in mainstream classes to explain about the unit and, if so, what? What training have mainstream teachers had and how have they altered their practice to accommodate the unit children, as a result?

6. How much time will the child spend in the special unit and how much in mainstream? The child must be able to manage in the mainstream classes as well as in the unit, or the purpose of inclusion is defeated. It will, therefore, be necessary to ask questions about the mainstream classes and curriculum as well as the special unit. If a child succeeds well in a unit but fails in mainstream, then, clearly, their needs are not being addressed.

7. What happens to the work that the child misses when they are in the special unit? How do they catch up or will they be following the same curriculum? If the unit has a number of different aged children, are lessons taught across the age ranges in the unit or will children be taught separately?

8. Is there sufficient staffing within the special unit for children to have 'time out' or to accompany children into their mainstream classes? Is the curriculum in the unit an adapted or supplemented curriculum rather than one that is an alternative to the mainstream classes? If the unit is for sensory needs, such as hearing impairment, will the specialist teacher of the deaf accompany the child into mainstream classes, or will they need to stay behind in the unit for other children?

9. What are the arrangements for playtimes and lunchtimes? Will the unit children have the same playtimes and lunchtimes? Will they be part of the mainstream school or be offered alternatives? Why was the host school chosen to house the special unit? Sometimes the unit

is excellent, but the host school has difficulties which may affect the overall placement. In the worst cases, host schools are sometimes chosen because they have declining numbers on roll or unused space and the children in the special unit have no particular links to the area or children served by the school.

10. Ask how any therapeutic or counselling input would be integrated into the special unit. Will any joint sessions be run in the special unit as a whole, such as social skills and, if so, do the other children form an appropriate peer group?

11. In addition to children integrating into mainstream classes, there may also be reverse integration with mainstream children being brought into the unit to provide help with academic work or mobility. Ask if this occurs.

12. What are the links between mainstream and unit staff on a day-to-day basis and how do unit staff know what is being taught, especially when they go and support a child within a lesson? Do they know what is being taught before they attend the lesson or is it all done 'on the hoof'? Can the unit staff pre-rehearse curriculum vocabulary with the child, if necessary?

13. Is the special unit also used as a resource for other children within the school? This is often positive as it will have the effect of ensuring that the children are not seen as different or segregated. On the other hand, if it is an autistic base, this might be quite difficult for the autistic children to accept.

14. The issue of social inclusion will be key to the eventual success of a unit placement. How does the school ensure social inclusion takes place? Who monitors whether the unit children are integrating with mainstream children? Does anyone track playground, lunchtime integration?

15. How will attendance in a special unit work at Key Stage 4 when the child needs to access examination courses? In many schools, attendance in the special unit decreases over the years as the child becomes more successfully integrated into mainstream classes. What happens if this does not occur?

16 Can the school show evidence either quantitatively or qualitatively that the children in the special unit achieve the outcomes predicted for them?

CHAPTER 29

Special Schools

Special schools which offer specialist provision for children with special educational needs, whose needs cannot be met in a mainstream school, may cater for a specific special need or, alternatively, may be more generic in their make up. There will be a need to establish whether a child requires a special school, such as a specialist autistic school, or whether, in fact, even if they do have autism, the child's needs will be more appropriately met in a school where they can mix with other children who do not have autism. With the move towards inclusion, it will be necessary to ascertain exactly why a special school is needed and, in particular, whether the outcomes are positive compared to the schooling they may receive, perhaps in a mainstream school.

It is important not to be confused by terminology, as there is now a *specialist* school's programme where mainstream schools are encouraged to consider specialist status in the arts, business and enterprise, engineering, humanities, languages, maths and computing, music, rural dimensions, science and technology fields. Some of these schools are referred to as special schools, shortened from specialist schools.

In view of the number of children with special educational needs, who are now being educated in mainstream schools, populations within special schools have been changing over time and this is often reflected in their designation by the Secretary of State. There are three main types of special schools:

- Maintained special schools.
- Non-maintained special schools.
- Independent special schools.

Despite inclusive policies, statistics over the years suggest the percentage of children educated in maintained special schools has remained fairly constant at around 1 per cent of the school population.

Special schools and mainstream schools measure a child's progress in terms of P (Performance) Scales, if the child's attainments have not yet reached Level 1 of the National Curriculum. P Scales are used for all the subjects of the National Curriculum, including religious education, citizenship and PSHE. The P Scales range from Level 1 to Level 8, with Level 8 being the highest level of attainment. There are other levels within the P Levels, which enable the teacher to break things down into even smaller chunks of learning using such schemes as B-Squared or PIVATS (Performance Indicators for Value-Added Target Setting). There are also assessments available to support schools using P Scales, such as Equals Pace.

All these schemes are able to provide or generate data showing attainment and 'value added' achievement.

QUESTIONS TO ASK ABOUT SPECIAL SCHOOLS

1. How many children are in the school? What is the age and gender balance? What is the designation of the school according to the DCSF? Describe the range of needs.

2. What provides the 'specialism' within the school?

3. Look at the facilities, the curriculum and the specialist qualifications of staff and ask what are the differences compared to any other special school or mainstream school. This will lead to a consideration of whether the school is specialist in any one area.

4. Consider the individual child's special educational needs and, in particular, whether a primary need has been identified, e.g. a child may have moderate learning difficulties, but also have a primary hearing impairment. It will be necessary to explore whether the resources within a special school for children with moderate learning difficulties can, at the same time, address the hearing impairment and, if not, whether a specialist school for children with hearing impairment may be preferable if they also take children with moderate learning difficulties. Ask the school these questions.

5. In all special schools, there should be opportunities for inclusion and it will be necessary to find out what these are and whether the children are included in reality or whether it is more of an exercise for the school in order to satisfy their own inclusion policies. Many special schools also operate outreach services for mainstream schools. Ask about these as this may indicate the specialist nature of the school and the way in which the teachers are used in the Local Authority or local community for training and their expertise.

6. A key question, when looking at special schools, is to determine whether all teachers share the specialism, or only some of them, e.g. if a child is placed in a specialist dyslexic school, will the child receive

lessons in history and geography at secondary level from specialist teachers in their subject area, who have also undertaken SpLD training? If not, one must consider whether the value of attending such a school outweighs a mainstream experience.

7. The age of the child may also dictate whether a special school should be tried immediately or whether there is time to assess different options, e.g. mainstream or dual placements. If a very young child is being placed, there would need to be sound reasons for opting for an immediate special school placement. Ask the special school whether they would consider input into other school environments to support a child, e.g. through mainstream or on a dual placement.

8. It is important to consider the question of transport, particularly if the special school is not in the child's Local Authority. Not all children qualify for transport, and this needs to be discussed further with the Local Authority. Is transport flexible, e.g. if the child wants to join in extra-curricular activities?

9. It will be necessary to ask specific questions about school to home communication, particularly if the child is using transport, as parents will not be going to the school on a daily basis, even for a young child. Does the school provide any support for parents at home? Does the school provide training for parents, e.g. on communication aids or signing systems used at school?

10. Given the agenda for inclusion, it is always worthwhile to ask whether there are any short- or long-term plans with regard to a special school, as some may be scheduled to close down or merge with other schools, changing their designation. It is also helpful to consider whether there are any planned building projects. This may be particularly difficult, for example, for children with ASD.

11. In the same way that questions need to be asked with regard to respect for children's cultural and religious needs in any school, in particular, a special school may need to adapt their approach and curriculum to ensure a level of understanding. Ask about this if it is important for the family.

12. Where a Statement names a special school, it cannot be assumed that the school will provide all the necessary input in terms of therapy that the child needs and these therapies should still be quantified in the Statement. As a consequence, it is very important to ask about the exact resources available within the school, in terms of therapeutic input (speech and language therapy, occupational therapy, physiotherapy plus any other therapies), and also ask exactly what the child will be receiving. If the child has come from a mainstream provision, it may be that they will be receiving less therapy than previously, but

the delivery of therapy may be different, so it is important to ask the right questions.

13. Similarly, even though the child may attend a special school, the special school may not supply everything the child needs, e.g. if a child with ASD is also dyslexic, the school may need to provide a teacher with SpLD qualifications from the Local Authority Advisory Service who does not normally work in that particular school.

14. Within a special school, small classes are more usual, but it is still important to ask about adult/child ratios. This may raise some issues, because, on the face of it, adult/child ratios may appear much higher. However, there may be children in the class who have 1:1 support and, in theory, as those assistants are dedicated to those children, the adult/child ratio, which seemed attractive, may be quite different than it first appears. When asking about adult/child ratio, always ask if any children in the class have 1:1 and then work out the ratios from there. It will also be important to ascertain what qualifications the staff have. If a child receives a lot of input from an assistant, rather than the teacher, what are the assistant's qualifications for the job?

15. Within a special school, it is necessary to ask about the peer group, as many schools take quite a varied number of children. If, for example, the child has strengths in social interaction, it is obviously important that they are in a class where other children interact socially and positively, rather than, perhaps, being placed with children who have social communication issues, such as autistic children. Similarly, if the child has a strength in language, ask how many of the children have good expressive language, and what communication needs they do have. Observation in a classroom may reveal this quite quickly. Sometimes a special school can be appropriate but the peer group may be completely wrong. This may not mean that the school should be rejected, but it will lead to questions about whether the child can be moved to a different class, spend some of the day integrated into a different class, or have some mainstream inclusion experience.

16. In addition to looking at the class, it is important to consider the school as a whole, and exactly how much time the child will spend with other children who may have very different needs in the playground or at lunchtime, or at whole-school events such as assemblies, etc. Many schools will operate different playtimes for different Key Stages, so that fewer children are in the playground. Ask about this.

17. Ask what role the regular staff adopt within the playground and at lunchtime. If different staff are employed on dinner duty, then ask about their training, particularly if a child may need extra input during unstructured social times.

18. Because of the nature of special schools, there may be small classes and the curriculum may be more restricted in some ways and this needs to be explored.

19. Ask about opportunities of work experience at Key Stage 4 and how the child will be supported, depending on their special needs.

20. Will there be appropriate behavioural role models in the class, particularly if the child is good at imitating bad behaviour? What strategies does the school use to address poor behaviour and reward good behaviour?

21. If the child is relatively young and placed in a special school, ask the school to provide statistics about how many children are phased back into mainstream school when they are older. This is particularly important, for example, in a specialist dyslexic placement, as many of these children would be able to access mainstream school once their literacy levels rise.

22. Ask about resources in the special school. Can equipment be used at home, e.g. laptops, OT equipment and if the equipment can be used at home, what are the arrangements for transporting it? Who will be responsible for insurance?

23. If a child is moving into a special school at Key Stage 3 or 4, ask about preparation for life after school and how the school will introduce life skills.

24. What extra-curricular activities are provided? Can children access them if they have to rely on school transport or is it dependent on parents collecting them?

25. Does the school offer an extended curriculum? What is it?

26. Ask questions about individual therapeutic intervention (see specific chapters).

CHAPTER 30

Dual Placements

Dual placement offers the possibility of opportunities for inclusion or as described by many parents, 'the best of both worlds'. For many children with special educational needs, decisions are made inevitably on a 'best fit' placement, and sometimes thinking laterally, together with professionals who exhibit a high level of expertise in making judgements, it is possible to think of children appropriately placed in a special school who would also benefit from attendance in a mainstream setting. It is also possible for this to work the other way, where the primary placement is in a mainstream setting, coupled with attendance at a special school. Depending on the practicalities, inclusion could take place in any mainstream school, not necessarily the school local to where the child lives, but it usually takes place in a mainstream school local to the special school. However, if the child attends each school on completely separate days, either possibility can be canvassed.

Most Local Authorities will want a dual placement noted in Part 4 of a Statement of Special Educational Needs, so that both the special school and the mainstream school are named. This will provide the appropriate funding. It will be necessary to clarify on which school roll the child is registered and whether they will count against the admission number. In most cases, the special school is the primary provider. Funding can be complicated and so the Local Authority and the schools need to be very clear how the money is being used, particularly in terms of support during the time at the mainstream school. It is important that details of the partnership programme are set out in the Statement. The Statement should confirm that both the mainstream school and the special school named on the Statement accept responsibility for the progress, attainment and well-being of the child, irrespective of the actual balance of time spent in each school. One school must take responsibility for holding all attainment records and take lead responsibility for reporting to parents, but always in partnership with the partner school. In most cases, this will be the responsibility of the special school.

It will also be essential to work out transport issues, particularly if the child has to take school-to-school transport during a school day, e.g. some children at primary level spend the morning working on formal skills in a special school placement and the afternoons at a mainstream placement where, perhaps, more informal activities are happening. This will involve transport costs and also raise issues about how the lunch hour is spent and where lunch will actually be eaten.

Where pre-school children appear to have complex difficulties, it is often difficult to decide whether a special or mainstream school will provide the most beneficial setting once compulsory education starts. By attending a special school nursery and a local nursery, a comprehensive assessment can be made across the two pre-school settings so that decisions can be taken using evidence gleaned from both provisions, once the compulsory phase of education begins.

For dual placements to work well there appear to be some important key features:

- Shared responsibility so that no decision about the child's educational programme can be made without consulting with both schools.
- Pro-active communication and communication networks that work effectively.
- Sharing of resources, expertise and joint commitment.
- Preparation and planning before starting on a dual placement with particular emphasis on timetabling.

It is unclear how many children are currently dual registered, but in 2003, 2000 children were on these types of placement (Wilson 2006), so it is possible that this number has significantly increased since then.

If a child attends a special school, some would view their education as reflecting a form of segregation. Others take the view that the more protected and supportive environment of a special school can enhance their self-identity or self-esteem. For some children in a special school, their self-confidence is increased whilst, for others, it has long-ranging consequences and they never feel able to compete in an employment market alongside their higher achieving peers. There are similar arguments posed about mainstream schools which can offer good or bad experiences for different children.

Frequently, the drive behind dual placements is for children to achieve a balance between forming effective social relationships on the one hand, whilst, on the other hand, receiving an appropriately tailored education with the over-arching idea that both aspects will help them to reach their potential academically and socially.

QUESTIONS TO ASK ABOUT A DUAL PLACEMENT

1. It will be important, before commencing a dual placement, to arrange that the child spends some time in both placements so that the child has some idea of both schools and also the schools can be in a position to address specific needs rather than just looking at paperwork.

2. When considering a dual placement, it will be necessary to think about how the child will adjust to transition and change. Attending two schools is a complex arrangement and not appropriate for every child. Having said that, if it is a very structured arrangement, even children who may have difficulty in dealing with unstructured times or unplanned changes to the timetable can benefit from such a placement and so one should not automatically assume that it will not work.

3. Before any discussion about curriculum or support, the arrangement has to be practical and both schools must agree on the practicalities and the limitations. If, for example, there is a changeover in the middle of the day, decisions need to be taken about where the child will eat lunch and who will be at the school to receive the child so they do not have to enter the busy school playground on their own, which may be quite daunting. If the schools have different uniforms, what will happen?

4. Be clear what the perceived objectives are from both placements. If attendance at mainstream is to experience social inclusion with local children from the community, it is important that this actually happens. Is the child attending clubs within school? Is the child integrating in the playground? How are mainstream teachers ensuring that they are part of a group session within the class they attend and are not left out?

5. It is very important that the teachers involved spend time in each other's settings. It cannot be assumed that school staff from either school have knowledge about the other school environment or curriculum.

6. How will communication take place between the schools and how will each school involve the parents? Sometimes the same learning support assistant supports the child in both placements and then becomes the key worker and liaises between the schools. If that is the case, it is important to ensure that the LSA has the qualifications for such a role and that not too much responsibility is put on the LSA's shoulders when, in fact, qualified teachers should be making the decisions.

7. One of the schools must adopt responsibility for the individual education plan, but it is essential that IEP meetings are organized so both schools can attend and that some of the targets that are set can be carried out in both schools.

8. It is more common to find that the therapeutic provision is situated in the special school rather than in the mainstream one. However, the therapists also need to visit and be aware of what the child is coping

with in a mainstream classroom which may be very different from the special school classroom and the therapists may need to address these aspects as part of their goals.

9. Mainstream teachers may not have the skills and knowledge about the necessary resources, particularly if a child is working well below the National Curriculum level of the classroom or working at P Levels. It is important that access to the necessary resources is available to them. This should be more straightforward in a dual placement because of the close working relationship between the two schools.

10. Do mainstream staff have the training to facilitate the child's progress and, if not, how will they obtain that training? Again, this may be quite simple, e.g. teachers from each school could join in-service training sessions at the other school or undertake visits.

11. It will be vital to measure the progress the child is making in their learning to ensure that things are not falling through the net because of the dual placement. In effect, the monitoring must be done even more carefully than usual. How will this occur?

12. It is well accepted that attitudes of school staff play a major role in how children are accepted into a school. The attitude of a class teacher can make or break the dual placement. Ask specifically how the class teacher feels about having the child in their class.

13. How will the child become involved in extra-curricular activities and what is available during the times they attend at each school? Given that the child will not be spending a full week in either school, it will be necessary for teachers to ensure that they are socially accepted in the class. The teacher may need to do some work with the peer group, helping them to understand that the child is a full member of the class even though they are not always there. Ask how this will be done.

14. If a child has been successful on a dual placement at primary school, it may be quite different at secondary level and many searching questions need to be asked before a dual placement is continued. It is, however, possible to maintain dual placements at secondary school, but it needs much more thinking about because of the number of teachers and the curriculum that the child will need to follow.

Dual placements can also be described as split placements, and there are also a number of link schemes and outreach services which may also fall under this umbrella. The most important thing about any of these schemes, which involve some kind of partial integration, is that they are not just seen as a 'token solution' to inclusion, but that the continuum of provision is fully explored and the benefits outweigh some of the limitations of this approach.

CHAPTER 31

Pupil Referral Units

Pupil Referral Units (PRUs) have had a checkered career. There are currently 70,000 children being taught in PRUs after being excluded from mainstream schools. Most are boys aged 11 to 15 years and just 1 per cent of all children get at least five C grade GCSEs. Over 60 per cent of children attending PRUs have special educational needs, many with BESD. Many of these PRUs were not planned or designed to be a long-term setting and, as a result, were not regarded as part of a Local Authority's range of planned SEN provision. Although the SEN Code of Practice gives Local Authorities the power to arrange for some or all of a child's special educational provision to be made either by attendance in school or 'otherwise' (paragraphs 8:91–8:96), placements, such as a PRU, were only to be used for relatively short periods of time, whilst a more appropriate placement was being arranged. As a result 'agreed, managed moves' should be high on any agenda for a child in a PRU to either move to a new school to give them a fresh start or to advise on further behaviour management strategies in a local school.

Managed moves should only take place with the agreement of the parents, head teachers, governors and the Local Authority and parents should not be pressurized into removing their child from school under the threat of permanent exclusion. Managed moves are more successful when they are arranged prior to permanent exclusion and they are part of a process which allows for a quick move from one school to another. PRUs have also been helpful in providing outreach services for mainstream schools to prevent the escalation of behavioural difficulties and arrangements complement and augment the SEAL Programme (Social and Emotional Aspects of Learning Curriculum). SEAL develops skills in self-awareness, managing feelings, empathy, motivation and social skills. It builds on work in the field of emotional literacy and helps children achieve the five outcomes of Every Child Matters.

The government has recently announced plans to replace Pupil Referral Units, which are referred to as 'outdated and unhelpful' and are consulting on a new name (the current preference is prospect schools) and propose a range of alternative provisions which will overhaul education for disengaged young people intended to ensure that children at mainstream schools receive a more appropriate curriculum, focusing on core subjects so they leave school with basic skills, but also introducing more creative programmes to motivate children to learn in a different kind of environment. Ideas currently being floated include a range of alternative provision, including charities and businesses, Studio Schools™, virtual schools and other projects.

One of the difficulties with PRUs is that they may include children who have been excluded together with children who are not attending school because of medical problems, pregnant schoolgirls, school-phobics or children awaiting placement in a maintained school. The amount of teaching available is variable, but children who have been permanently excluded from school must receive full-time education, i.e. a minimum of 25 hours per week for children at Key Stage 4 from the sixth day following the head teacher's decision to exclude. However, a full timetable for an excluded child may look very different from one provided within a school, as it could involve direct and indirect education with providers from further education colleges, employers or work-based trainers. Some children are dual-registered at both a mainstream school and a PRU. Legally, a PRU is defined as a form of 'education otherwise' (a school is any educational institution that provides full-time education for five or more children of compulsory school age) and, as a result, a PRU is not subject to all legislative requirements that apply to mainstream and special schools. The key differences that distinguish PRUs from mainstream schools are:

1. Management committees – most Local Authorities set up management committees to oversee the work of PRUs, which may consist of Authority officers, head teachers from maintained schools, SENCos, local governors, elected members, Connexions Personal Advisors and parents, amongst others.

2. Curriculum – PRUs do not have to teach the full National Curriculum, but they must offer a balanced and broadly based curriculum in accordance with national guidelines from the Qualifications and Curriculum Authority.

3. Staffing – PRU staff must be qualified teachers or instructors. It is usually suggested that there should be at least two qualified members of staff on site to provide support in case of disruption and to give respite to other staff during the day.

4. Premises – PRUs do not have to provide a head teacher's room, playing fields or staff accommodation for teachers to use for both work and social purposes.

PRUs are different to each other and no 'one size fits all'. In considering the kinds of questions that might be asked, it is recognized that children will be placed in PRUs for different reasons and not all questions will be appropriate to every PRU or, indeed, every child who attends there.

PRUs are inspected by Ofsted in the same way as other schools and so this would be a helpful starting point to consider the provision on offer.

QUESTIONS TO ASK ABOUT A PUPIL REFERRAL UNIT

1. Why has the child been placed in the PRU? What is the history that has led to placement and the behaviour strategies that have been implemented so far? Why did the Pastoral Support Plan (PSP)* fail? What will the PRU now do differently and what strategies will be attempted?

2. Does the PRU have a full description of the child's needs in every area, not only behaviour? This should include interests, extra-curricular activities, favourite subjects, likes and dislikes, as well as descriptions of any behavioural incidents and special educational needs.

3. What curriculum will be delivered and what are the target levels in the core subjects? In addition to academic subjects, what else will be contained in the curriculum in terms of behavioural, social and emotional needs and who will be delivering these?

4. What are the qualifications of the teachers and assistants and any therapists who will also be present?

5. If the child has been out of school for a long time, what was the child's level of attainment at the time of exclusion rather than more recently as standards may be quite different?

6. How can the family support the interventions at the PRU and how will discussions take place to ensure consistency of approach? What peer group will there be and how will the PRU ensure that an appropriate peer group will be available, either within the PRU or as a result of links with mainstream placements?

7. If a child has had to leave school part way through a GCSE course, how will any coursework be done, and any results already gained, be taken into consideration?

8. Will a Risk Assessment take place? What other agencies have been or are currently involved? Have any trigger events happened within the family?

---

* A Pastoral Support Plan (PSP) is a school-based, co-ordinated plan to help children with social, emotional and behavioural needs to manage their own behaviour more effectively and to improve their attendance.

9. Will a multi-professional meeting take place prior to transfer and, if so, who will be invited?

10. How will the child's views and hopes be taken into account?

11. What help does the child feel they need and how will that be different from anything they have received in the past? It may be helpful for the child to draw up what has been successful and unsuccessful. What will be the exit strategy and the reintegration plans for the child and is the PRU able to put any time limits on this?

12. How will progress be measured? Ask if a Personal Learning Plan (PLP) is in place. These plans will focus on outcomes and progression (school, college and employment) and set out the steps to achieve this end.

13. Given that 80 per cent of children in PRUs are deemed to have special educational needs, children with Statements of Special Educational Needs should not be admitted without appropriate decisions having been taken about long-term placement and how the PRU will meet the provision in the Statement. What decisions are being made and who will be involved with the decision-making process?

14. Will the physical conditions of the PRU meet the needs of children with special educational needs? Consider the physical environment and the outside play or relaxation areas.

15. Staff recruitment and retention may be a difficulty for a PRU and it is important to ask about this. How frequently do staff change and why?

16. If a child is being transferred back to a mainstream school, how will the behavioural support be maintained or replaced once this move occurs?

17. What is the PRU's record on attendance and punctuality and how are children followed up if these are a problem? What systems are in place for registering children for lessons?

The Pastoral Support Plan (PSP) should act as a preventative measure for children at risk of exclusion in a mainstream school. If a child already has an IEP, a separate PSP should not be set up. Instead, behavioural targets should be included in the IEP.

A PSP should be set up for a child:

- who has several fixed period exclusions that may be leading to a permanent exclusion
- who is identified as being at risk of failure at school through disaffection
- where the situation is complex and a range of agencies are required to support the child.

CHAPTER 32

Residential Schools

There may be many complex reasons why a residential school for children with special educational needs may be favoured, and most residential schools will now be very aware of the necessity to be inclusive and look for opportunities for social integration within the community where appropriate. Residential schools cover a wide range of need, spanning all the special educational needs categories, including:

- communication difficulties, such as autism
- speech and language disorders
- learning difficulties
- emotional, behavioural and social difficulties
- physical difficulties
- sensory impairments
- specific learning difficulties.

It will be important to look at the Ofsted Inspections carried out both for the school and residential aspect.

The terms '24-hour curriculum' or 'waking day curriculum' are used interchangeably. In some cases, where there are sleep disorders, it may well be a real 24-hour curriculum, but the normal preference is to use 'waking-day curriculum'. The primary argument for a residential school is usually that the child's needs extend beyond the school day and throughout the waking day, and that the educational provision could not be made by the parents. Under the UN Convention on the Rights of the Child, a child does have the right to a family life and a home life as well as a right to education. The need for a waking-day curriculum will not necessarily mean that a child will have to attend a residential school. Some Local Authorities will already have provision for extending the school day and/or supporting the family at home through social care packages.

There is no formal definition of a waking-day curriculum, but, by inference, it suggests that not all formal learning takes place within the school day and further teaching and learning must take place at the end of the normal school day, thereby extending the hours to the residential care side. The aim of a waking-day curriculum will be to maximize the learning potential of the individual child so that all staff can view learning as seamless between school and the care setting and the community as a whole. The reasons for a residential placement may be varied. The child may need a consistent behaviour management programme across the waking-day, which cannot be provided at home. It may be that the child's language development requires specific input and continuity, backed up by augmentative communication. Sometimes, placement in a residential school occurs because there is no specialist school meeting the needs of the particular child within daily travelling time and distance. Schools can offer weekly, fortnightly, termly or 52 weeks accommodation. In some schools, holidays are more evenly distributed, so the long summer break is more limited. It will be necessary to establish what the residential arrangements actually are.

The amount of consistent time spent at the school may relate to the child's need for continuity of management. In effective residential schools, individual care plans and individual education plans will be cross-referenced to target behavioural, personal and social targets in both settings and planning will take place which will reinforce learning and independence usually involving therapeutic input in some form.

In addition to the questions one would normally ask of a day school, there are additional questions that one would ask specifically when visiting a residential school focusing on the care arrangements:

QUESTIONS FOR THE CARE SIDE OF A RESIDENTIAL SCHOOL
Care

1. What is the relationship between care staff and school staff? Is there a plan that transcends both parts of the school to ensure an effective waking day curriculum? Ask to see examples.

2. Do the staff have the necessary experience, expertise and knowledge to care for the child with a particular need? What recent training courses have they been on?

3. Do the care staff go on their own training courses, or do they rely on the head of care feeding back to them? Do care staff ever do training together with the school/education staff?

4. What is the turnover of staff like, and how long have most of the staff been at the school? How do care staff liaise with school staff? Do they

both spend time in the different settings that the child experiences and, therefore, have a good understanding of the whole world of the child?

5. How many agency staff are usually employed? How many staff are on duty each night? Where are they located? Are they waking-night staff or do they sleep? Are there sufficient staff on duty after school and at the weekend to give children choices of activities?

6. How is a key worker appointed and if the child does not like the key worker, can they be changed?

7. What kind of Risk Assessment is undertaken for activities which the child might be asked to do? How do the care staff ensure that all children can access outings and leisure activities?

8. What happens if a parent is not happy with something that is going on in relation to the child's care?

9. Will the child be able to sleep in a single or shared room, and if the latter, how are choices of rooms made? How will the staff know if a child has left their room at night?

10. How will the school celebrate birthdays or other events happening at home?

11. How do the children get the opportunity to choose which television programmes they watch, what music they listen to or what they do when school finishes for the day? How do the care staff deal with conflicts of taste in music, television programmes or children who do not like a lot of noise?

12. Is there sufficient space for children to leave the main lounge, and, if so, are there sufficient adults around to accompany them outside or to other areas? Many children require 'time out' periods or calm relaxation opportunities but may still need supervision.

13. What can children bring into the residential side with them and how are these things kept safe, particularly if they are very special to them, such as favourite books/games/toys?

14. Do the bedrooms look homely and clean? Are the bedrooms tidy? Will the child be expected to make their own beds as part of a living plan?

15. How are children able to express their individual tastes? If religion or culture is important, how does the school respond to this?

16. What are the range of activities or outings that children can do at weekends and after school, and what happens if children do not want to join in these activities? Can they choose to opt out and, if so, what will be the alternatives?

17. How will the school ensure that the child who has specific needs, perhaps physical or sensory needs, can join in the same activities as other children or go on trips?

18. Some residential schools are in large country houses; what is the access like and are community facilities nearby for all children to use, such as local youth clubs, the cinema, local shops and sports centres?

19. If the child has any particular care needs, such as a special diet, bedding or a particular piece of equipment, e.g. a particular type of seat or hoist, will the school be able to positively respond to these very individual needs and will the equipment be available? Do therapists, such as speech and language therapists, occupational therapists and physiotherapists spend any time in the care side and how do they advise staff on programmes or strategies?

20. What arrangements are there for reassessing the child's equipment needs and for updating the equipment?

21. Does the school have particular policies concerning lifting and how will these affect the child? What are the policies for restraint?

22. What sort of training is given on independent living and travelling skills? Are older children taught to budget, shop, cook, wash, iron, mix and socialize with the wider community?

23. What other skills appropriate for the child's level of abilities are taught, e.g. how to fill in forms, how to use a post office or access libraries and other resources? Is help given to use a telephone and telephone directory? What help is offered to develop communication skills using the internet and ICT?

Food

1. Where are meals taken? Do the children have lunch in school or do they have lunch in the care environment? What are the reasons for the choice of venue?

2. Do children have a choice of food? How much of a choice and how are they given that choice? Can a child access the menu with their level of communication difficulty, e.g. is a pictorial format available? Ask to see a typical week's menu.

3. Can the school cater for a child's particular dietary needs and will the school respect cultural/religious issues relating to food? Can the school cater for a child's particular likes and dislikes?

4. What happens if a child does not want to finish a meal?

5. Do children who need help to eat receive 1:1 help? Who gives this help? Will they be familiar with the child's needs and feeding programme, if relevant?

6. Do staff eat the same food as the children? Do staff and children eat at the same time (this may be a good or bad idea, depending on the child's needs)?

7. What programmes are in place for developing independent skills in feeding or choosing food (this may be particularly relevant for children on a very limited diet, e.g. with autism)?

8. Do therapists who work with children in the school day, also see them on the care side? Do they help set up and monitor feeding programmes (the input from a speech and language therapist and occupational therapist may be crucial here) and other self-help programmes?

Safety

In addition to the formal inspections that are carried out by Ofsted, ask:

1. What is the staff/child ratio when they go out after school or at weekends? Is this adequate for the child in question?

2. Does the school have regular fire practices?

3. How do the care staff ensure that the children are supervised enough to keep them safe?

4. Does the school keep an accident book for all incidents, however small?

5. Has the school had any serious incidents recently?

6. If the child is vulnerable to the possibilities of abuse of any kind, how does the school teach children about their rights to be safe? How does the school ensure that every child feels they have someone they can trust and confide in (especially if the child is non-verbal or has complex learning difficulties)?

7. If the child runs away, is the site secure? Go over safety and risk situations at entry and exit points, particularly if the child is an expert escape artist!

Health

1. Will the child see a GP at school or receive a regular check-up and what are the arrangements for informing parents?

2. Do children see a dentist?

3. Do children have eye tests?

4. Is there always a qualified first-aider on site at all times?

5. If there is a need for regular medication, what records are kept?

6. If the child requires occasional medication, what procedures will be followed for deciding when this happens and will the parent be informed?

7. Is medication ever administered without agreement from parents and, if so, in what circumstances?

8. What happens when the child is ill and cannot attend school? Who looks after the child?

Parent contact

1. How will the child keep in contact with a parent, particularly if they are not able to use a telephone? Are there web-cams?

2. Can a parent go and visit at any time? What sort of notice does the school require and is there somewhere to stay overnight if necessary?

3. When a parent visits, is there somewhere private to go with the child or can they take the child off premises?

4. Is the school happy for siblings (and extended family members) to visit as well?

5. What do staff do when children are homesick?

6. How do staff ensure that the child is communicating their feelings accurately?

7. How often do parents receive a written report and how is feedback sent from school during a normal week?

The other children

1. Do children seem happy? Are they smiling or laughing?

2. What does the rapport appear to be between staff and children?

3. Do staff members know the names of children they see in passing?

4. Are there children with whom the child in question could be friends?

5. Are there children who might pose a threat to the child's safety?

6. If the child is in a minority because of their particular impairment, religion, culture or background, will they fit in and be able to make friends?

7. How do teachers and care staff protect children from bullying and how do children report bullying?

Adapted from *The Right Place? A Parent's Guide to Choosing a Residential Special School* by Jenny Morris, published in 2003 by the Joseph Rowntree Foundation. Reproduced by kind permission of the Joseph Rowntree Foundation.

CHAPTER 33

Home Education

Home education (also referred to as 'homeschooling' in the USA, Elective Home Education or Education Otherwise) is the education of school-aged children in locations other than at school. This includes any arrangements for the education of a child at home (but also, for example, in a Pupil Referral Unit). Home education is an alternative to school and any family can choose this option for their children. Parents do have the right, in law, to adopt primary responsibility for the education of their children instead of delegating it to a school, and many thousands of families in the UK and worldwide do exercise that right. There are many reasons why families may decide to home educate, and they do not have to follow a curriculum or work a regular school day. There is no requirement to study for formal qualifications, but many families choose to do so. If a parent wishes to remove a child from the school roll, in order to home educate, then they must go through a deregistration process which involves writing to the head teacher of the school. Guidance on these regulations are issued and parents do not have to give any reasons for their decisions, or details about their plan. There is no requirement for parents to obtain the schools' and Local Authorities' agreement to educate their children at home, and likewise, schools and Local Authorities should not seek to prevent parents from doing so.

There are no official figures on how many children are home educated in the UK, but it is suggested that it is around 50,000 children (0.5%) of compulsory educational age. Elective home education is distinct from the home tuition provided by advisors or tutors appointed by the Local Authority when a child cannot attend school because of, for example, illness, or where the child attends a Pupil Referral Unit.

The elective home education guidelines for Local Authorities sets out their statutory responsibilities in relation to children whose families choose to educate them at home and provides guidance for parents about these responsibilities. It clearly states that the responsibility for a child's education rests with the parents. In England, education is compulsory, but school is not.

It is certainly advisable to contact the Local Authority to find out about their duties and what support they may be able to provide.

The regulations, however, do not apply to children who have been placed by the Local Authority in special schools and in this situation a child cannot be deregistered without the Local Authority's consent. This is in place to ensure that the child's special educational needs are met and because the Local Authority has a duty towards the child, but parents do have the right to educate their children at home even with special educational needs (see also Chapter 8).

The law (Section 7, Education Act 1996) does state that:

> The parent of every child of compulsory school age shall cause him to receive efficient full-time education suitable – (a) to his age, ability and aptitude and (b) to any special educational needs he may have, either by regular attendance at school or otherwise.

The terms 'efficient' and 'suitable' education are not defined in the Education Act 1996, but 'efficient' has been broadly described in case law as an education that 'achieves that which it sets out to achieve'. It is, therefore, recommended by parent groups that parents should set out their aims and what they hope to achieve, so that they can be judged as being 'efficient' if they achieve these aims.

'Suitable' education is one that:

> primarily equips a child for life within the community of which he is a member, rather than the way of life in the country as a whole, as long as it does not foreclose the child's options in later years to adopt some other form of life if he wishes to do so. (Mr Justice Woolf in the case of R v Secretary of State for Education and Science 1985)

There is currently no legal definition of 'full-time'. Children normally attend school for between 22 and 25 hours a week for 38 weeks of the year, but this measurement of 'contact time' is not comparable to the almost constant 1:1 contact for children being educated at home and education can easily take place outside normal school hours.

Home educating parents are not required to:

- teach the National Curriculum
- provide a broad and balanced education
- have a timetable
- have premises equipped to any particular standard
- set hours during which education will take place
- have any specific qualifications
- make detailed plans in advance

- observe school hours, days or terms
- give formal lessons
- mark work done by their child
- formally assess progress or set developmental objectives
- reproduce school-type peer group socialization
- match school-based, age-specific standards.

However, Local Authorities should offer advice and support to parents on these matters if requested.

The role of the Local Authority is such that it can make informal enquiries of parents who are educating their children at home to establish that a suitable education is being provided. Local Authorities have no statutory duties in relation to monitoring the quality of home education on a routine basis. However, parents, in turn, may choose to provide evidence that their child is receiving an efficient and suitable education by the following means:

- Writing a report about their child's progress and curriculum.
- Keeping a running sample of work which can then be made into an annotated folder.
- Inviting the Local Authority's representative to the house with, or without, the child being present.
- Meeting the Local Authority's representative somewhere other than the house, with or without the child being present (there is no automatic right of access to the home environment).

Most Local Authorities, having made an initial visit to satisfy themselves that the child is receiving a suitable education may only keep in touch on a yearly basis.

If it appears to the Local Authority that a child is not receiving a suitable education, then it can serve a school attendance order.

If a child has a Statement of Special Educational Needs and is being home educated, then the Local Authority still has a statutory duty to undertake an annual review. This review will include assessing whether the Statement is still appropriate and it may be possible to alter or even cease to maintain the Statement depending on the current circumstances and the provision being made.

Parents of children with special educational needs do not need to have any special qualifications or training to assume direct responsibility for their children's education, but the Local Authority does have a legal duty to ensure the child's needs are being met and, ultimately, if there is a disagreement, then it will need to be resolved by the Special Educational Needs and Disability Tribunal (SEND Tribunal) and in the same way as a child within school, the Local Authority has a duty to inform the parents of their right to appeal.

There are many different styles to home education and different philosophies used. Parents do not have to subscribe to a recognized belief system or an educational method. Possible approaches are:

- Accelerated learning.
- Autonomous education (with an emphasis on individual self-expression and self-motivation).
- A recognized pedagogical approach, such as Steiner, which derives from the work done by Rudolf Steiner (where there is an emphasis on natural materials, no television, computers, plastic toys, etc., no pressure to learn to read or write, up to the age of 7 years. Older children do the same sort of things at the same time each day – academic work in the mornings, studying one subject at a time, history every day for two or three weeks, etc. They maintain contact with nature, modern languages can be learnt by reading good literature in the original version and there is a classical approach to maths, geometry, algebra and trigonometry), or Montessori (not having televisions and computer games in the home, not feeding children junk food, having toys that involve the imagination).
- Specific home-based programmes related to special educational needs, such as Son-Rise, Applied Behavioural Analysis and others, which may address aspects of autism.

QUESTIONS A PARENT MAY WANT TO ASK OF THEMSELVES ABOUT HOME EDUCATION

1. How are resources built up for home education? This may include:
   - access to the internet at home or in the library
   - access to public libraries or to school libraries where the Local Authority permits this
   - contact with other home educating families on a local basis, or via membership of a national support organization or via the internet support lists to share educational ideas – this is particularly helpful as it will enable new home educators to benefit from the experience of others and also to provide socialization opportunities
   - access to interested supportive adults who can add to the child's learning by providing experience and opportunities that the parent does not have
   - trips and outings to stimulate or follow-up a particular interest in a subject

- access to materials for reading and writing on a personalized level
- linking in with virtual classrooms
- educational toys, resources and books at jumble sales, second-hand bookshops and car boot sales.

It is certainly not necessary to 'reinvent the wheel' as there are many packaged resources for home education now available through several home education websites.

2. How will socialization be built up at home? There are two main aspects of socializing in schools. The first is learning to co-operate with others in class. Any group activity may yield the same results that a child will get in school and for many home educators, having two or three children playing in the back garden can develop the same skills. Alternatively, there are more structured group activities, such as joining extra-curricular clubs or groups. The other aspect of socializing at school is the unstructured play at lunchtime and playtime. For some children, this is a positive experience when they develop friends and learn about each other, but for others it may be isolating and may result in bullying or experiences where self-esteem is reduced. Home educators will build up skills and positive characteristics of their children in a way that helps them to cope with situations within the community. Visiting libraries, museums, shops, elderly neighbours and hospitals, as well as participating in other activities can all contribute to a child becoming more confident within a larger group situation.

3. How is success measured? The main philosophy behind home education is an acknowledgement that children learn in different ways, at different rates and, as a result, teaching and testing will be individualized. If parents are confident with the reasons they have chosen to home educate, then they are likely to be successful. However, things sometimes do not work out in home education as one expects them to, but this may be considered a strength as much as a weakness and educators will use these opportunities to move things along in a positive way.

4. How will the child take public examinations? If a parent decides that a child needs to take GCSEs, perhaps because they will be useful for future career options, there appear to be three main ways in which home educated children have taken GCSEs:

- by correspondence courses/virtual classrooms
- by enrolling at a local college or adult-education class
- at home doing their own research, choosing appropriate books and buying past exam papers.

5. There is also a flexi-schooling option, where a child can register in a school, perhaps part time, as they approach GCSEs. The older the child, the more control they may want to take and the child can then decide whether or not they want to work for exams, what subjects to study or what correspondence courses to follow.

6. It is important to be aware that home educators are in a similar position to parents who send their children to private schools, in that there is no funding available to support them. In some areas there are charitable trusts which may exist, which might make awards to families who meet specific criteria, e.g. if a child has special educational needs, and registers of charities can be checked at a local library.

7. How do parents get support? Research into the support needs of parents who educate their children at home results in a complex picture with some parents feeling a lack of support and some isolation. Families need to consider the impact on the whole of their family life and not just, perhaps, on one child who is being home educated. It is helpful to talk to others who have walked down this road, perhaps before embarking on the journey.

8. If the child has special educational needs, parents need to feel confident they can meet all the child's needs. Ask the Local Authority to provide help and speak to the educational psychologist.

It should be noted that a recent review of home education has recommended that there should be compulsory annual registration which should be administered by Local Authorities. It will be necessary to consider the current situation if the findings of this review are put into practice.

THE QUESTION OF SOCIAL INCLUSION: DOES IT MATTER WHERE CHILDREN ARE TAUGHT?

The general issues about inclusion are covered in previous chapters, but social inclusion is also mentioned here in the context of home education, with specific reference to children with special educational needs.

It is known that children with special educational needs can experience rejection and bullying in mainstream schools and some parents would argue that a child in a special school will have a more inclusive experience. For other children, being educated in a specialist environment may prove to be an enduring barrier both within education and later in life. Decisions about whether a child will be accepted or rejected by other children may well depend on their own social competence as much as the ability of the school to include them. For some parents, the lack of social inclusion within school is a trigger for the decision to home educate.

The following questions are posed to ensure that parents and professionals have fully considered whether social inclusion can be improved in a particular school.

QUESTIONS ON SOCIAL INCLUSION

1. What are the child's social competencies? Does the child have effective social and problem-solving skills and are they willing to engage with other children?

2. Does the school have an inclusive culture with positive staff attitudes to inclusion and explicit whole-school arrangements to encourage positive peer attitudes?

3. How does the school teach friendship skills and, if necessary, assertiveness?

4. How does the school monitor appropriate interactions with peers?

5. If a child is not interested in social interaction, or not motivated to develop social skills, does the school and/or parent still feel that social integration is a good thing and, if so, how will it be achieved?

6. How will the school include the child in the classroom, e.g. are there facilities for group work?

7. How will the child be included in the playground and in unstructured activities, such as extra-curricular clubs?

8. Will the school become involved and work with the parents to monitor after-school friendships, as this is often desired by the child and is a more problematic area for the school to become involved in?

9. What effective strategies are being used by the school to ensure inclusion and will these work with the particular child, given their special educational needs?

10. Can any peer preparation be undertaken if the child is starting a new class or a new school?

11. Who will be involved in teaching the necessary strategies the child needs and will this involve outside professionals, such as the educational psychologist, therapists, etc.?

12. Discuss with the school what is practically achievable in terms of developing social skills. It may be necessary to draw up some targets; such as increasing confidence and self-esteem, developing independence and thinking about what is needed to reach the goals and whether that is possible in the school's environment.

13. Will the child have appropriate role models to develop new skills and the possibility of practising them in a small group before joining a larger group? Will the school pair the child up with a supportive friend or with someone with similar difficulties and which option would be preferable?

14. If the child presents with inappropriate behaviours, how will the school try and establish what is triggering this behaviour and whether or not it is related to difficulties they may have with inclusion? Will the school draw up a Pastoral Support Plan?

Clearly, depending on the type of school and the stage of the child's development, expectations with regard to social skills will be quite different. It is important when assessing whether social inclusion has been successful to determine what efforts have been needed (both on behalf of the child and the school) and whether the advantages and outcomes continue to outweigh the disadvantages.

If parents are uncertain about home education, because of the possibility of the child becoming socially isolated, at least these questions will offer ideas and strategies to discuss with the school before the step is taken to home educate.

CHAPTER 34

Hospital Schools

There are a number of hospital schools which provide access to the National Curriculum whilst a child is in hospital. Some are located and run in a specific hospital, whilst others provide services to a number of different hospitals. The schools are funded by the local authority but have their own governing body and budget. Some hospital schools provide a limited number of places for children who are not in-patients, but who are receiving medical or mental health services and who could benefit from attending the hospital school. Some hospital schools have developed outreach support to mainstream schools to meet certain medical and mental health needs.

About 14 per cent of children between 4 and 16 have a chronic illness; however the majority of these children will not have a Statement of Special Educational Needs. For some children with medical needs, it may be a one-off incident. If the condition is chronic, then the hospital school will work more in partnership with other agencies and the child's own school. The government policy on education and illness states:

> Each Local Authority shall make arrangements for the provision of suitable education at school or otherwise than at school for those children of compulsory school age, who by reason of illness, exclusion from school or otherwise, may not for any period receive suitable education unless such arrangements are made for them. (Section 19, Education Act 1996)

The statutory guidance on access to education for children and young people with medical needs sets out minimum national standards of education for these children who cannot attend school because of medical needs. Hospital schools or hospital teaching services provide part of an integrated hospital/home education service for children.

Hospital schools are subjected to the same Ofsted Reports as other schools, although it is acknowledged that once a child is in hospital there are no choices about the school they attend.

QUESTIONS TO ASK ABOUT HOSPITAL SCHOOLS

In addition to the usual questions one might ask of a school, the following points may be helpful to raise:

1. Will the hospital school link with the SENCo of the child's school and discuss the way in which a smooth return back to school can be facilitated, especially if the child has been out of school for some time?

2. If the child leaves hospital with symptoms or the need for medication or further treatment, ensure that the school nurse and/or teachers are aware of this and the impact that this might have on a normal school day. Some medications can alter the mood or appearance of a child. Identify how this information will be passed from one school to the next.

3. Ask to meet with hospital staff to find out what impact the child's condition will have on every-day activities, such as PE, or whether the child may need to eat regular snacks throughout the day or hand in homework a bit later. This will need to be reported back to the school.

4. If the child has been through a traumatic episode, it may be necessary to ensure that when they return to school, they have some extra time from a teacher or other adult to talk through their experiences. In some cases, this may need to involve a counsellor and/or CAMHS. If there is a need to request any special arrangements in advance of GCSE examinations or SATs, ensure that contact is made with an appropriately qualified teacher, in order for teacher assessments to be made where possible.

5. If a child is in hospital, ask the teacher at school to ensure that peers do not forget about the child, as peer support is vital throughout this period and this will help successful reintegration following an illness.

6. Because of the nature of hospitals, it may be that the child has had an unstable peer group in a hospital school and will need some time to readjust. Discuss this with the teachers at the hospital school, the parents and the receiving school and find ways to make the transition as non-problematic as possible.

7. Even though the child may not have had a Statement of Special Educational Needs before entering hospital, it is possible that this process may be required when leaving hospital, depending on what the child's needs are at the time. Ask who will help a parent through that process.

8. If a child has had a lengthy absence and missed a lot of work through illness, depending on what stage of their education they are working

at, it may be necessary to discuss how the child will catch up on the work missed. Will the child require additional teaching? How will this be fitted in? Will the child have to drop a subject to compensate for extra help?

9. If a child is over compulsory school age, but under 18, and has missed a lot of school, it is possible for a Local Authority to arrange continuing education perhaps by arranging for the child to repeat a year. This should be discussed with the child as well as with the school, as the child may have their own thoughts on this.

CHAPTER 35

Studio Schools™ and Virtual Schools

STUDIO SCHOOLS™

The Studio Schools™ concept has been developed by the Young Foundation. Studio Schools™ have been designed to help 14–19-year-olds better prepare for the world of work. Their website states: 'They will be small schools of around 300 children that will teach the National Curriculum through interdisciplinary, enterprise themed projects, but will have a very different style and ethos to most existing schools with a strong emphasis on practical work and enterprise.'* The schools will look and feel like a cluster of businesses and the children will be as much workers as students. Every child will have a personal coach, there will be mixed-aged teams and the schools will have many of the features of a workplace. The staff will comprise a mix of teachers and non-teachers with business expertise. Studio Schools™ aim to complement existing secondary schools by providing an alternative approach for young people who may be alienated by traditional schools or who are looking for a different approach. They will try to address the challenge of disengagement and provide a more attractive route to practical education for troubled children whose needs are not currently being successfully addressed. Some of these children could have Statements for behavioural, emotional and social difficulties (BESD).

As this is a new 'untried and untested' venture, it is too early to pose specific questions, but questions can be adapted from this book.

---

* Reproduced by kind permission of the *Young Foundation*, www.launchpad.youngfoundation. org.

VIRTUAL SCHOOLS

New technology has now opened up an area of schooling for children who previously were unable or unwilling to attend a real school and virtual schooling is increasingly being floated as a possibility, even for children with special educational needs.

It is not known how many children are out of school at any one time as there are no official public figures. Estimates vary greatly, between 10,000 to 100,000 school-aged children missing from the education system nationally. There are many reasons why children may not attend school. These include children who are:

- suffering from medical problems
- permanently excluded or who are on fixed term exclusions from school
- already working in a PRU but who receive some education at home
- school-phobic or school refusers
- teenage mothers
- bullied
- looked-after children
- suffering from mental health issues
- travellers
- recent arrivals to the UK and who are waiting for school places
- carers for their parents or siblings
- educated out of school through choice.

Children can now attend virtual classrooms that may better suit their needs than a normal classroom. For some children, the virtual classroom removes the stress and becomes a place where there is just a focus on learning and where there is no peer group to encourage bad behaviour. Whilst there are concerns about missing out on the social aspects of school, children meet online or via voice and text messaging and do form friendships. If the Local Authority is recommending virtual schooling, then they need to be sure that the child has a multi-media package which will include an appropriate computer, printer, digital camera, broadband and a set of resources on whichever home package the Local Authority is working with. Children can work on assignments or blogs, view curriculum materials and discuss them via email or online chat-rooms. There is often a greater emphasis on more creative forms of learning; with online galleries which can showcase paintings, photographs, audios and movies. One of the difficulties is that parents are expected to supervise work and would also need to be at home because of health and safety issues. This type of education is, therefore, very dependent on support from home, although there are now examples of PRUs who allow children to work from home on one day a week and to set their own curriculum.

There are many advertisements for virtual schools on the internet, and it is extremely difficult to know how to evaluate them and their particular strengths and weaknesses. Most will highlight that their education meets the requirements of the National Curriculum and emphasize the flexible teaching methods which allow children to work at their own pace and levels that suit them. Most will advertise personally assigned subject tutors who are qualified teachers and who provide feedback and ongoing assignments. Clearly, whilst a virtual school will be able to meet some needs for specific children, if this scheme is being recommended by a Local Authority for a child with special educational needs, they will need to confirm how the child's special educational needs will be met in their entirety through virtual schooling, e.g. if they require therapy input or social inclusion as part of their provision.

A typical timetable may include logging onto the internet and chatting to classmates in the 'school hall' at the start of the day, followed by three hour-long lessons divided by break and lunchtime.

Virtual schools need to solve the difficulties that arise because of lack of eye contact. Methods for rewarding, disciplining and resolving conflict are challenges. For good work, teachers may send pictures across the screen and they have the option of reprimanding a child privately by clicking on their user name only, or in public, in a shared access window where everyone can read the child's excuses. One advantage of this method is that every interaction between children and teachers is on record, but there are downsides, such as no physical exercise or eye contact, little verbal and physical communication and no chances to learn how to handle the bustle and bullying in the playground (which some may see as an advantage!).

Sitting in front of a computer for hours on end may be a parent's nightmare and could have some side-effects, so parents really have to consider how they will introduce compensatory activities into the child's life or there is the risk of isolation.

Ofsted have surveyed how virtual learning environments are generally developing across schools and colleges. Their report, published in January 2009, noted that Visual Learning Environments (VLEs) are still in the early stages of development and although learners with learning difficulties used computers to support their learning in class, the 'ready availability of a supportive tutor in class was seen as a greater factor in their learning' (p.15).

QUESTIONS TO ASK ON VIRTUAL SCHOOLING

1. If a virtual school has been recommended for a child with a Statement of Special Educational Needs, it is important to find out the reasons for this and, in particular, how the provision on the Statement will be met.

2. As this is a relatively new form of education, ask what experience the Local Authority has with any of the online educational providers and why they prefer one provider over another.

3. Look at the levels of engagement and, in particular, the amount of time the child will be expected to sit in front of a computer.

4. Who will be supervising the child, both in a practical sense and also in terms of their learning? If parents are expected to support the virtual classroom, are they onside and, if so, what is the expectation in terms of them being there all the time? If parents cannot supervise the child, are there health and safety issues, insurance issues or other aspects that a Local Authority would need to consider? Is it advisable for parents and children to be together at home for extended periods, if the child has special educational needs? Has a psychologist been consulted on this aspect?

5. If a child has a Statement of Special Educational Needs, how will the Local Authority provide for all their needs?

6. What about social inclusion? What success rates can the virtual school report on, both in terms of academic success, but also as a method of returning children to mainstream schooling (if appropriate)? Will the child get together with other children also in virtual schools, and how will this be organized?

7. Who will provide the necessary equipment and what happens when repairs are needed?

8. Are there other ways in which the child can link with a mainstream classroom, e.g. using the virtual classroom linked to an actual classroom so that the child can hear classmates talking and in discussion (this may be suitable for children on long-term medical absence who are away from a class which they would normally attend)?

9. For some children who have rejected the whole notion of school, virtual schooling can reduce some of the school-like vocabulary by avoidance of using words such as teacher, pupil, lessons, etc. If this is important to a child, ask whether this is the case with the particular online provider.

10. Question whether the child is considered eligible for the particular provider. Some providers will not accept children who view it only as short-term or temporary provision, and if they are expected to benefit from alternative provision within six months, they will not be accepted into the programme.

11. How will funding be given?

PART 7

SUMMARY

CHAPTER 36

Evaluating the Findings

Reference has already been made to recording opinions, but this chapter deals with evaluations. How do you know whether what you have observed or heard during a school visit is important and if it is important, what priority should you give to the information? As always, the response is that it depends on the individual child and the extent to which the observations will have an impact on their particular special educational needs. If, for example, you observe a busy lively school, this may be very detrimental to a child with sensory issues related to autism, but very positive for a child who finds such an atmosphere helpful in establishing social relationships and creating other learning opportunities. Consider the following questions once the visit is over:

1. What are the school's strengths and weaknesses?
2. In your view, does the school have the motivation and willingness to listen to the issues raised and effect change?
3. Have things worked out in the past? If not, why not?
4. What are the good practice issues that you have been able to identify and can these be built on?
5. Does the school give the impression of fresh thinking and working with parents and in their contacts with external agencies?
6. Has the school had any experience of meeting the needs of a child like the one you are discussing? If so, can the school determine what their own strengths and weaknesses are?
7. Through observation, does it appear that the school is inclusive and other children accept children with special educational needs?

In any evaluation, it is important to back up your viewpoint with observations and facts, using evidence you have gained from your school visit. It is also necessary to show impartiality and to present a balanced argument, and where there are good things, these need to be stated as well.

Categorize your points into specific topics, such as written material, observation and therapeutic support, and constantly ask yourself the question 'what does it all come down to'?

Make sure you have considered all aspects of the school:

- the curriculum
- classroom organization and grouping of children within the class that the child will be part of
- access to all school facilities, including sports and extra-curricular activities
- breaks and lunchtimes
- interaction with peers and social inclusion
- homework
- management of behaviour
- assessment and exam arrangements
- links with therapists and other professionals
- links with other provisions, such as special units or special schools
- outreach work
- in-service training
- arrangements for partnership with parents
- potential for extending the curriculum beyond school hours.

Key considerations, whether in a mainstream or special provision, will be the make up of the specific class the child will join, the range of needs in the class, their National Curriculum levels, the teacher/child ratio, the physical environment and the range and level of the therapeutic input.

SUMMARY

If various chapters in this book have been followed, you should now be able to answer the following key questions:

1. How suitable is the school's policy and structure, in particular, does the child's needs match the admissions' criteria?
2. How suitable is the general physical environment?

3. How suitable is the specific class that the child will be joining?

4. How understanding are the staff?

5. How knowledgeable and well trained are the staff in being able to plan and provide for the education of the child?

6. Is this school conversant with the particular special needs of the child? If not, can the school receive training? Does the school want to train?

7. How suitable is the general curriculum? Can it be enhanced or extended? Are resources available?

8. How detailed and individually appropriate is the special provision offered?

9. What therapy is available and how will it be delivered and where? Who will deliver the therapy and what is their background and training? Is it appropriately matched to the child's needs?

10. What strengths of the child will be enhanced?

11. What long-term objectives would the child be able to aim for, both in terms of academic achievements and social skills? Will this provision result in fast or slow gains?

12. Can the school competently meet the child's special educational needs and can they maintain the required provision?

13. Will the child be academically and socially included and will their cultural, religious and ethnic needs be respected?

CHARTING THE RESULTS

Please use the photocopiable blank chart at the end of this chapter to chart your results. (The example on p.268 may be helpful as a guide.)

1. List the child's special educational needs, preferably from Part 2 of the Statement, if applicable, or from the available professional reports.

2. List the provision required to meet the needs, preferably from Part 3 of the Statement, if applicable, or from the available professional reports.

3. List how the school could meet the child's needs and whether the provision is currently available.

4. Make notes about the areas where the needs and provision could not be met at the present time. Where are the gaps?

5. Identify whether any additional provision would be required (it may be possible for the Local Authority or school to increase the level of provision).

6. Note anything about the child's special educational needs which would make it difficult for the school to teach other children (this may be identified by the school or it may be identified by observation, e.g. bulky equipment in an already crowded space).

7. If you need to consider the question of whether the provision suggested takes due account of the efficient use of all resources, then you will need to find out the costs of each placement (plus any extra resources or provision) per year, and compare the costs of different placements.

8. If considering residential provision, you may need to consider the following additional questions:

    a. Is there an alternative appropriate day local provision, which could offer a place?

    b. Is there an educational need for a residential placement?

Accept or reject the school on the basis of your evaluation. Your decision should be based on factual evidence where possible. Try to be impartial.

The following pages can be photocopied for personal use only.

CHARTING THE RESULTS

Suggested headings (if the child has a Statement, the headings may differ under Part 2)	What are the child's special educational needs?	What provision does the child need to meet these needs?	What can the school provide?	What are the gaps?	Can these gaps be filled? If so, how? If not, is the school appropriate?
1. Educational					
Cognitive functioning					
Acquisition of concepts					
Literacy/numeracy					
Approaches/attitudes to learning					
Educational attainment (include National Curriculum levels)					
2. Communication					
Listening/speaking					
Receptive/expressive language					
Social use of language					

3. Behavioural, social and emotional					
Behaviour					
Interpersonal skills					
Emotional development					
4. Motor and sensory skills					
Gross motor skills					
Fine motor skills					
Sensory integration					
5. Independence and self-help skills					
Self-help skills					
Independent skills					
Awareness of danger					

AN EXAMPLE OF A YEAR 9 CHILD IN A MAINSTREAM SCHOOL

What are the child's special educational needs?	What provision does the child need to meet these needs?	What can the school provide?	What are the gaps?	Can these gaps be filled? If so, how? If not, is the school appropriate?
1. Educational				
Moderate learning difficulties	Modified curriculum	Differentiation in all lessons Limited LSA support in lessons	Teachers/SENCo need to prepare and provide worksheets. Need dedicated LSA hours SENCo to source books and equipment from local special school	School willing but has no previous experience so will need training plus funding SENCo needs time to do this
Literacy P8 Numeracy P8/ Level 1	Access to lessons in Year 9; specific teaching for basic skills	Limited LSA support in lessons	No specialist teaching for basic skills at P Levels in mainstream secondary school	Is there a special school outreach teacher who can provide this input?
Poor concentration	Small groups and catch-up work	Some flexibility to take small groups out on withdrawal basis	Room available? Teacher or teaching assistant available? Peers of similar standards? Can school allow child to drop some subjects?	Physical space in school on regular basis will need to be timetabled
2. Communication				
Specific language impairment	1:1 weekly SaLT session plus programme through week	No provision at school Referral to Primary Care Trust (PCT)	School would need to rely on PCT Has school worked with SaLT?	If SaLT provision not available through PCT, is a private service available? Training needed by SaLT

	Group social skills session with peers with similar language difficulties plus role models with normal language	Language teacher from Local Authority Advisory Service	Is there a group?	Group work not viable unless child joins existing Year 7 SULP group
Limited social use of language				
3. Behavioural, social and emotional				
Emotional reliance	Peer mentoring	School has existing peer-mentoring system	None	Yes
Poor interpersonal skills	Structured activities during breaktime or access to quiet in-school area	Access to in-school area but no additional staff resources for outside areas	Additional teaching assistants – need funding	School can provide extra teaching assistants
4. Motor and sensory skills				
Poor fine motor skills	1:1 OT for 30 minutes per week Motor skills handwriting programme to be carried out throughout week by teaching assistant	School has no experience of working with OT No provision Referral to PCT	School would need to rely on PCT OT; no OTs available in area – school knows this	Is private OT possible? How will this fit into secondary timetable?
Sensory integration needs	Sensory Diet	Can regular physical breaks be taken?	School could not accommodate this	No large room available for sensory integration work
5. Independence and self-help skills				
No awareness of danger	Life skills programme in community	School would need support from local special school and teaching assistant	Resources would need to be available This could not take place in school	Not been tried before Is an extended day possible?

In this case, there are many gaps to fill and there is a lack of experience in this mainstream school. However, it is possible that with additional resources and training, mainstream provision could still work. Decisions about placement should take into consideration that this child is in Year 9 and it will be necessary to consider what Key Stage 4 possibilities exist for him as well.

Bibliography

Advisory Centre for Education (ACE) (2008) *Applying for a School: A Practical Guide to Parents' Legal Rights* (original work published 1997 & 2007).

Anzalone, M. (2001) Sensory Integration and Self Regulation in Infants and Toddlers. Washington, DC: Zero to Three.

Barthel, K. *Connections: Treatment of Sensory Processing Disorders*. Booklet distributed at conference (attended by OT) on 22–23 July 2008. Labyrinth Journeys.

Bondy, A. and Frost, L. (2001) 'The Picture Exchange Communication System.' *Behaviour Manipulation 25*, 5, 725–744.

Booth, T. and Ainscow, M. (2002) *Index for Inclusion: Developing Learning and Participation in Schools*. Bristol: Centre for Studies on Inclusive Education (CSIE).

Booth, T., Ainscow, M. and Kingston, D. (2006) *Index for Inclusion: Developing Play, Learning and Participation in Early Years and Childcare*. Bristol: CSIE.

Booth, T., Ainscow, M., Black-Hawkens, K., Vaughan, M. and Shaw, L. (2000) *Index for Inclusion: Developing Learning and Participation in Schools*. Bristol: CSIE.

Bray, M. and Todd, C. (2005) *Speech and Language: Clinical Process and Practice*. Oxford: Wiley-Blackwell Publishers.

British Council for School Environments and Morgan Ashurst (2008) *Family Guide to School Environments*. London: BCSE and Morgan Ashurst.

British Dyslexia Association (BDA) (2009) 'What is dyslexia?' Available at www.bdadyslexia.org.uk/about-dyslexia/faqs, accessed 8 October 2009.

British Psychological Society (1999) *Dyslexia, Literacy and Psychological Assessment*. Leicester: British Psychological Society.

Case Study AskAce (2008) 'Advisory Centre for Education.' *Magazine of the Advisory Centre for Education 2*, 1, 24–25.

Conti-Ramsden, G., Botting, N., Knox, E. and Simkin, Z. (2002) 'Different school placements following language unit attendance: which factors affect language outcome?' *International Journal of Communication Disorders 37*, 2, 185–195.

Corbett, C. and Perepa, P. (2007) *Missing Out? Autism, Education and Ethnicity: The Reality for Families Today*. London: The National Autistic Society.

Crystal, D. (1989) *Listen to Your Child: A Parent's Guide to Children's Language*. London: Penguin Health Books.

Crystal, D. and Varley, R. (1998) *Introduction to Language Pathology*. Oxford: Whurr Publishers.

DCSF (2001) *Good Practice Guidelines for Learning Mentors*. DfES Publications. London: The Stationery Office.

DCSF (2007) *Elective Home Education: Guidelines for Local Authorities*. London: The Stationery Office.

DCSF (2007) *Inclusion Development Programme (IDP)*. London: The Stationery Office.

DCSF (2007) *The New Arrivals Excellence Programme; Primary and Secondary National Strategies*. London: The Stationery Office.

DCSF (2008) *Special Educational Needs in England*. London: The Stationery Office.

DfES (2001) *Special Educational Needs Code of Practice*. London: The Stationery Office.

DfES (2001) *Access to Education for Children and Young People with Medical Needs*. London: The Stationery Office.

DfES (2001) *Inclusive Schooling – Children with Special Educational Needs*. London: The Stationery Office.

DfES (2001) *National Numeracy Strategy.* London: The Stationery Office.

DfES (2004) *Every Child Matters: Change for Children.* London: The Stationery Office.

DfES (2006) *Every Child Matters: Looking for a School Nurse?* London: The Stationery Office.

Elliott, C. D., Smith, P. and McCulloch, K. (1996) *British Ability Scales II.* Cheltenham: NFeR-Nelson Publishing Company.

Goleman, D. (1995) *Emotional Intelligence – Why it can Matter More than IQ.* London: Bloomsbury Publishers.

Kersner, M. and Wright, J. (2004) *Speech and Language Therapy: The Decision Making Process When Working with Children.* London: David Fulton Publishers.

Kranowitz, C. S. (2005) *The Out of Sync Child.* New York: Perigee.

Le Couteur, A. (Chair, Core Working Group) (2003) *National Autism Plan for Children (NAPC)* produced by NIASA (National Initiative for Autism: Screening and Assessment). Copyright The National Autistic Society.

Miller, L. J. (2006) *Sensational Kids.* New York: Perigee.

McKeown, S. (June/July 2008) 'Education outside school.' *Special Children Magazine,* 17.

Morris, J. (2003) *The Right Place? A Parent's Guide to Choosing a Residential Special School.* York: Joseph Rowntree Foundation.

Office for Advice, Assistance, Support and Information on Special Needs (2008) *Finding a Special Needs School/Home Learning.* Brockenhurst: OAASIS.

Ofsted (2000) *Evaluating Educational Inclusion – Guidance for Inspectors and Schools.* London: Ofsted.

Ofsted (2003) *The Education of Pupils with Medical Needs.* London: Ofsted.

Ofsted (2005) *Every Child Matters. Framework for the Inspection of Children's Services.* London: Ofsted.

Ofsted (2005) *Removing barriers: A 'Can-do' Attitude. A report on developing good practice for children with special needs in early years childcare and education in the private and voluntary sectors.* London: Ofsted.

Ofsted Survey (2008) *How Well New Teachers are Prepared to Teach Pupils with Learning Difficulties and/or Disabilities.* London: Ofsted.

Ofsted (2009) *Virtual Learning Environments: An Evaluation of their Development in a Sample of Educational Settings.* London: Ofsted.

Pepper, J. and Weitzman, E. (2004) *It Takes Two to Talk: A Practical Guide for Parents of Children with Language Delays* (3rd edn). Hanen Centre.

Qualifications and Curriculum Authority (1999) *Statutory Inclusion Statement of the National Curriculum.* London: QCA.

Reebye, P. and Stalker, A. (2008) *Understanding Regulation Disorders of Sensory Processing in Children.* London: Jessica Kingsley Publishers.

Rinaldi, W. (2001) *Social Use of Language programme (SULP) Revised.* NFER-Nelson.

Royal National Institute for Deaf People (2004) *Equipment for Deaf Learners Factsheet.* London: RNID.

Scope (2001) *Introduction to Cerebral Palsy (information sheet).* Available at www.scope.org.uk/information/factsheets/introcp, accessed on 11 September 2009.

Shaw, S. (1995) *Bilingual Pupils and Special Educational Needs – A Teacher's Guide to Appropriate Support and Referral.* London: Royal Borough of Kingston upon Thames.

Teachernet (2009) *Managing Medicines in Schools* (reproduced under the terms of the Click-Use Licence). London: The Stationery Office.

Teodorescu, I. (1998) *Write from the Start: Unique Programme to Develop the Fine Motor and Perceptual Skills Necessary for Effective Handwriting.* LDA.

Tutt, R. (December 2008/January 2009) 'Fit for purpose.' *Special Children Magazine.*

Warnock Report (1978) *Special Educational Needs.* Report of the Committee of Enquiry into the Education of Handicapped Children and Young People. London: Her Majesty's Stationery Office.

Wechsler, D. (2004) *Wechsler Intelligence Scale for Children.* Fourth Edition. (WISC-IV). Oxford: Harcourt Assessment, The Psychological Corporation.

Wilbarger, P. and Wilbarger, J.L. (1991) *Sensory Defensiveness in Children Aged 2–12: An Intervention Guide for Parents and Other Caretakers.* Van Nuys, CA: Avanti Educational Programs.

Wilson, C. (2006) *The Best of Both Worlds? Parents' Views on Dual Placements.* Submitted for the Degree of Masters of Arts in Disability Studies.

Cases

A v SENDIST and London Borough of Barnet – QBD 25 November 2003 – [2004] ELR 293.
R v Secretary of State for Education and Science, ex parte Talmud Torah Machzikei Hadass School Trust [1985].

Acts

Care Standards Act (2002) London: HMSO.
Children Act (2004) London: HMSO.
Data Protection Act (1998) London: HMSO.
Disability Discrimination Act (1995) London: HMSO.
Disability Discrimination Act (2002) London: HMSO.
Disability Discrimination Act (2005) London: HMSO.
Education and Inspections Act (2006) London: HMSO.
Education Act (1996) London: HMSO.
Education Act (1998) London: HMSO.
Education Act (2002) London: HMSO.
Freedom of Information Act (2000) London: HMSO.
Human Rights Act (1998) London: HMSO.
Race Relations (Amendment) Act (2000) London: HMSO.

(Acts reproduced under the terms of the Click-Use Licence)

Resources and Useful Organizations

Alert Program: How does your Engine Run

An innovative program that supports children, teachers, parents and therapists to change or maintain states of alertness and regulate their arousal states ('engine levels').

7200 Montgomery NE
Ste B9, Box 397
Albuquerque
NM 87109
USA
www.alertprogram.com (accessed June 2009)

Applied Behavioural Analysis (see NAS)

An intervention programme teaching linguistic, cognitive, social and self-help skills enabling learning and development in autistic children. (Lovaas Therapy is an early intensive ABA approach.)

Bobath Therapy

Used for children suffering from neurological impairment with an aim to improve or restore the child's ability to function and facilitate more normal movement.

The Bobath Centre
Bradbury House
250 East End Road
London
N2 8AU
www.bobath.org.uk (accessed June 2009)

Brain Gym

A series of simple movement-based activities developed by Dr Paul Dennison to prepare children with the physical skills for learning.

12 Golders Rise
Hendon
London
NW4 2HR
www.braingym.org.uk (accessed June 2009)
Edu-Kinesthetics, Inc.
PO Box 3395
Ventura

CA 93006–3395
USA
www.braingym.com

British Sign Language

BSL is the first and preferred language of deaf people. Signers primarily use their hands, body and facial movements as a visual means of communication.

www.britishsignlanguage.com (accessed June 2009)

British Society for Music Therapy

BSMT acts as an advisory body and is a centre of information on all aspects of music therapy.

24–27 White Lion Street
London
N1 9PD
Tel: 020 7837 6100; Email: info@bsmt.org
www.bsmt.org (accessed June 2009)

The Foundation for Conductive Education

FCE is a national charity with an international reach, with an aim to develop and advance the science and skill of CE.

Cannon Hill House
Russell Road
Moseley
Birmingham
B13 8RD
www.conductive-education.org.uk (accessed June 2009)

The Frenchay E-tran Frame

The E-tran (Eye-Transfer) Frame is a low-tech communication aid for people who have difficulty with speech.

70 Alston Drive
Bradwell Abbey
Milton Keynes
MK13 9HG
www.speechmark.net (accessed June 2009)

The Hanen Program

Provides parents and educators with training to apply language facilitation strategies flexibly across many contexts so that intervention becomes a natural part of their daily interactions with their child.

The Hanen Centre
Suite 515–1075 Bay Street
Toronto
Ontario
Canada
M55 2BI
www.hanen.org (accessed June 2009)

Intensive Interaction

An approach to teaching pre-speech fundamentals of communication to children and adults with severe learning difficulties and/or autism.

www.intensiveinteraction.co.uk

Jump Ahead Programme (West Sussex Grid for Learning 2005)

A graded intervention programme devised for children with motor co-ordination difficulties.

West Sussex County Council
Children and Adults
County Hall
Chichester
PO19 1RF
Search http://wsgfl.westsussex.gov.uk

The Listening Program™

A music-based auditory stimulation approach that gently trains the auditory system to accurately process sound.

The Villa
1 Hollingwood Lane
Bradford
West Yorkshire
BD7 2RE
5748 South Adams Avenue Parkway
Ogden
UT 84405
USA
www.thelisteningprogram.com (accessed June 2009)

Makaton®

A unique language programme which uses speech, gestures and written signs to provide visual representations of language to increase understanding and ease expressive communication.

Manor House
46 London Road
Blackwater
Camberley
Surrey
GU17 0AA
www.makaton.org (accessed June 2009)

National Autistic Society

NAS champion the rights and interests of all people with autism and aims to provide individuals with autism and their families with help, support and services which can make a positive difference to their lives.

393 City Road
London
EC1V 1NG
www.autism.org.uk (accessed June 2009)

Paget Gorman

A grammatical sign system which reflects normal patterns of English, used by many speech and language-impaired children.

2 Downlands Bungalows
Downlands Lane
Smallfield
Surrey
RH6 9SD
www.pgss.org (accessed June 2009)

Pyramid Educational Consultants (PECS)

Pyramid is the source for PECS, an alternative/augmentative communication system that teaches students to initiate spontaneous communication in a social context from the outset.

Pavilion House
6 Old Steine
Brighton
BN1 1EJ
www.pecs.org.uk (accessed June 2009)

Rebound Therapy

Used to facilitate movement, promote balance, relaxation and sensory integration, and to improve fitness, exercise tolerance and communication skills.

www.reboundtherapy.org (accessed June 2009)

Social and Emotional Aspects of Learning (SEAL) (DCSF)

A curriculum resource to develop the underpinning qualities and skills that help promote positive behaviour and effective learning. It focuses on five social and emotional aspects of learning: self-awareness, managing feelings, motivation, empathy and social skills.

http://nationalstrategies.standards.dcsf.gov.uk/node/87009 (accessed June 2009)

Social Use of Language Programme (SULP)

Developed by Wendy Rinaldi, the SULP was devised to assist younger children with the development of pragmatic awareness and to introduce concepts that are fundamental to any communicative situation.

www.wendyrinaldi.com (accessed June 2009)

Son Rise Program

A treatment for children and adults challenged by autism spectrum disorders and other developmental difficulties.

www.autismtreatmentcenter.org (accessed June 2009)

The Place2B

An innovative award-winning charity that works inside schools to improve the emotional well-being of children, their families and the whole school community, helping to build 'mentally healthy' schools where all children can thrive.

13/14 Angel Gate
326 City Road
London
EC1V 2PT
www.theplace2b.org.uk (accessed June 2009)

Therapeutic Story Writing

By working with the metaphor in stories – written both by the child and the teacher – SEN teachers support children to address emotional issues in a way that does not overwhelm the child.

Centre for Therapeutic Story Writing
59 Florence Road
Brighton
BN1 6DL
www.therapeuticstorywriting.com (accessed June 2009)

Treatment and Education of Autistic and related Communication-handicapped CHildren (TEACCH)

A programme to help prepare people with autism to live and work more effectively at home, at school and in the community. Emphasis is on structured teaching and organizing the physical environment to develop schedules and work systems to make the autistic child as independent as possible.

www.teacch.com (accessed June 2009)

The Wilbarger Deep Pressure and Proprioceptive Technique and Oral Tactile Technique (OTT) (formerly Wilberger Brushing Protocol (WBP))

To promote embodied, comprehensive and person-centred practices by providing resources for collaboration, support and education.

41 East Street
Southampton
MA 01073
USA
www.ot-innovations.com (accessed June 2009)

Write from the Start (previously The Teodorescu Perceptuo-Motor Programme)

Over 400 carefully graded exercises and activities to develop hand/eye co-ordination, form constancy, spatial organization, figure-ground discrimination, orientation and laterality necessary for effective handwriting. By Ion Teodorescu and Lois Addy.

LDA
Duke Street
Wisbech
Cambs
PE13 2AE

Websites

Afasic
The UK charity representing children and young adults with speech, language and communication impairments, working for their inclusion in society and supporting their parents and carers.
www.afasic.org.uk (accessed June 2009)

Anaphylaxis Campaign
Provides information and support to the growing number of people at risk from life-threatening allergic reactions (anaphylaxis) and works vigorously to achieve a safer environment for all those with severe allergies.
www.anaphylaxis.org.uk (accessed June 2009)

Angelman Syndrome
Angelman Syndrome Support, Education and Research Trust (ASSERT) is a United Kingdom based support group. It is run by volunteers who have direct contact with people with Angelman Syndrome. The majority of the trustees are parents or relatives of children or adults with Angelman Syndrome.
www.angelmanuk.org (accessed June 2009)

Association of Child Psychotherapists (ACP)
The professional body for psychoanalytically-trained child and adolescent psychotherapists in the UK.
www.childpsychotherapy.org.uk (accessed June 2009)

Association of Educational Psychologists (AEP)
The professional association and trade union for educational psychologists practising in the UK.
www.aep.org.uk (accessed June 2009)

Association of Speech and Language Therapists in Independent Practice (ASLTIP)
ASLTIP provides information on independent speech and language therapy throughout the United Kingdom and supports speech and language therapists in independent practice.
www.helpwithtalking.com (accessed June 2009)

Asthma UK
The charity dedicated to improving the health and well-being of the 5.4 million people in the UK whose lives are affected by asthma.
www.asthma.org.uk (accessed June 2009)

Bristol Healthy Schools Programme
Bristol Health Schools Programme supports Bristol schools in achieving National Healthy Schools Status.
www.bristolhealthyschools.nhs.uk (accessed June 2009)

British Association for Counselling and Psychotherapy (BACP)
BACP can provide advice on a range of services to help meet the needs of anyone seeking information about counselling and psychotherapy. It is a service which will enable potential clients to find a suitable counsellor with whom they feel comfortable, in their particular area and seek to remove the anxiety that may be associated with choosing a counsellor.
www.bacp.co.uk (accessed June 2009)

British Association of Art Therapists (BAAT)
The professional organization for art therapists in the United Kingdom, it maintains a comprehensive directory of qualified art therapists and works to promote art therapy in the UK.
www.baat.org (accessed June 2009)

British Association of Dramatherapists (BADth)
BADth is the professional body for Dramatherapists in the United Kingdom. Through the work of its executive officers, sub-committees and individual members, it represents Dramatherapists' interests in numerous ways: for example, with employing authorities, government departments, professional bodies and the media.
www.badth.org.uk (accessed February 2009)

British Association of Occupational Therapists (BAOT)
The professional body and trade union for occupational therapy staff in the UK, with over 29,000 members.
www.baot.org.uk (accessed June 2009)

British Association of Play Therapists (BAPT)
BAPT is the first and foremost professional association for Play Therapy in the UK.
www.bapt.info (accessed June 2009)

British Association of Teachers of the Deaf (BATOD)
BATOD is the sole UK Association representing the interests of teachers of the deaf. The website is a rich source of information about all aspects of education of deaf children and young people – a resource meeting the aims of the Association – to promote excellence in deaf education.
www.batod.org.uk (accessed June 2009)

British Dyslexia Association (BDA)
The BDA is the voice of dyslexic people. They aim to influence government and other institutions to promote a dyslexia-friendly society.
www.bdadyslexia.org.uk (accessed June 2009)

British Psychological Society (BPS)
The British Psychological Society is the representative body for psychology and psychologists in the UK.
www.bps.org.uk (accessed June 2009)

Chartered Society of Physiotherapy (CSP)
The professional educational and trade union body for the UK's 48,000 chartered physiotherapists, physiotherapy students and assistants.
www.csp.org.uk (accessed June 2009)

College of Occupational Therapists (COT)

The College of Occupational Therapists is a wholly owned subsidiary of BAOT and operates as a registered charity. It represents the profession nationally and internationally, and contributes widely to policy consultations throughout the UK. The College sets the professional and educational standards for occupational therapy. It provides leadership, guidance and information relating to research and development, education, practice and lifelong learning. In addition, 11 accredited specialist sections support expert clinical practice.
www.cot.org.uk (accessed June 2009)

Council for the Registration of Schools Teaching Dyslexic Pupils (CReSTeD)

CReSTeD provides a list of schools approved for their SpLD (dyslexia) provision. For full information and a list of schools, Tel: 01242 604 852; Email: admin@crested.org.uk
www.crested.org.uk (accessed June 2009)

Criminal Records Bureau (CRB)

The CRB's aim is to help organizations in the public, private and voluntary sectors by identifying candidates who may be unsuitable to work with children or other vulnerable members of society.
www.crb.gov.uk (accessed June 2009)

Department for Children, Schools and Families (DCSF)

The DCSF wants to make this country the best place in the world for children and young people to grow up. Our Children's Plan sets out how we can achieve our ambitions.
www.dcsf.gov.uk (accessed June 2009) (reproduced under the terms of the Click-Use Licence)

Diabetes UK

Diabetes UK is the largest organization in the UK working for people with diabetes, funding research, campaigning and helping people live with the condition.
www.diabetes.org.uk (accessed June 2009)

Dyslexia Action and Dyslexia Institute

Dyslexia Action is a national charity and the UK's leading provider of services and support for people with dyslexia and literacy difficulties.
www.dyslexiaaction.org.uk (accessed June 2009)

Dyspraxia Foundation

The Foundation seeks every opportunity to increase understanding of dyspraxia, particularly among professionals in health and education and encourages its local groups to do the same.
www.dyspraxiafoundation.org.uk (accessed June 2009)

EduBase (also known as School Lookup) and maintained by the DCSF

From nurseries through to colleges, EduBase lets you search for establishments by name, location or type. So, whether you're looking for a specific single school or college or for more than one establishment meeting your criteria, EduBase can help.
www.edubase.gov.uk (accessed June 2009) (reproduced under the terms of the Click-Use Licence)

EPNET: The Educational Psychology List

A forum for the exchange of information and advice among university research/teaching staff working in the field of educational psychology and educational psychologists throughout the UK and elsewhere.

Guide to Psychology and its Practice – Raymond Lloyd Richmond, PhD

A common-sense approach to some common questions and concerns about the practice of clinical psychology.
www.guidetopsychology.com (accessed June 2009)

Health Professions Council (HPC)
The HPC is a regulator set up to protect the public. It keeps a register of health professionals who meet standards for their training, professional skills, behaviour and health.
www.hpc-uk.org (accessed June 2009)

Independent Schools Council Information Service (ISC)
The ISC represents 1280 independent schools educating more than 500,000 children. Schools are accredited by the Independent Schools Inspectorate (ISI) and the Head of each ISC school is a member of one of their Heads' Associations. ISC schools cover the entire academic range. They also cover a wide social range, with nearly a third of children receiving help with their school fees.
www.isc.co.uk (accessed June 2009)

Landau Kleffner Syndrome (LKS)
FOLKS (Friends of Landau Kleffner Syndrome) is a UK registered charity for children with LKS, their families and interested professionals.
www.friendsoflks.com (accessed June 2009)

Mentoring and Befriending Foundation (MBF)
The Mentoring and Befriending Foundation (MBF) provides guidance and support to organizations and practitioners involved in mentoring and befriending.
www.mandbf.org.uk (accessed June 2009)

Montessori Schools
The Montessori approach is holistic and aims to develop the whole child. Fundamental to the approach is the belief that a child's early years from birth to six are the period when they have the greatest capacity to learn.
www.montessori.org.uk (accessed June 2009)

National Association for Small Schools (NASS)
NASS is a campaigning organization who advise and support small schools at risk of closure, lobby on behalf of small schools and humanity of scale in education and promote the virtues of small schools and known best practice.
www.smallschools.org.uk (accessed June 2009)

National Autistic Society (NAS)
The NAS champions the rights and interests of all people with autism and aims to provide individuals with autism and their families with help, support and services that they can access, trust and rely upon and which can make a positive difference to their lives.
www.nas.org.uk (accessed June 2009)

National Deaf Children's Society (NDCS)
The NDCS is the national charity dedicated to creating a world without barriers for deaf children and young people.
www.ndcs.org.uk (accessed June 2009)

National Institute for Health and Clinical Excellence (NICE)
NICE is an independent organization responsible for providing national guidance on promoting good health and preventing and treating ill health.
www.nice.org.uk (accessed June 2009)

National Organization for Pupil Referral Units
Will provide a collective voice in the future for PRUs and influence debate and policy in the area to improve the quality of educational provision for pupils at risk of social exclusion.
www.prus.org.uk (accessed June 2009)

National Society for Epilepsy
The leading national epilepsy medical charity working for everyone affected by epilepsy, through their cutting edge research, awareness campaigns and expert care.
www.epilepsysociety.org.uk (accessed June 2009)

Office for Advice, Assistance, Support and Information on Special Needs (OAASIS)
A resource for parents and professionals caring for children with autism/Asperger's syndrome and other learning disabilities.
www.oaasis.co.uk (accessed June 2009)

Ofsted
Ofsted inspects and regulates care for children and young people, and inspects education and training for learners of all ages. They raise aspirations and contribute to the long-term achievement of ambitious standards and better life chances for service users. Their educational, economic and social well-being will in turn promote England's national success.
www.ofsted.gov.uk (accessed June 2009) (reproduced under the terms of the Click-Use Licence)

Prader–Willi Syndrome (PWS)
A registered charity and the only organization in the UK which is dedicated to supporting people with PWS, their families, carers and the professionals who work with them.
www.pwsa.co.uk (accessed June 2009)

Professional Association of Teachers of Students with Specific Learning Difficulties (PATOSS)
As a professional association of teachers of students with specific learning difficulties, PATOSS is for all those concerned with the teaching and support of pupils with SpLD: dyslexic, dyspraxic, ADD, and Asperger's syndrome.
www.patoss-dyslexia.org (accessed June 2009)

Rett Syndrome
A national charity seeking to make change happen for people living with Rett syndrome.
www.rettsyndrome.org.uk (accessed June 2009)

Royal College of Speech and Language Therapists (RCSLT)
The professional body for speech and language therapists and support workers to promote excellence in practice and influence health, education and social care policies
www.rcslt.org (accessed June 2009)

Royal National Institute for the Blind (RNIB)
RNIB provides a range of services for children with visual impairment, including education advice, support and training for professional staff.
www.rnib.org.uk/learning (accessed June 2009)

Royal National Institute for the Deaf (RNID)
RNID is the largest charity working to change the world for the UK's 9 million deaf and hard of hearing people.
www.rnid.org.uk (accessed June 2009)

Scope
Scope is the disability organization in England and Wales whose focus is people with cerebral palsy. Their aim is that disabled people achieve equality: a society in which they are as valued and have the same human and civil rights as everyone else.
www.scope.org.uk (accessed June 2009)

Sense for deafblind people

Sense is the leading national charity that supports and campaigns for children and adults who are deafblind. It provides expert advice and information as well as specialist services to deafblind people, their families, carers and the professionals who work with them. Sense also supports people who have sensory impairments with additional disabilities.
www.sense.org.uk (accessed June 2009)

Special Educational Needs and Disability (SEND) Tribunal

SEND Tribunal considers parents' appeals against the decisions of Local Authorities (LAs) about children's special educational needs if parents cannot reach agreement with the LA.
www.sendist.gov.uk (accessed June 2009)

Steiner Schools

Steiner education is based on the work of Dr Rudolf Steiner (1861–1925). The priority of the Steiner ethos is to provide an unhurried and creative learning environment where children can find the joy in learning and experience the richness of childhood rather than early specialization or academic hot-housing. The core subjects of the curriculum are taught in thematic blocks and all lessons include a balance of artistic, practical and intellectual content. Whole class, mixed ability teaching is the norm.
www.steinerwaldorf.org (accessed June 2009)

Studio Schools™

The Young Foundation undertakes research to understand social needs and then develops practical initiatives and institutions to address them. Visit www.youngfoundation.org for further information.
www.launchpad.youngfoundation.org/node/128 (accessed June 2009)

Teachernet

Developed by the Department for Children, Schools and Families as a resource to support the education profession. It carries information about teaching and learning, teaching strategy, teaching and learning tips, learning psychology and links to thousands of resources.
www.teachernet.gov.uk (accessed June 2009) (reproduced under the terms of the Click-Use Licence)

United Nations Convention on the Rights of the Child (UNICEF)

UNICEF is the leading advocate for children's rights, active in 190 countries through country programmes and National Committees.
www.unicef.org (accessed June 2009)

Williams Syndrome Foundation

The Williams Syndrome Foundation is run for parents by parents. The foundation is supported by a panel of eminent medical and professional advisers.
www.williams-syndrome.org.uk (accessed June 2009)

World Federation of Occupational Therapists (WFOT)

WFOT is the key international representative for occupational therapists and occupational therapy around the world and the official international organization for the promotion of occupational therapy.
www.wfot.com (accessed June 2009)

Young Minds Schools Outreach Service

YoungMinds is the UK's only national charity committed to improving the mental health and emotional well-being of all children and young people.
www.youngminds.org.uk (accessed June 2009)

Index